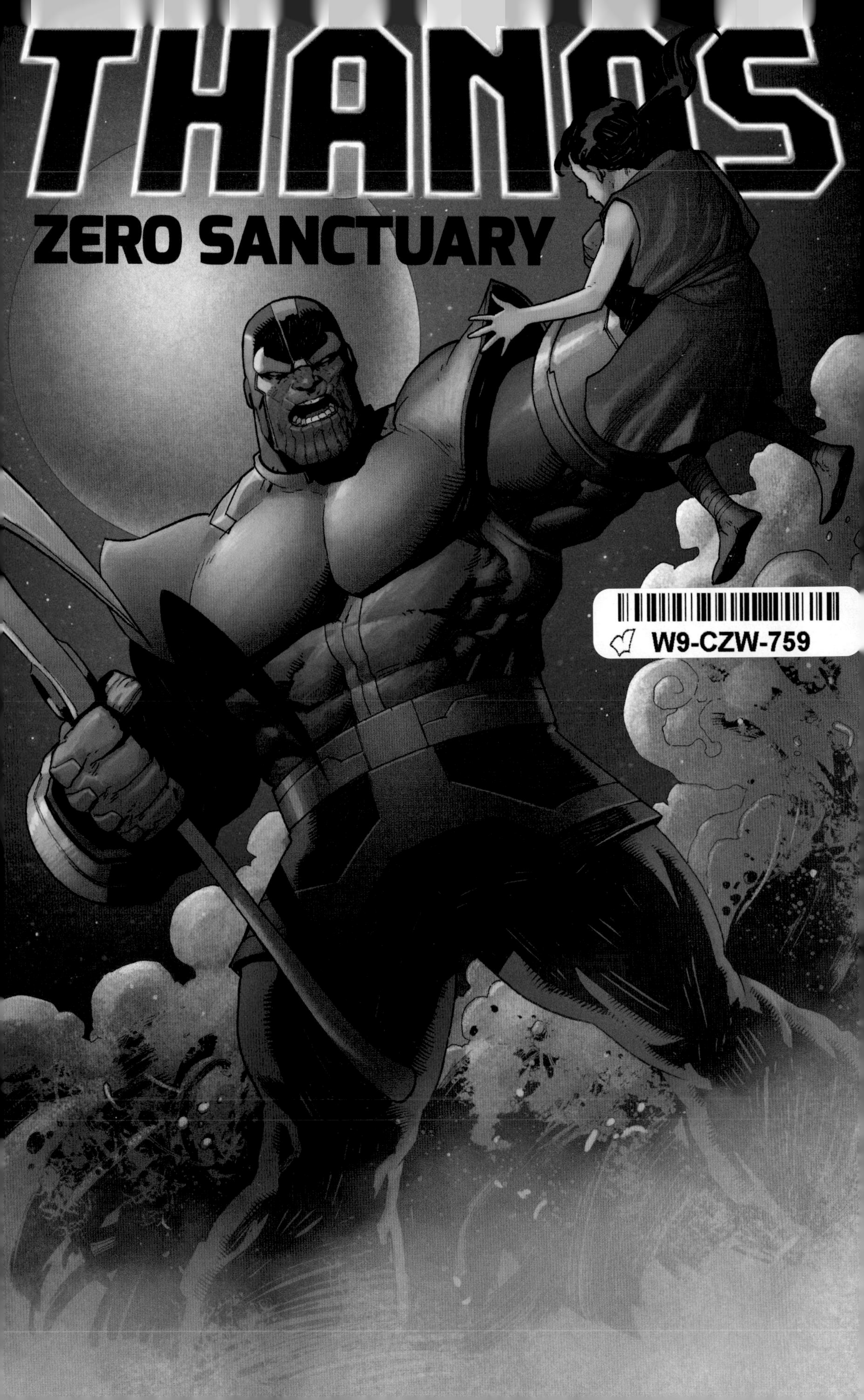
THANOS
ZERO SANCTUARY

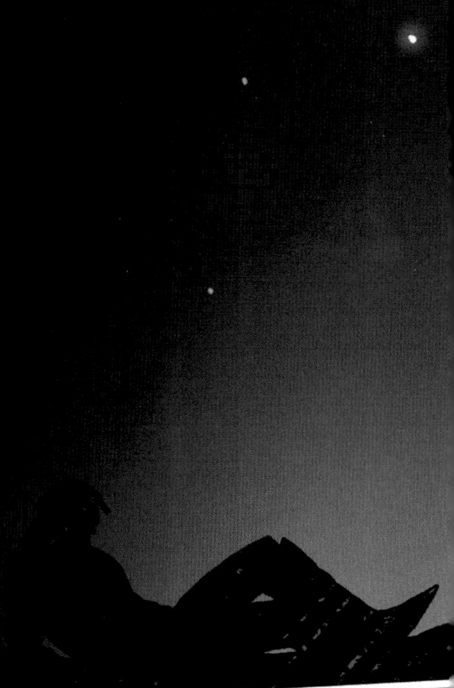

THE MAD TITAN KNOWN AS THANOS IS OBSESSED WITH TWO THINGS: POWER AND DEATH.

WHEN THANOS WAS A CHILD, HIS FASCINATION WITH KILLING WAS KINDLED BY A GIRL WHOM THANOS GREW TO LOVE. AS THEY GOT OLDER, THE GIRL PROMISED TO RETURN HIS LOVE IF ONLY HE COULD PROVE HIMSELF TO HER. HOWEVER, NO MATTER HOW HIGH THANOS' DEATH TOLL ROSE, SHE ALWAYS DEMANDED MORE. REALIZING THAT HE WAS THE ONLY PERSON WHO COULD SEE HIS PARAMOUR, THANOS DISCOVERED THAT SHE WAS NO MERE WOMAN, BUT THE INCARNATION OF DEATH ITSELF.

FOR YEARS, THANOS' INFATUATION WITH DEATH COMPELLED HIM ACROSS THE COSMOS, BRINGING RUIN AND DESTRUCTION IN HIS WAKE. THAT IS, UNTIL HE WAS EXECUTED BY THE DEADLIEST ASSASSIN IN THE GALAXY…HIS ADOPTED DAUGHTER GAMORA. BUT BEFORE THEIR RELATIONSHIP CAME TO A BLOODY END, HOW DID IT BEGIN?

COLLECTION EDITOR **JENNIFER GRÜNWALD**
ASSISTANT EDITOR **CAITLIN O'CONNELL**
ASSOCIATE MANAGING EDITOR **KATERI WOODY**
EDITOR, SPECIAL PROJECTS **MARK D. BEAZLEY**
VP PRODUCTION & SPECIAL PROJECTS **JEFF YOUNGQUIST**
BOOK DESIGNER **SALENA MAHINA**

SVP PRINT, SALES & MARKETING **DAVID GABRIEL**
DIRECTOR, LICENSED PUBLISHING **SVEN LARSEN**
EDITOR IN CHIEF **C.B. CEBULSKI**
CHIEF CREATIVE OFFICER **JOE QUESADA**
PRESIDENT **DAN BUCKLEY**
EXECUTIVE PRODUCER **ALAN FINE**

THANOS: ZERO SANCTUARY. Contains material originally published in magazine form as THANOS (2019) #1-6. First printing 2019. ISBN 978-1-302-91770-8. Published by MARVEL WORLDWIDE, INC., a subsidiary of MARVEL ENTERTAINMENT, LLC. OFFICE OF PUBLICATION. 135 West 50th Street, New York, NY 10020. © 2019 MARVEL No similarity between any of the names, characters, persons, and/or institutions in this magazine with those of any living or dead person or institution is intended, and any such similarity which may exist is purely coincidental. **Printed in the U.S.A.** DAN BUCKLEY, President, Marvel Entertainment; JOHN NEE, Publisher; JOE QUESADA, Chief Creative Officer; TOM BREVOORT, SVP of Publishing; DAVID BOGART, Associate Publisher & SVP of Talent Affairs: DAVID GABRIEL, VP of Print & Digital Publishing; JEFF YOUNGQUIST, VP of Production & Special Projects; DAN CARR, Executive Director of Publishing Technology; ALEX MORALES, Director of Publishing Operations; DAN EDINGTON, Managing Editor; SUSAN CRESPI, Production Manager; STAN LEE, Chairman Emeritus. For information regarding advertising in Marvel Comics or on Marvel.com, please contact Vit DeBellis, Custom Solutions & Integrated Advertising Manager, at vdebellis@marvel.com. For Marvel subscription inquiries, please call 888-511-5480. Manufactured between 10/4/2019 and 11/5/2019 by LSC COMMUNICATIONS INC., KENDALLVILLE, IN, USA.

THANOS
ZERO SANCTUARY

TINI HOWARD
WRITER

ARIEL OLIVETTI
ARTIST

ANTONIO FABELA
COLOR ARTIST

VC'S JOE CARAMAGNA
LETTERER

JEFF DEKAL
COVER ART

LAUREN AMARO
ASSISTANT EDITOR

DARREN SHAN
EDITOR

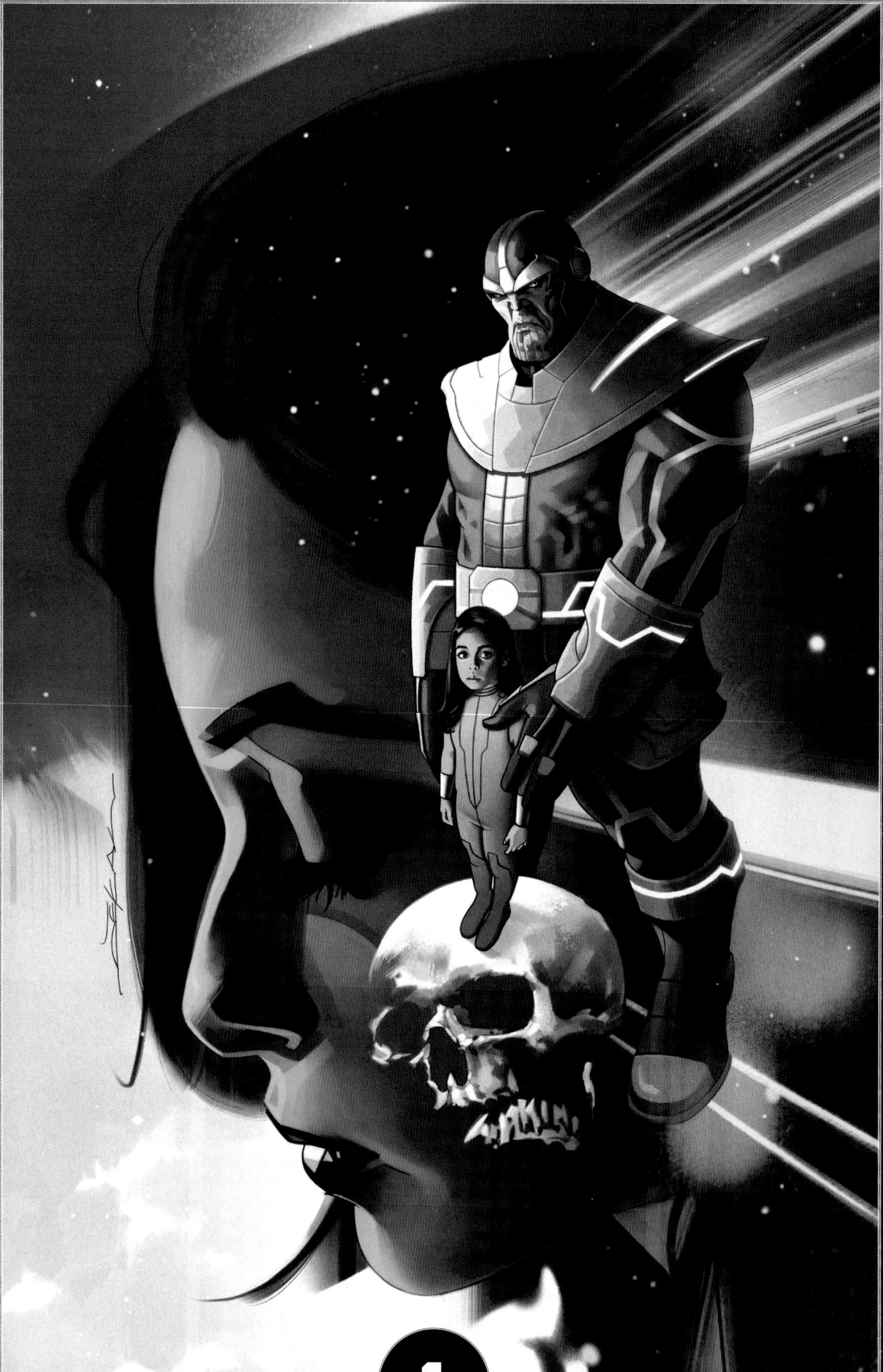

1

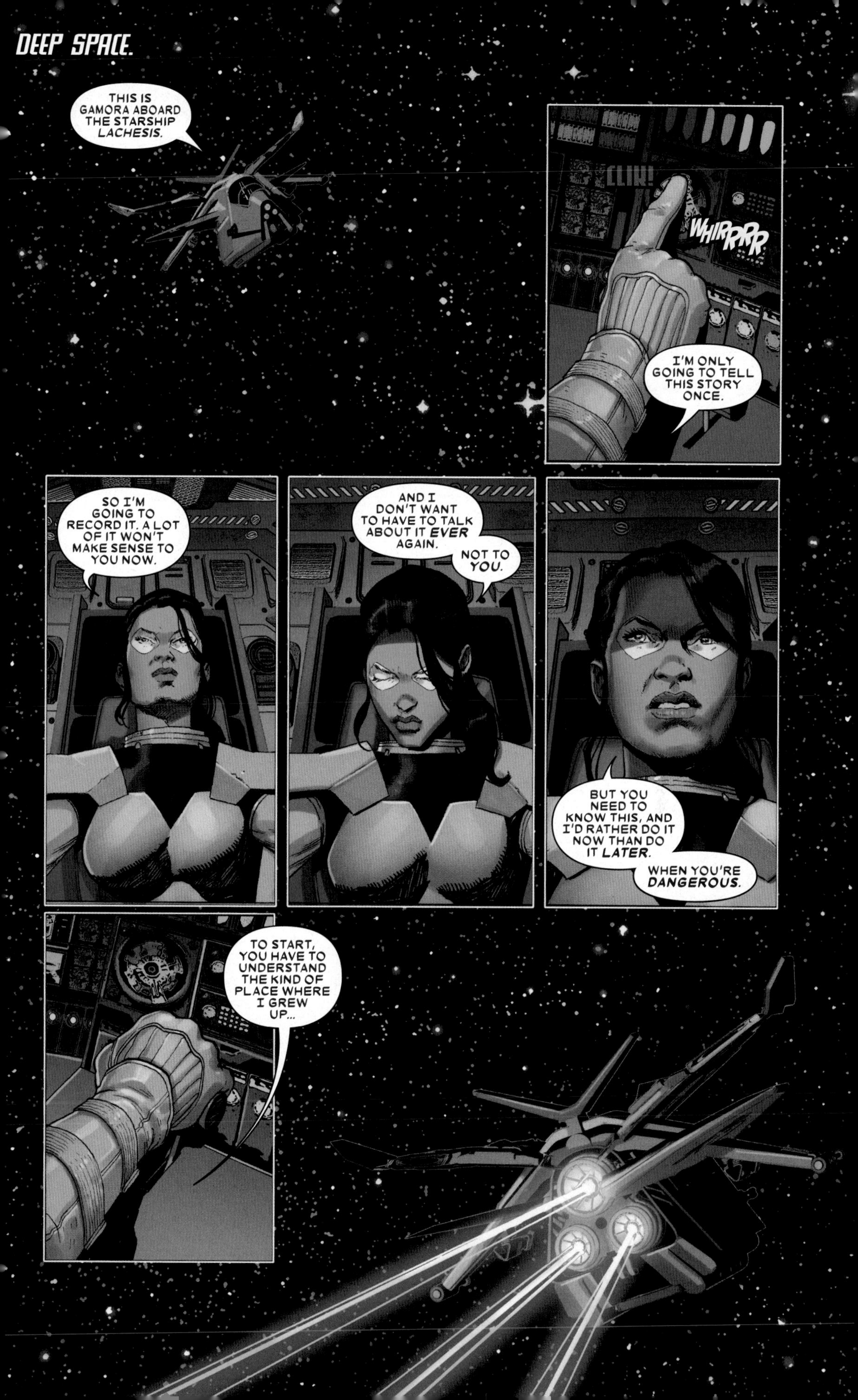
DEEP SPACE.
THIS IS GAMORA ABOARD THE STARSHIP LACHESIS.
CLIK!
WHIRRRR
I'M ONLY GOING TO TELL THIS STORY ONCE.
SO I'M GOING TO RECORD IT. A LOT OF IT WON'T MAKE SENSE TO YOU NOW.
AND I DON'T WANT TO HAVE TO TALK ABOUT IT EVER AGAIN.
NOT TO YOU.
BUT YOU NEED TO KNOW THIS, AND I'D RATHER DO IT NOW THAN DO IT LATER.
WHEN YOU'RE DANGEROUS.
TO START, YOU HAVE TO UNDERSTAND THE KIND OF PLACE WHERE I GREW UP...

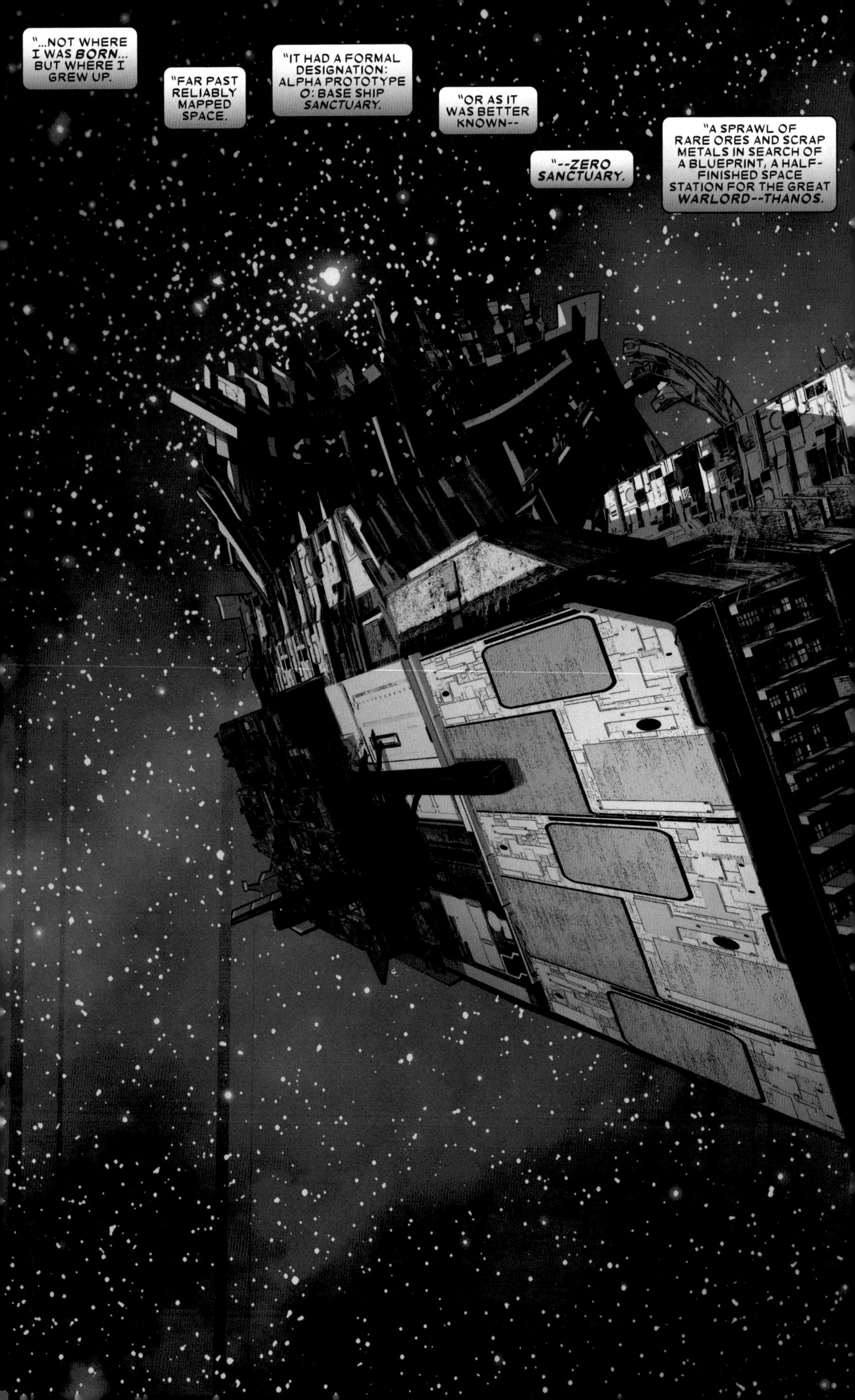
"...NOT WHERE I WAS *BORN*... BUT WHERE I GREW UP.
"FAR PAST RELIABLY MAPPED SPACE.
"IT HAD A FORMAL DESIGNATION: ALPHA PROTOTYPE O: BASE SHIP *SANCTUARY*.
"OR AS IT WAS BETTER KNOWN--
"--*ZERO SANCTUARY*.
"A SPRAWL OF RARE ORES AND SCRAP METALS IN SEARCH OF A BLUEPRINT, A HALF-FINISHED SPACE STATION FOR THE GREAT *WARLORD--THANOS*.

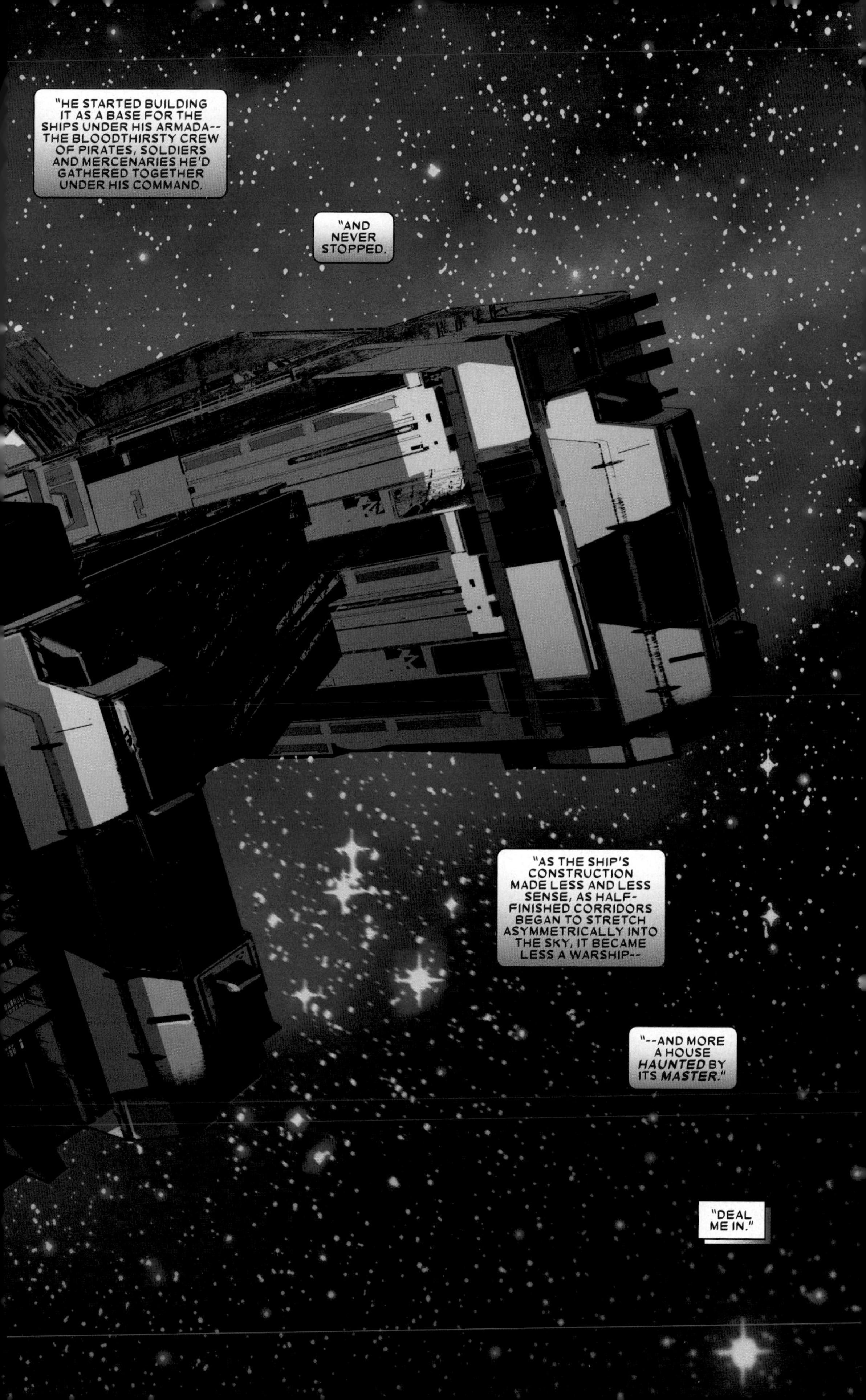
"HE STARTED BUILDING IT AS A BASE FOR THE SHIPS UNDER HIS ARMADA--THE BLOODTHIRSTY CREW OF PIRATES, SOLDIERS AND MERCENARIES HE'D GATHERED TOGETHER UNDER HIS COMMAND.
"AND NEVER STOPPED.
"AS THE SHIP'S CONSTRUCTION MADE LESS AND LESS SENSE, AS HALF-FINISHED CORRIDORS BEGAN TO STRETCH ASYMMETRICALLY INTO THE SKY, IT BECAME LESS A WARSHIP--
"--AND MORE A HOUSE *HAUNTED* BY ITS *MASTER*."
"DEAL ME IN."

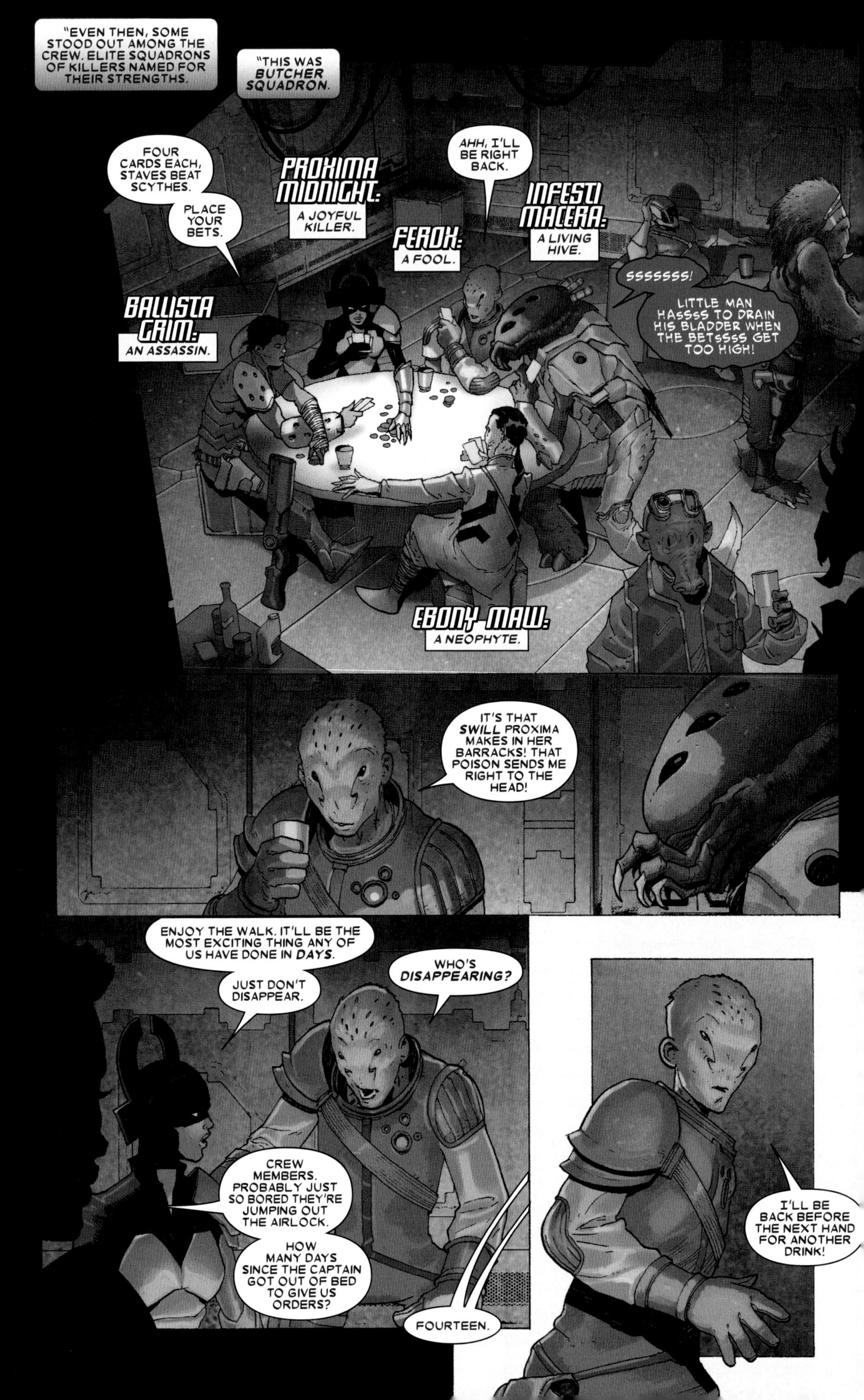

"EVEN THEN, SOME STOOD OUT AMONG THE CREW. ELITE SQUADRONS OF KILLERS NAMED FOR THEIR STRENGTHS.
"THIS WAS BUTCHER SQUADRON.
FOUR CARDS EACH, STAVES BEAT SCYTHES.
PLACE YOUR BETS.
BALLISTA GRIM: AN ASSASSIN.
PROXIMA MIDNIGHT: A JOYFUL KILLER.
AHH, I'LL BE RIGHT BACK.
FEROX: A FOOL.
INFESTI MACERA: A LIVING HIVE.
SSSSSSS!
LITTLE MAN HASSSS TO DRAIN HIS BLADDER WHEN THE BETSSSS GET TOO HIGH!
EBONY MAW: A NEOPHYTE.
IT'S THAT SWILL PROXIMA MAKES IN HER BARRACKS! THAT POISON SENDS ME RIGHT TO THE HEAD!
ENJOY THE WALK. IT'LL BE THE MOST EXCITING THING ANY OF US HAVE DONE IN DAYS.
JUST DON'T DISAPPEAR.
WHO'S DISAPPEARING?
CREW MEMBERS. PROBABLY JUST SO BORED THEY'RE JUMPING OUT THE AIRLOCK.
HOW MANY DAYS SINCE THE CAPTAIN GOT OUT OF BED TO GIVE US ORDERS?
FOURTEEN.
I'LL BE BACK BEFORE THE NEXT HAND FOR ANOTHER DRINK!

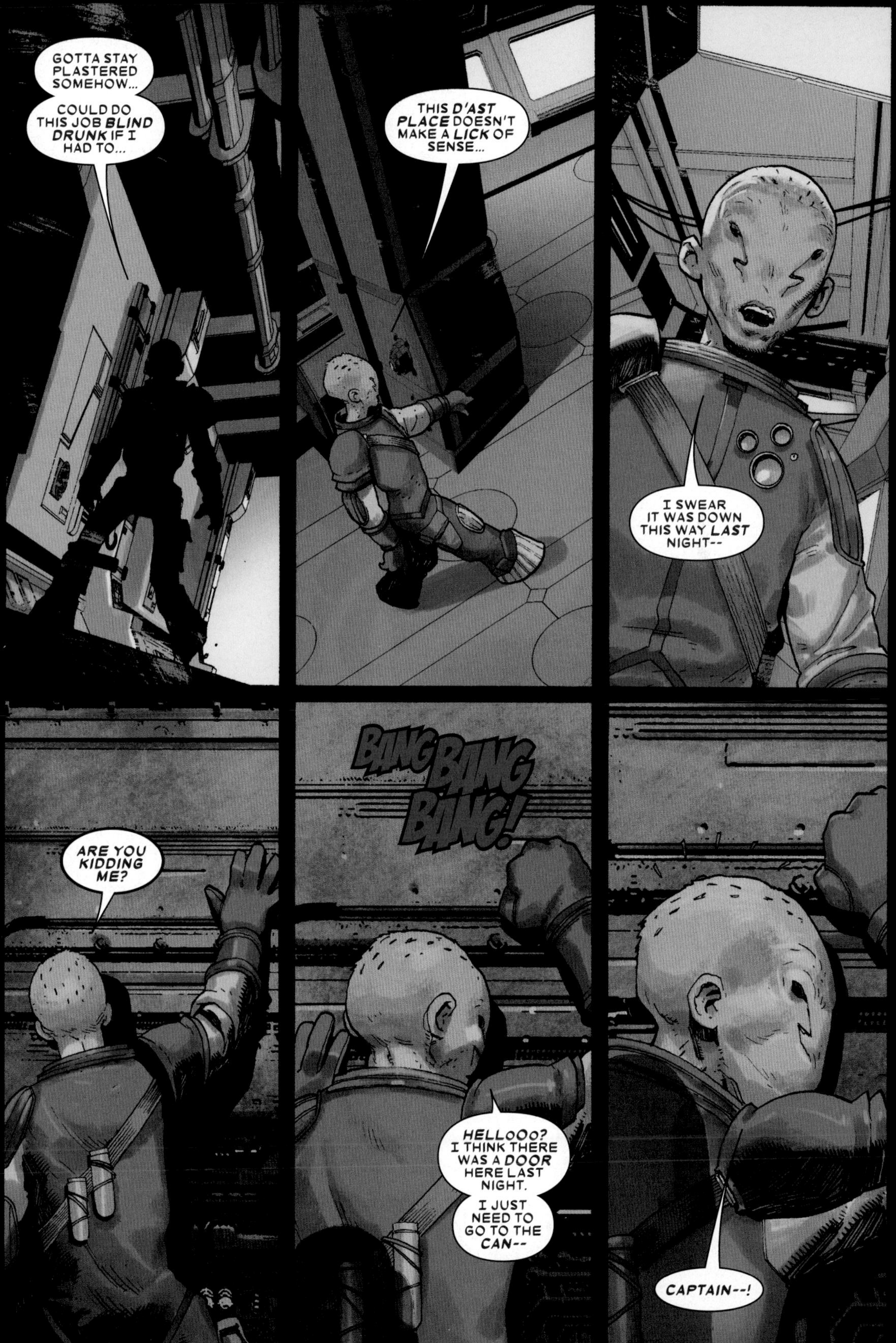
GOTTA STAY PLASTERED SOMEHOW...
COULD DO THIS JOB BLIND DRUNK IF I HAD TO...
THIS D'AST PLACE DOESN'T MAKE A LICK OF SENSE...
I SWEAR IT WAS DOWN THIS WAY LAST NIGHT--
ARE YOU KIDDING ME?
BANG BANG BANG!
HELLOOO? I THINK THERE WAS A DOOR HERE LAST NIGHT.
I JUST NEED TO GO TO THE CAN--
CAPTAIN--!

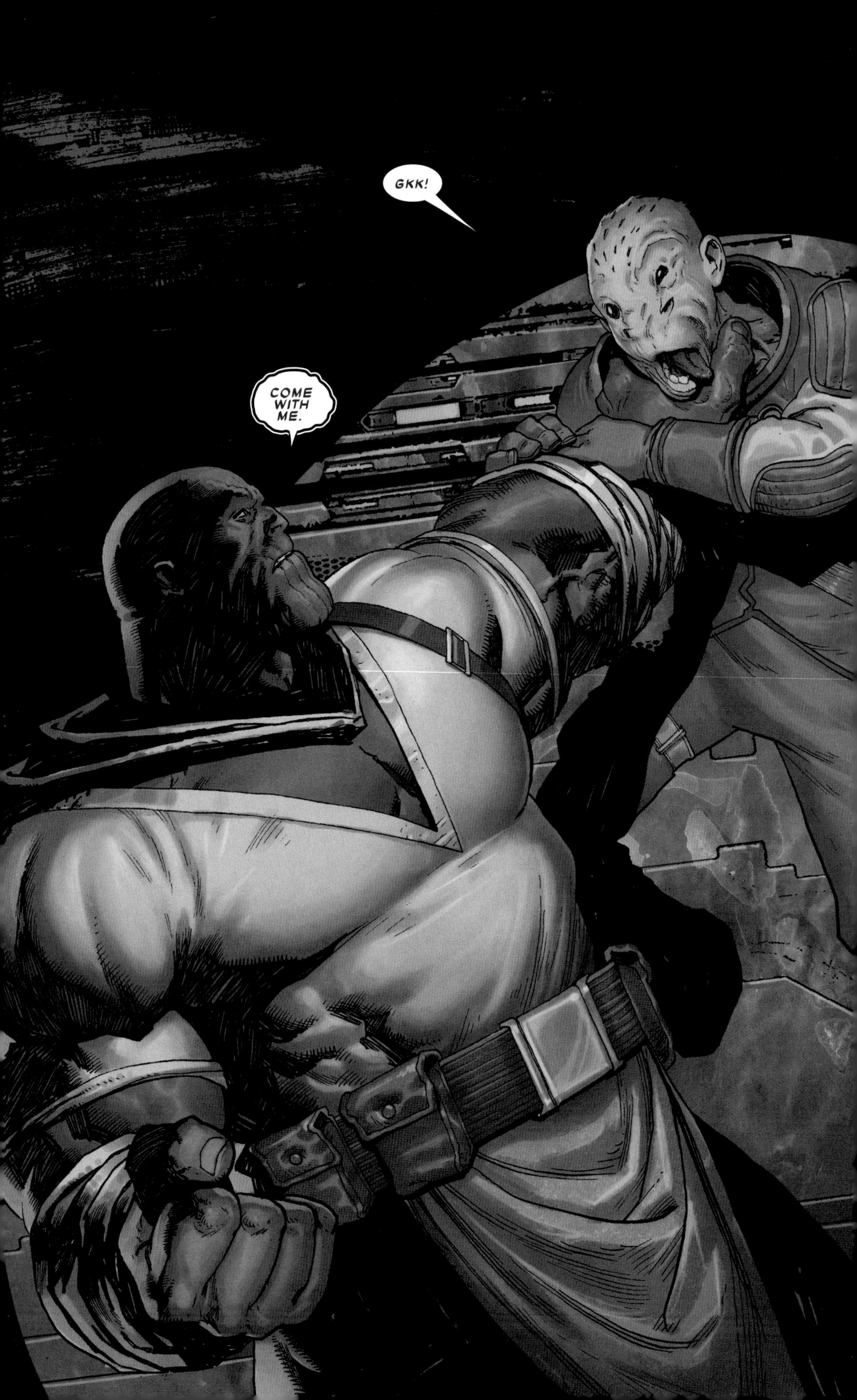
GKK!
COME WITH ME.

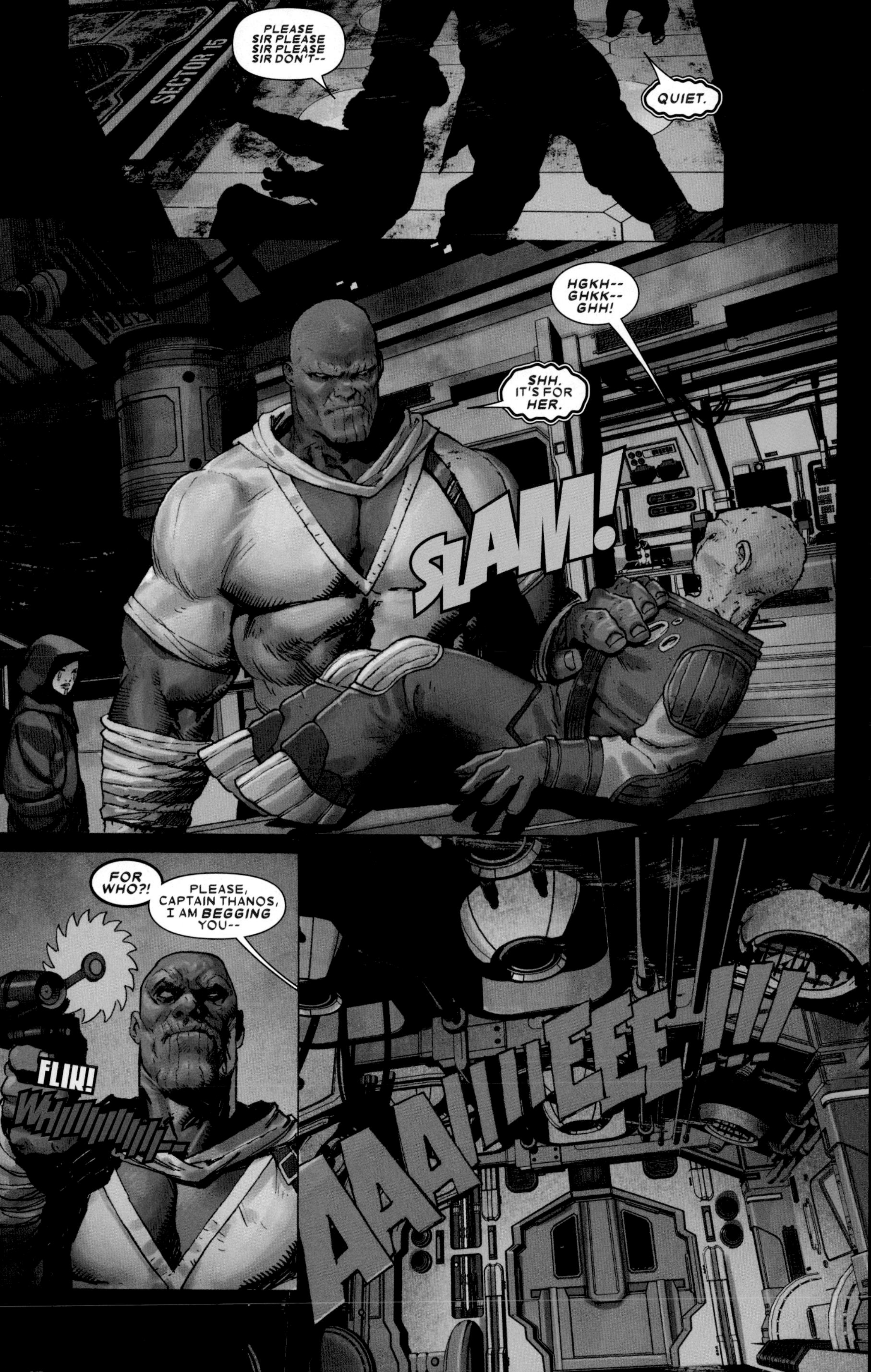
SECTOR 15
PLEASE SIR PLEASE SIR PLEASE SIR DON'T--
QUIET.
HGKH-- GHKK-- GHH!
SHH. IT'S FOR HER.
SLAM!
FOR WHO?!
PLEASE, CAPTAIN THANOS, I AM BEGGING YOU--
FLIK!
AAIIIIEEE!!!

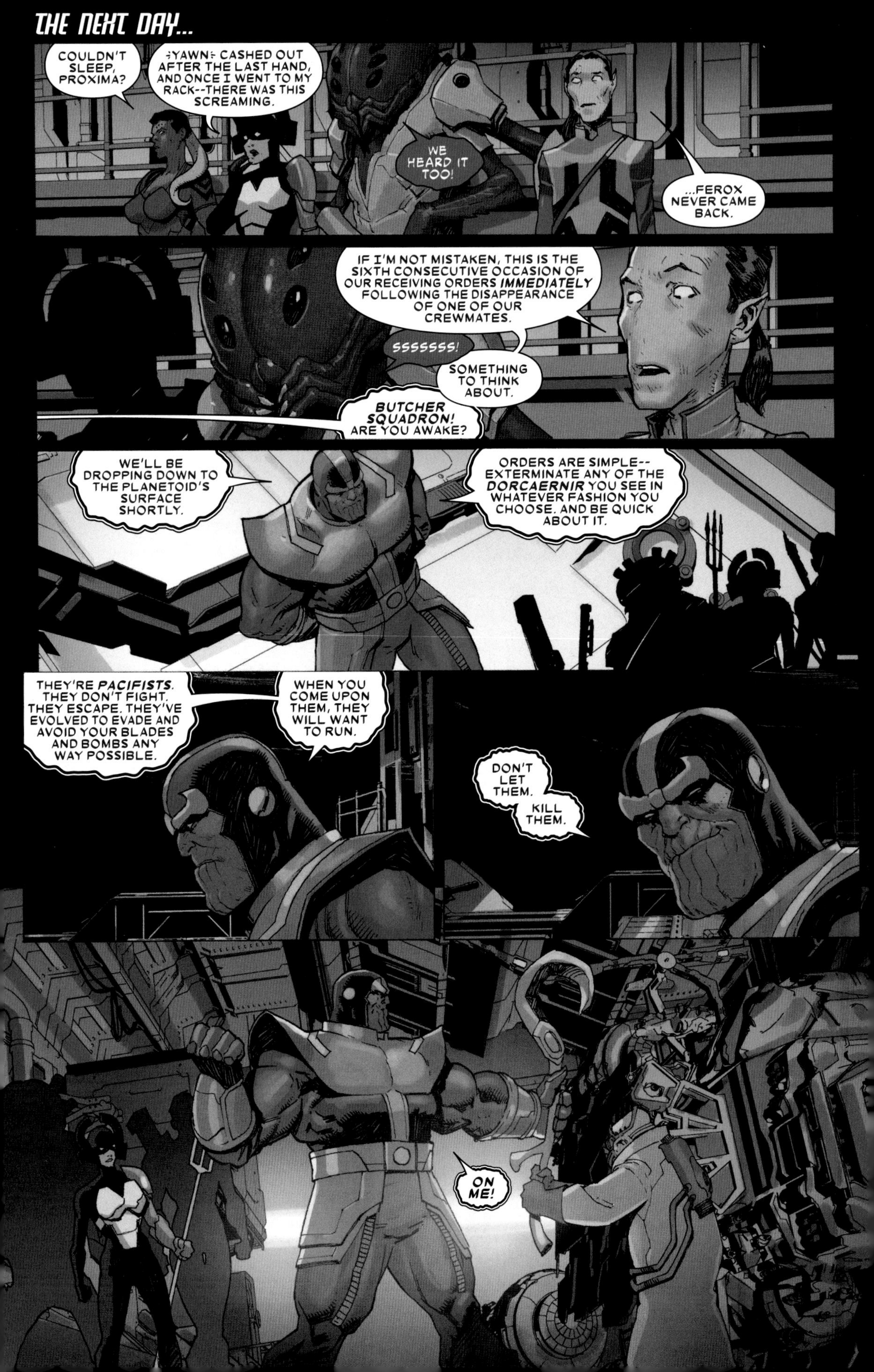
THE NEXT DAY...
COULDN'T SLEEP, PROXIMA?
-YAWN- CASHED OUT AFTER THE LAST HAND, AND ONCE I WENT TO MY RACK--THERE WAS THIS SCREAMING.
WE HEARD IT TOO!
...FEROX NEVER CAME BACK.
IF I'M NOT MISTAKEN, THIS IS THE SIXTH CONSECUTIVE OCCASION OF OUR RECEIVING ORDERS IMMEDIATELY FOLLOWING THE DISAPPEARANCE OF ONE OF OUR CREWMATES.
SSSSSSS!
SOMETHING TO THINK ABOUT.
BUTCHER SQUADRON! ARE YOU AWAKE?
WE'LL BE DROPPING DOWN TO THE PLANETOID'S SURFACE SHORTLY.
ORDERS ARE SIMPLE-- EXTERMINATE ANY OF THE DORCAERNIR YOU SEE IN WHATEVER FASHION YOU CHOOSE. AND BE QUICK ABOUT IT.
THEY'RE PACIFISTS. THEY DON'T FIGHT. THEY ESCAPE. THEY'VE EVOLVED TO EVADE AND AVOID YOUR BLADES AND BOMBS ANY WAY POSSIBLE.
WHEN YOU COME UPON THEM, THEY WILL WANT TO RUN.
DON'T LET THEM.
KILL THEM.
ON ME!

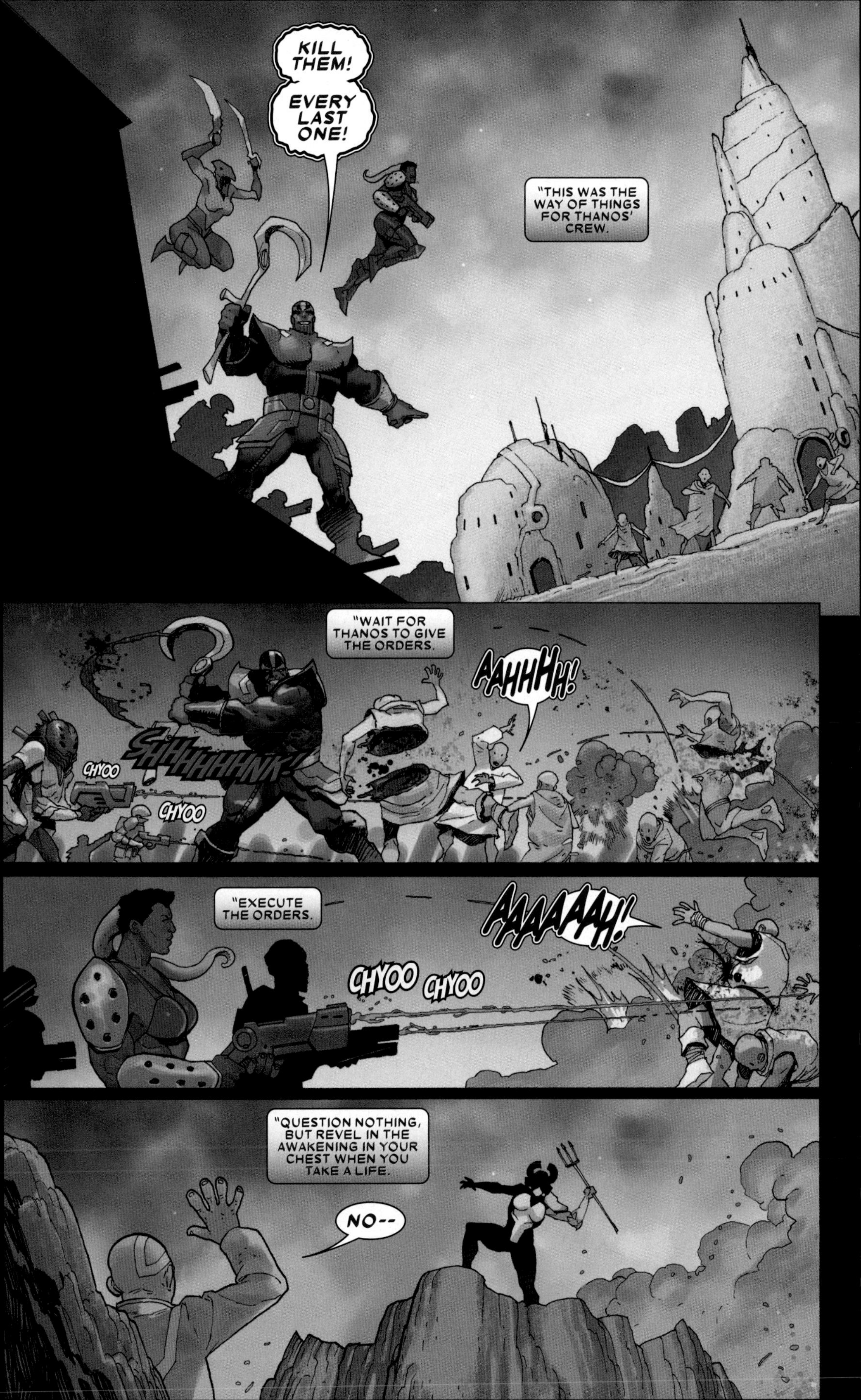
KILL THEM!
EVERY LAST ONE!
"THIS WAS THE WAY OF THINGS FOR THANOS' CREW.
"WAIT FOR THANOS TO GIVE THE ORDERS.
SHHHHHNK!
AAHHHH!
CHYOO
CHYOO
"EXECUTE THE ORDERS.
AAAAAAH!
CHYOO
CHYOO
"QUESTION NOTHING, BUT REVEL IN THE AWAKENING IN YOUR CHEST WHEN YOU TAKE A LIFE.
NO--

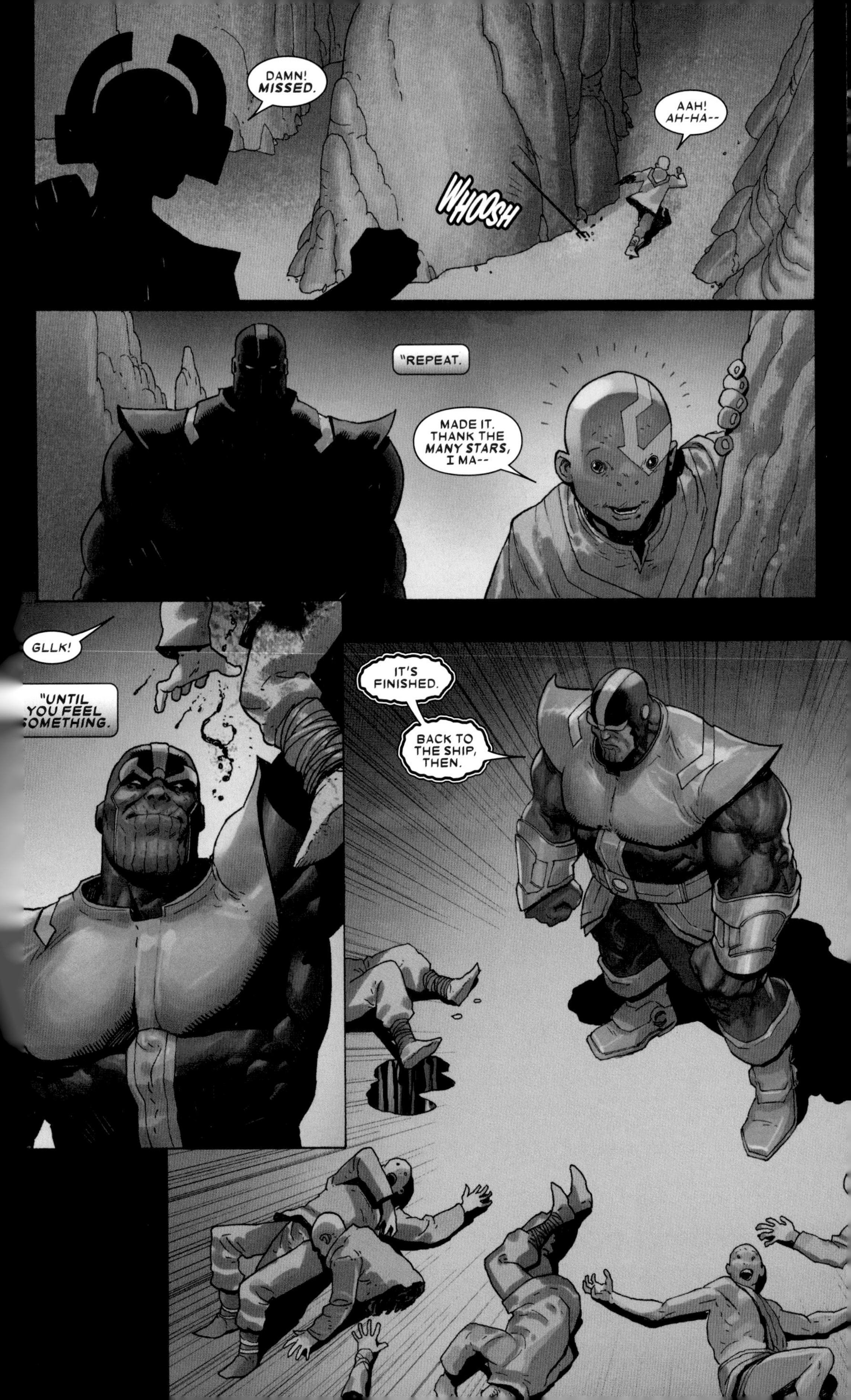

DAMN! MISSED.
AAH! AH-HA--
WHOOSH
"REPEAT.
MADE IT. THANK THE MANY STARS, I MA--
GLLK!
"UNTIL YOU FEEL SOMETHING.
IT'S FINISHED.
BACK TO THE SHIP, THEN.

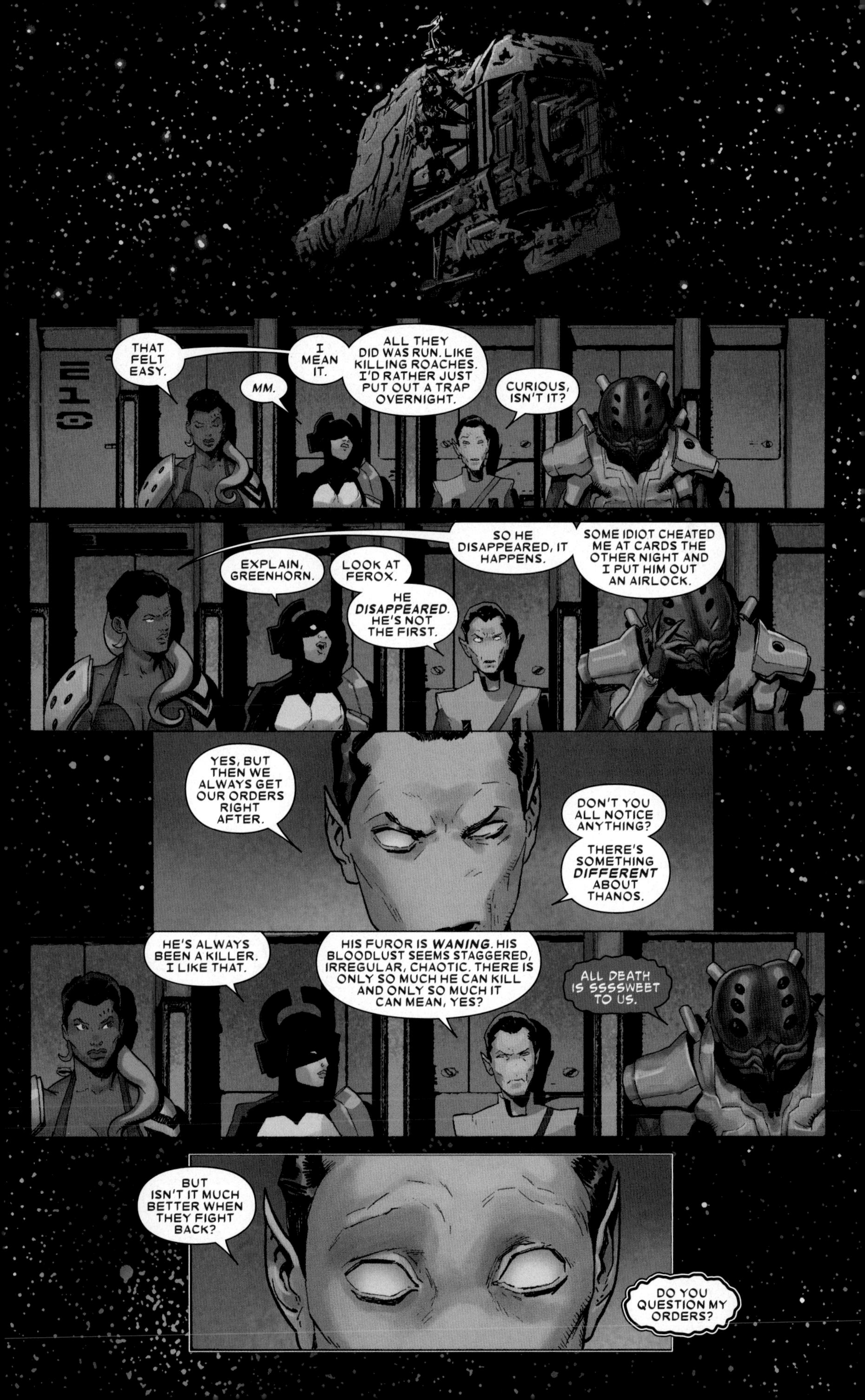

THAT FELT EASY.
MM.
I MEAN IT.
ALL THEY DID WAS RUN. LIKE KILLING ROACHES. I'D RATHER JUST PUT OUT A TRAP OVERNIGHT.
CURIOUS, ISN'T IT?
EXPLAIN, GREENHORN.
LOOK AT FEROX.
HE *DISAPPEARED*. HE'S NOT THE FIRST.
SO HE DISAPPEARED, IT HAPPENS.
SOME IDIOT CHEATED ME AT CARDS THE OTHER NIGHT AND I PUT HIM OUT AN AIRLOCK.
YES, BUT THEN WE ALWAYS GET OUR ORDERS RIGHT AFTER.
DON'T YOU ALL NOTICE ANYTHING?
THERE'S SOMETHING *DIFFERENT* ABOUT THANOS.
HE'S ALWAYS BEEN A KILLER. I LIKE THAT.
HIS FUROR IS *WANING*. HIS BLOODLUST SEEMS STAGGERED, IRREGULAR, CHAOTIC. THERE IS ONLY SO MUCH HE CAN KILL AND ONLY SO MUCH IT CAN MEAN, YES?
ALL DEATH IS SSSSWEET TO US.
BUT ISN'T IT MUCH BETTER WHEN THEY FIGHT BACK?
DO YOU QUESTION MY ORDERS?

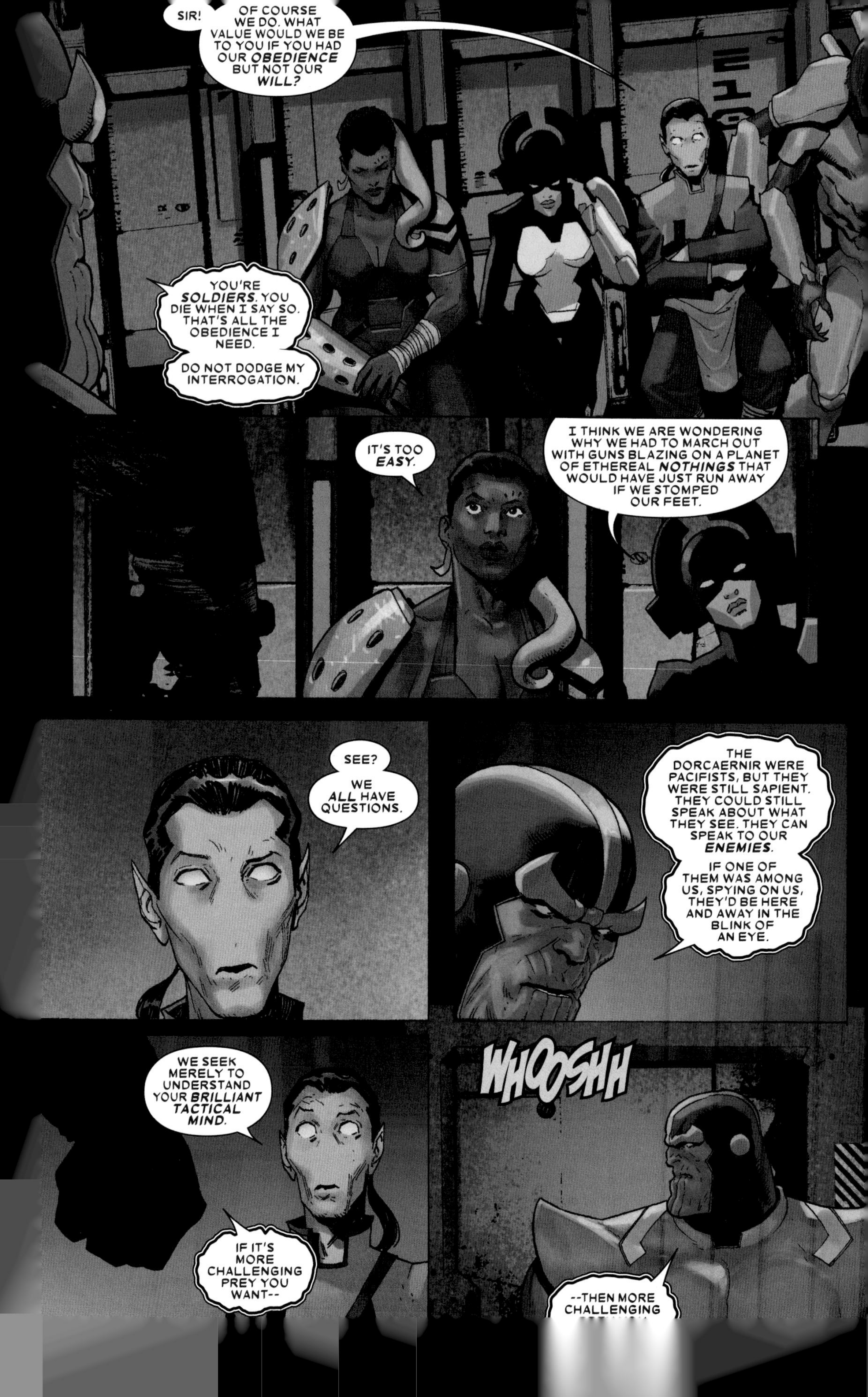
SIR!
OF COURSE WE DO. WHAT VALUE WOULD WE BE TO YOU IF YOU HAD OUR OBEDIENCE BUT NOT OUR WILL?
YOU'RE SOLDIERS. YOU DIE WHEN I SAY SO. THAT'S ALL THE OBEDIENCE I NEED.
DO NOT DODGE MY INTERROGATION.
IT'S TOO EASY.
I THINK WE ARE WONDERING WHY WE HAD TO MARCH OUT WITH GUNS BLAZING ON A PLANET OF ETHEREAL NOTHINGS THAT WOULD HAVE JUST RUN AWAY IF WE STOMPED OUR FEET.
SEE?
WE ALL HAVE QUESTIONS.
THE DORCAERNIR WERE PACIFISTS, BUT THEY WERE STILL SAPIENT. THEY COULD STILL SPEAK ABOUT WHAT THEY SEE. THEY CAN SPEAK TO OUR ENEMIES.
IF ONE OF THEM WAS AMONG US, SPYING ON US, THEY'D BE HERE AND AWAY IN THE BLINK OF AN EYE.
WE SEEK MERELY TO UNDERSTAND YOUR BRILLIANT TACTICAL MIND.
IF IT'S MORE CHALLENGING PREY YOU WANT--
WHOOSHH
--THEN MORE CHALLENGING

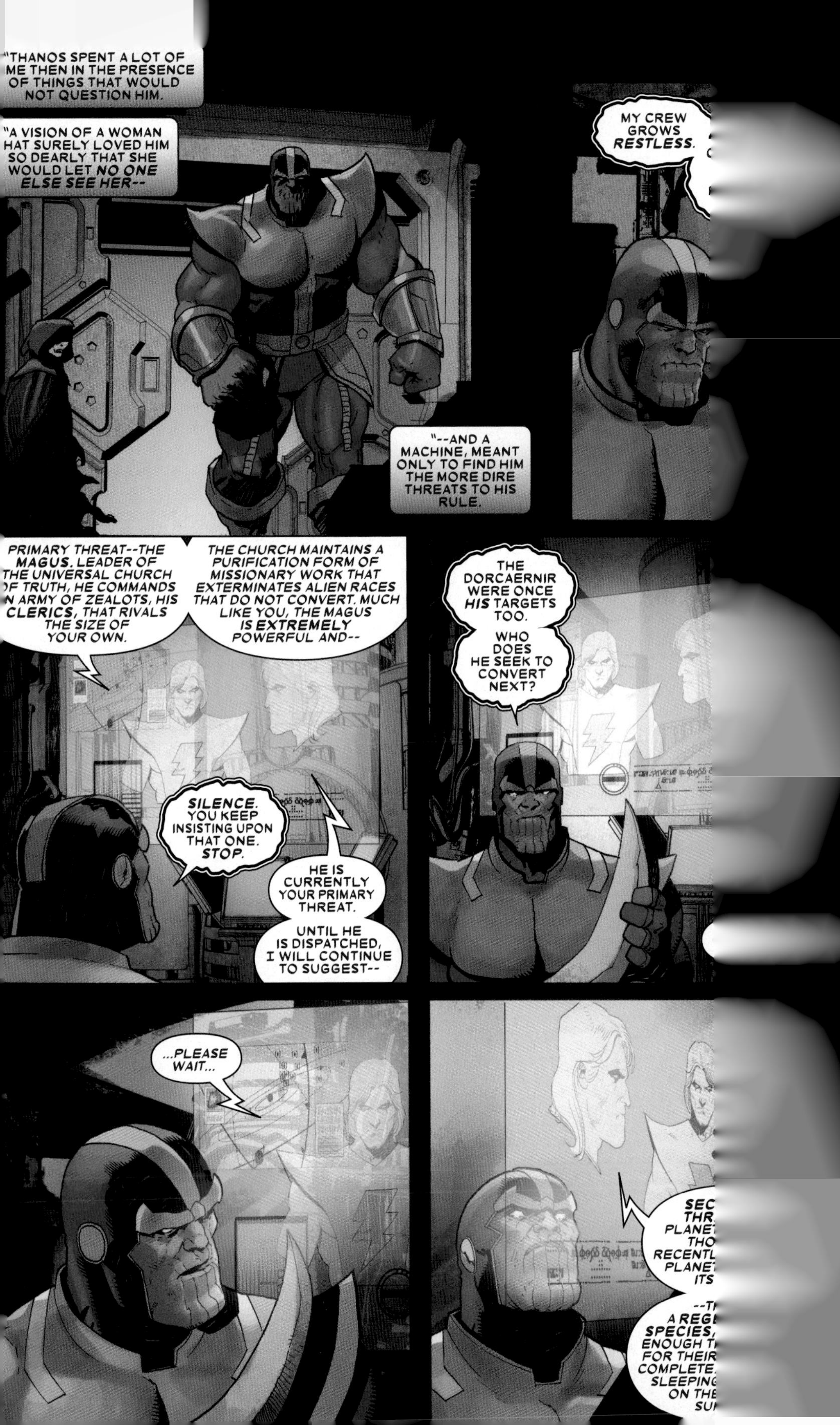
"THANOS SPENT A LOT OF ME THEN IN THE PRESENCE OF THINGS THAT WOULD NOT QUESTION HIM.
"A VISION OF A WOMAN HAT SURELY LOVED HIM SO DEARLY THAT SHE WOULD LET NO ONE ELSE SEE HER--
"--AND A MACHINE, MEANT ONLY TO FIND HIM THE MORE DIRE THREATS TO HIS RULE.
MY CREW GROWS RESTLESS.
PRIMARY THREAT--THE MAGUS. LEADER OF THE UNIVERSAL CHURCH OF TRUTH, HE COMMANDS N ARMY OF ZEALOTS, HIS CLERICS, THAT RIVALS THE SIZE OF YOUR OWN.
THE CHURCH MAINTAINS A PURIFICATION FORM OF MISSIONARY WORK THAT EXTERMINATES ALIEN RACES THAT DO NOT CONVERT. MUCH LIKE YOU, THE MAGUS IS EXTREMELY POWERFUL AND--
SILENCE. YOU KEEP INSISTING UPON THAT ONE. STOP.
HE IS CURRENTLY YOUR PRIMARY THREAT.
UNTIL HE IS DISPATCHED, I WILL CONTINUE TO SUGGEST--
THE DORCAERNIR WERE ONCE HIS TARGETS TOO.
WHO DOES HE SEEK TO CONVERT NEXT?
...PLEASE WAIT...

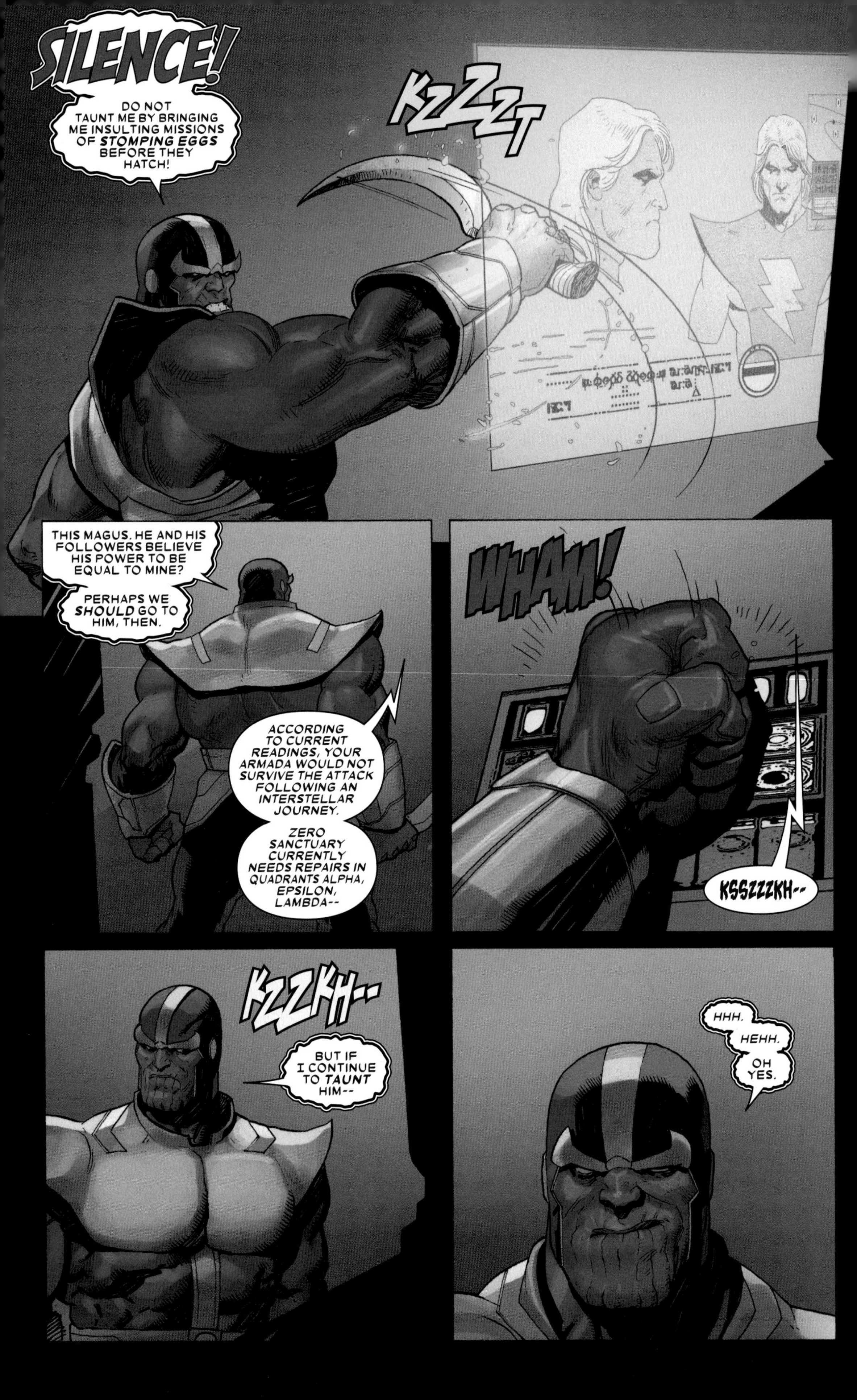
SILENCE!
DO NOT TAUNT ME BY BRINGING ME INSULTING MISSIONS OF STOMPING EGGS BEFORE THEY HATCH!
KZZZT
THIS MAGUS. HE AND HIS FOLLOWERS BELIEVE HIS POWER TO BE EQUAL TO MINE?
PERHAPS WE SHOULD GO TO HIM, THEN.
ACCORDING TO CURRENT READINGS, YOUR ARMADA WOULD NOT SURVIVE THE ATTACK FOLLOWING AN INTERSTELLAR JOURNEY.
ZERO SANCTUARY CURRENTLY NEEDS REPAIRS IN QUADRANTS ALPHA, EPSILON, LAMBDA--
WHAM!
KSSZZZKH--
KZZKH--
BUT IF I CONTINUE TO TAUNT HIM--
HHH.
HEHH.
OH YES.

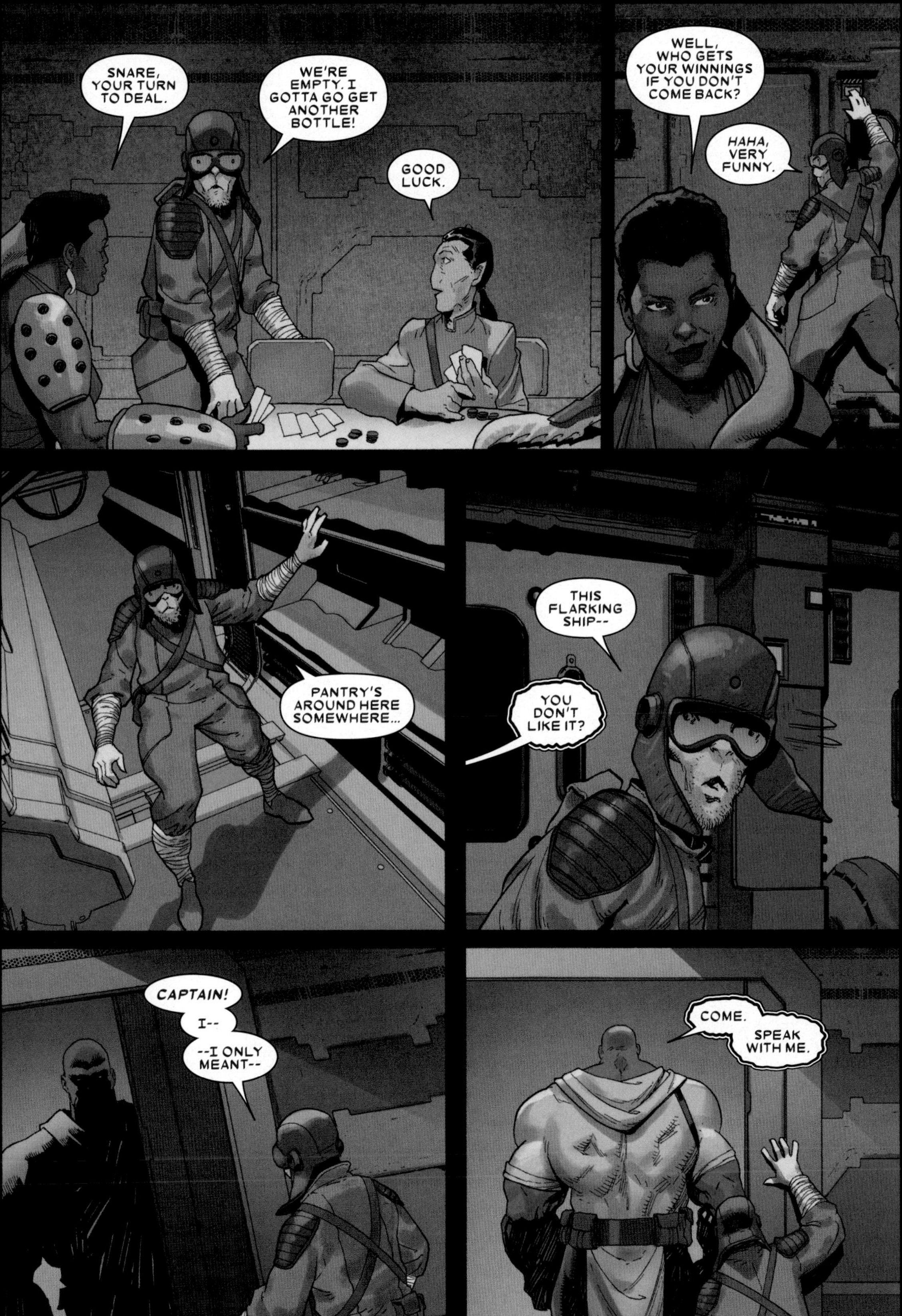
SNARE, YOUR TURN TO DEAL.
WE'RE EMPTY. I GOTTA GO GET ANOTHER BOTTLE!
GOOD LUCK.
WELL, WHO GETS YOUR WINNINGS IF YOU DON'T COME BACK?
HAHA, VERY FUNNY.
PANTRY'S AROUND HERE SOMEWHERE...
THIS FLARKING SHIP--
YOU DON'T LIKE IT?
CAPTAIN!
I--
--I ONLY MEANT--
COME.
SPEAK WITH ME.

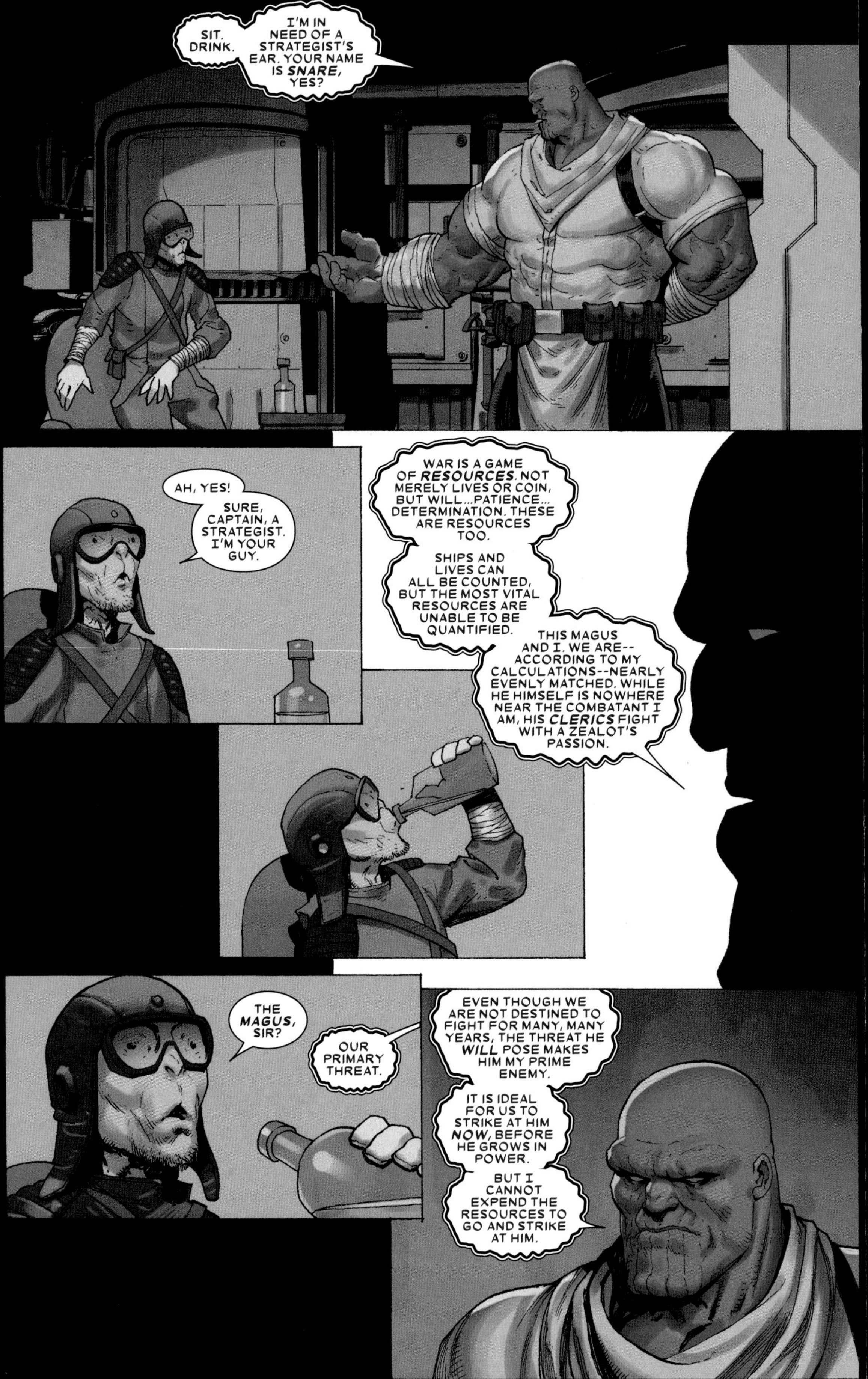

SIT. DRINK.
I'M IN NEED OF A STRATEGIST'S EAR. YOUR NAME IS SNARE, YES?
AH, YES!
SURE, CAPTAIN, A STRATEGIST. I'M YOUR GUY.
WAR IS A GAME OF RESOURCES. NOT MERELY LIVES OR COIN, BUT WILL...PATIENCE... DETERMINATION. THESE ARE RESOURCES TOO.
SHIPS AND LIVES CAN ALL BE COUNTED, BUT THE MOST VITAL RESOURCES ARE UNABLE TO BE QUANTIFIED.
THIS MAGUS AND I. WE ARE--ACCORDING TO MY CALCULATIONS--NEARLY EVENLY MATCHED. WHILE HE HIMSELF IS NOWHERE NEAR THE COMBATANT I AM, HIS CLERICS FIGHT WITH A ZEALOT'S PASSION.
THE MAGUS, SIR?
OUR PRIMARY THREAT.
EVEN THOUGH WE ARE NOT DESTINED TO FIGHT FOR MANY, MANY YEARS, THE THREAT HE WILL POSE MAKES HIM MY PRIME ENEMY.
IT IS IDEAL FOR US TO STRIKE AT HIM NOW, BEFORE HE GROWS IN POWER.
BUT I CANNOT EXPEND THE RESOURCES TO GO AND STRIKE AT HIM.

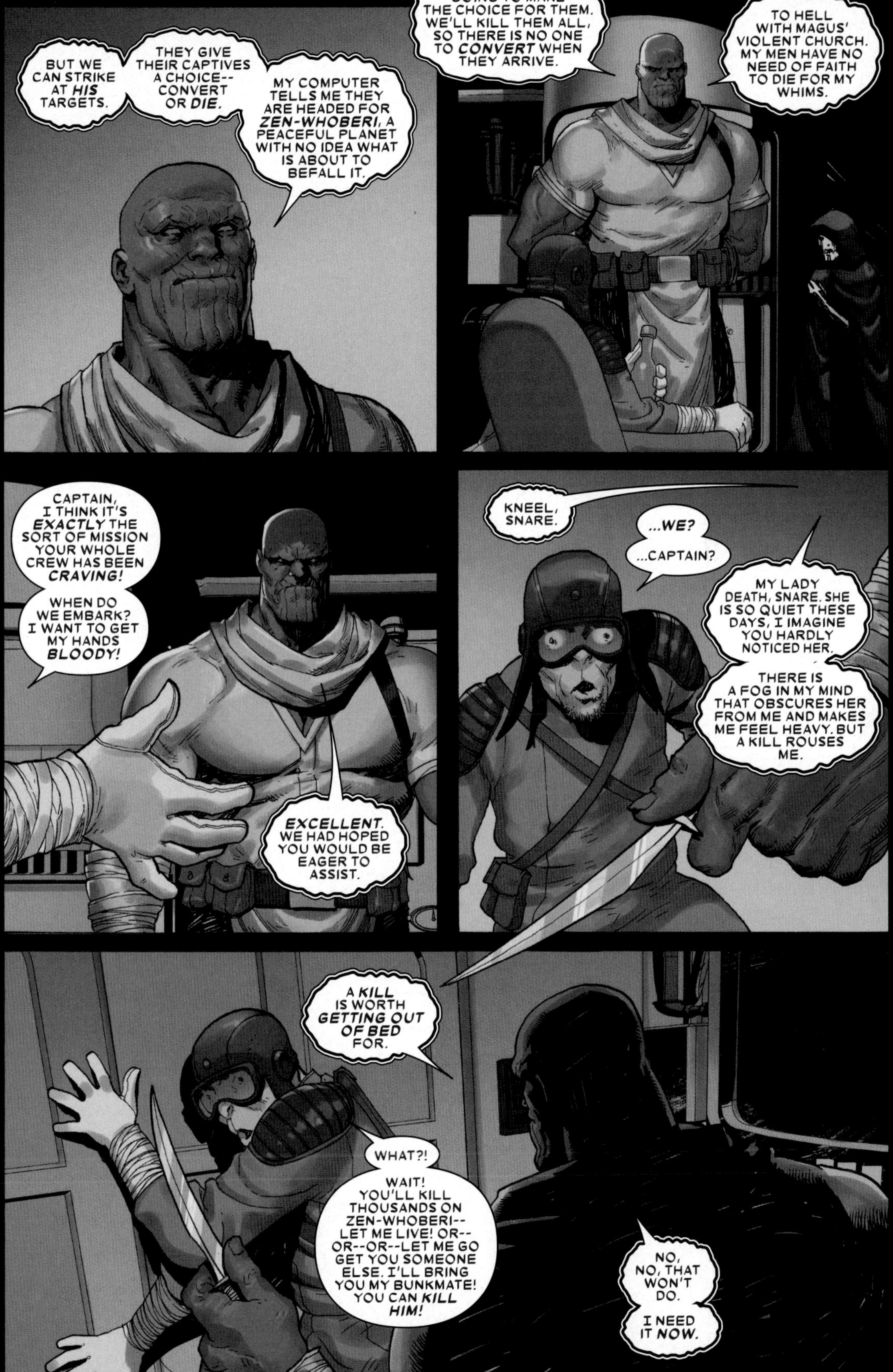
BUT WE CAN STRIKE AT HIS TARGETS.
THEY GIVE THEIR CAPTIVES A CHOICE-- CONVERT OR DIE.
MY COMPUTER TELLS ME THEY ARE HEADED FOR ZEN-WHOBERI, A PEACEFUL PLANET WITH NO IDEA WHAT IS ABOUT TO BEFALL IT.
WE'RE GOING TO MAKE THE CHOICE FOR THEM. WE'LL KILL THEM ALL, SO THERE IS NO ONE TO CONVERT WHEN THEY ARRIVE.
TO HELL WITH MAGUS' VIOLENT CHURCH. MY MEN HAVE NO NEED OF FAITH TO DIE FOR MY WHIMS.
CAPTAIN, I THINK IT'S EXACTLY THE SORT OF MISSION YOUR WHOLE CREW HAS BEEN CRAVING!
WHEN DO WE EMBARK? I WANT TO GET MY HANDS BLOODY!
EXCELLENT. WE HAD HOPED YOU WOULD BE EAGER TO ASSIST.
KNEEL, SNARE.
...WE?
...CAPTAIN?
MY LADY DEATH, SNARE. SHE IS SO QUIET THESE DAYS, I IMAGINE YOU HARDLY NOTICED HER.
THERE IS A FOG IN MY MIND THAT OBSCURES HER FROM ME AND MAKES ME FEEL HEAVY. BUT A KILL ROUSES ME.
A KILL IS WORTH GETTING OUT OF BED FOR.
WHAT?!
WAIT! YOU'LL KILL THOUSANDS ON ZEN-WHOBERI-- LET ME LIVE! OR-- OR--OR--LET ME GO GET YOU SOMEONE ELSE. I'LL BRING YOU MY BUNKMATE! YOU CAN KILL HIM!
NO, NO, THAT WON'T DO.
I NEED IT NOW.

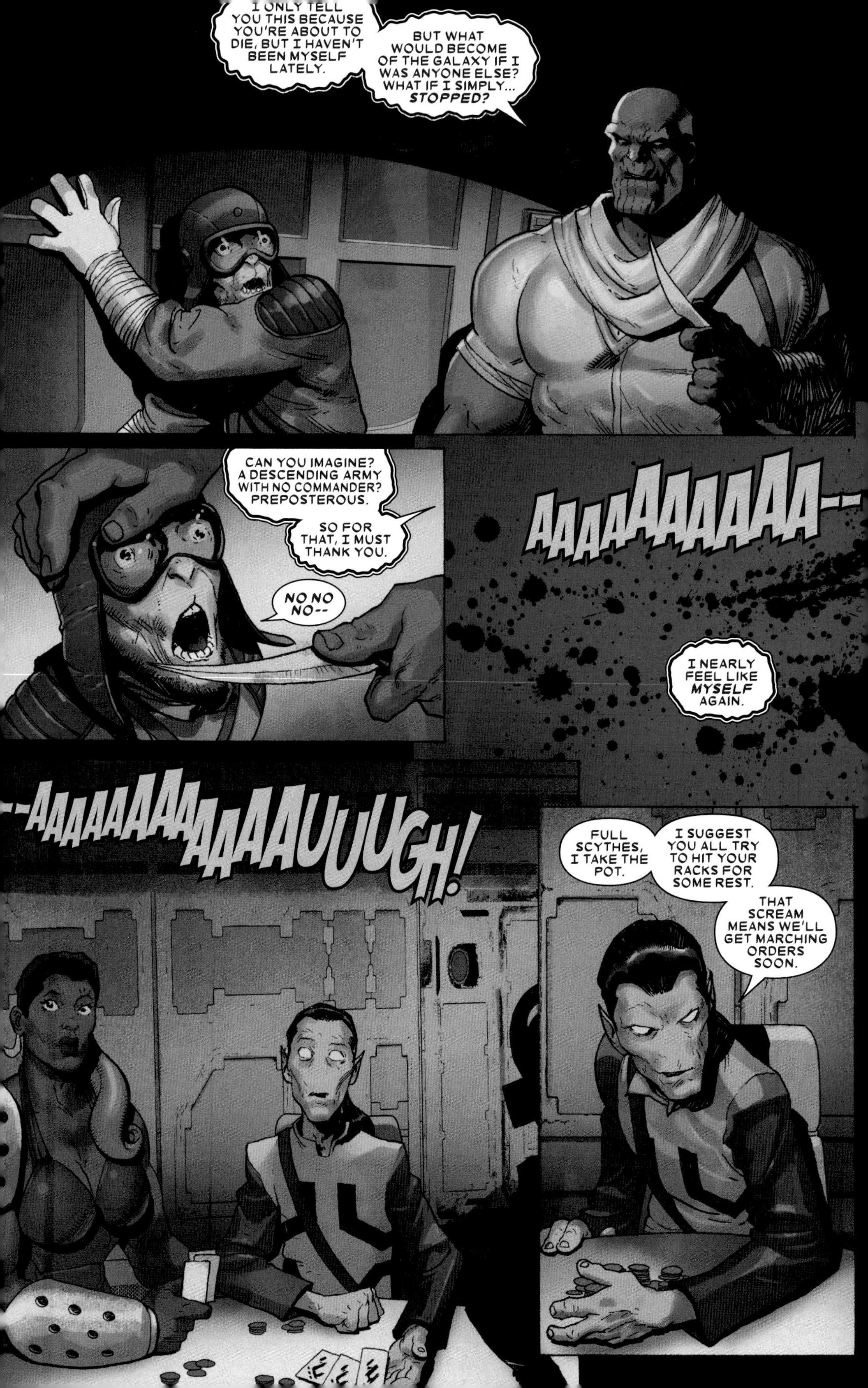
I ONLY TELL YOU THIS BECAUSE YOU'RE ABOUT TO DIE, BUT I HAVEN'T BEEN MYSELF LATELY.
BUT WHAT WOULD BECOME OF THE GALAXY IF I WAS ANYONE ELSE? WHAT IF I SIMPLY... STOPPED?
CAN YOU IMAGINE? A DESCENDING ARMY WITH NO COMMANDER? PREPOSTEROUS.
SO FOR THAT, I MUST THANK YOU.
NO NO NO--
AAAAAAAAAA--
I NEARLY FEEL LIKE MYSELF AGAIN.
--AAAAAAAAAAAAAUUUUGH!
FULL SCYTHES, I TAKE THE POT.
I SUGGEST YOU ALL TRY TO HIT YOUR RACKS FOR SOME REST.
THAT SCREAM MEANS WE'LL GET MARCHING ORDERS SOON.

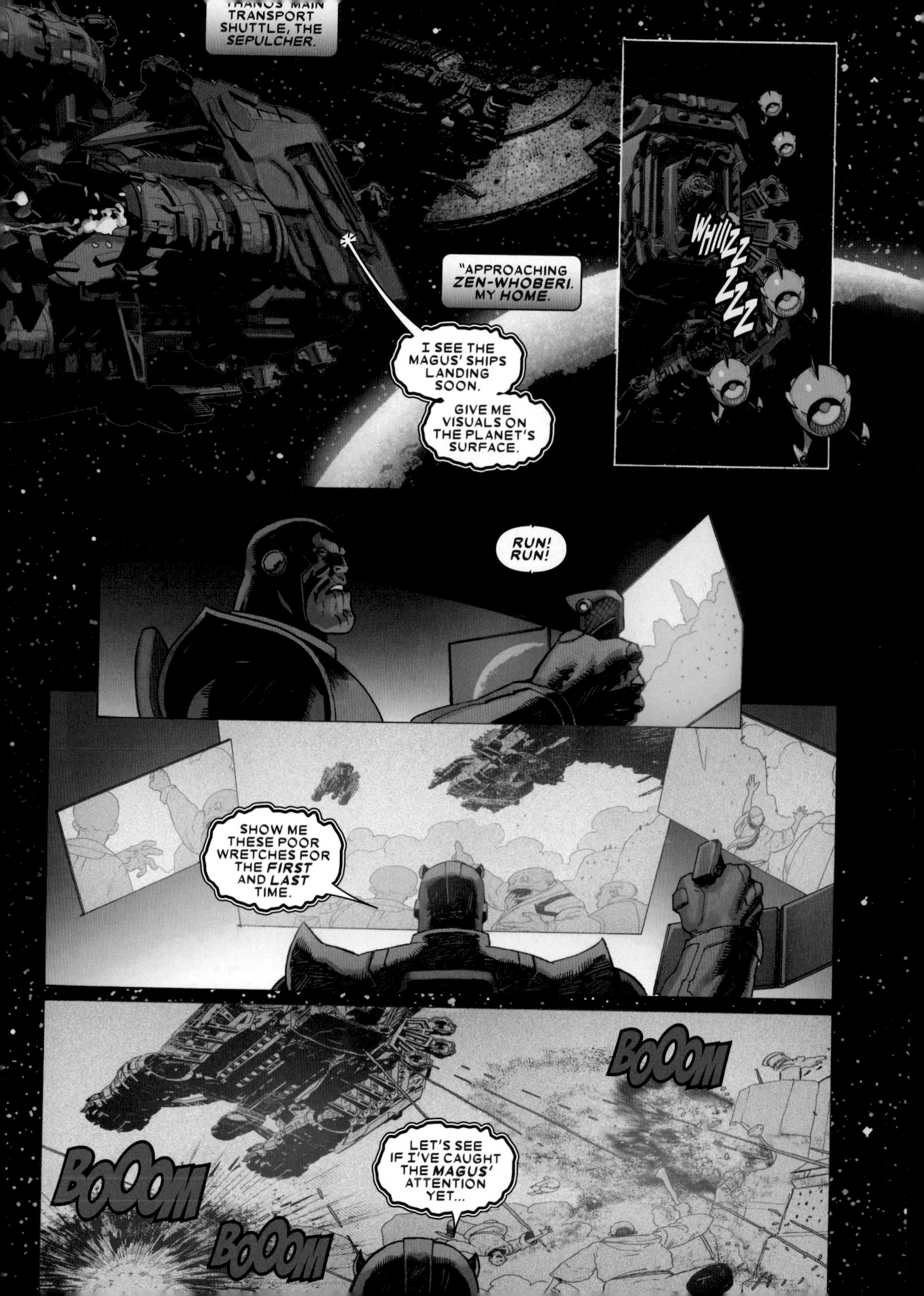
THANOS' MAIN TRANSPORT SHUTTLE, THE SEPULCHER.
"APPROACHING ZEN-WHOBERI. MY HOME.
I SEE THE MAGUS' SHIPS LANDING SOON.
GIVE ME VISUALS ON THE PLANET'S SURFACE.
WHIIIZZZZZ
RUN! RUN!
SHOW ME THESE POOR WRETCHES FOR THE FIRST AND LAST TIME.
BOOOM
BOOOM
LET'S SEE IF I'VE CAUGHT THE MAGUS' ATTENTION YET...
BOOOM

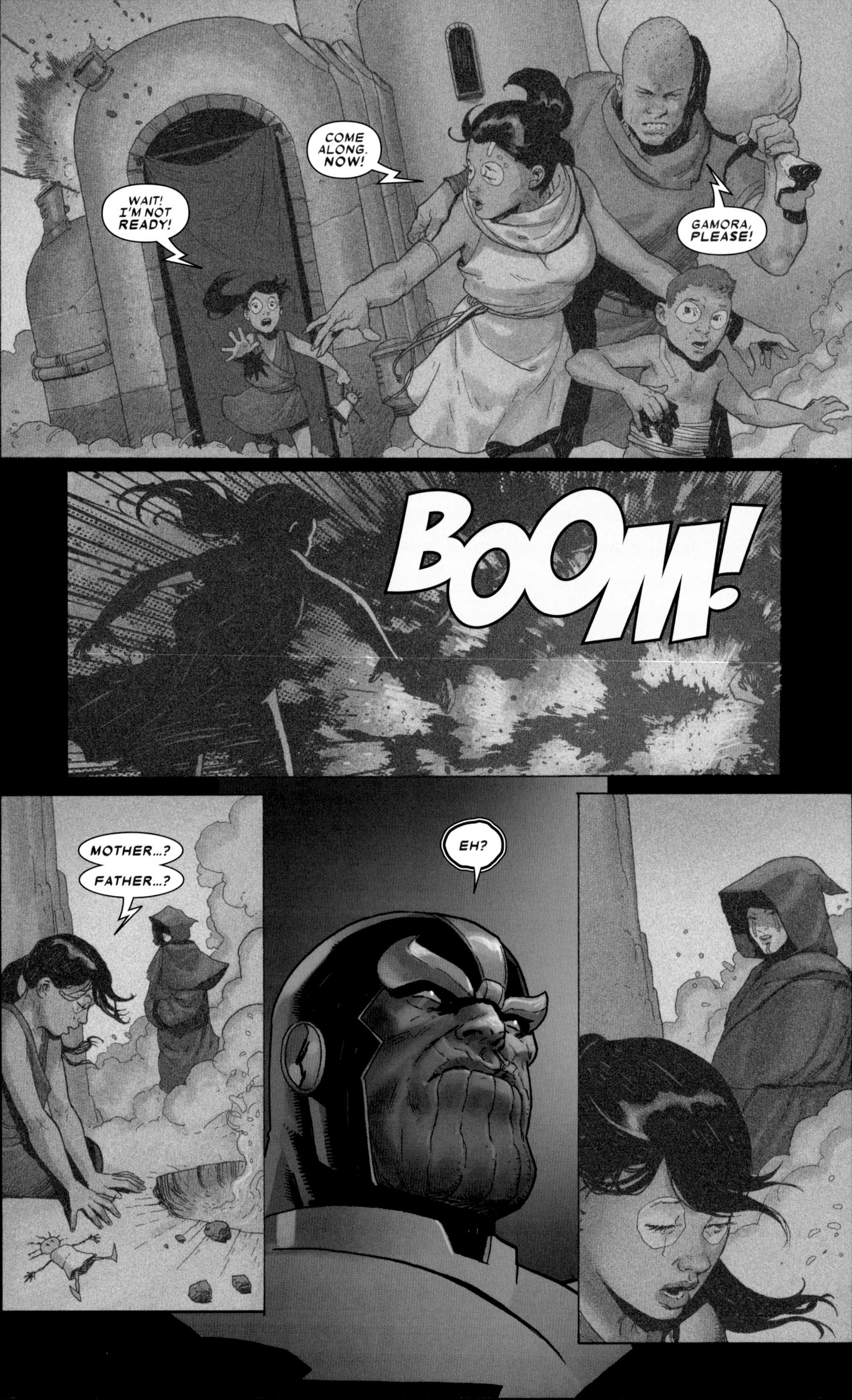
WAIT! I'M NOT READY!
COME ALONG. NOW!
GAMORA, PLEASE!
BOOM!
MOTHER...?
FATHER...?
EH?

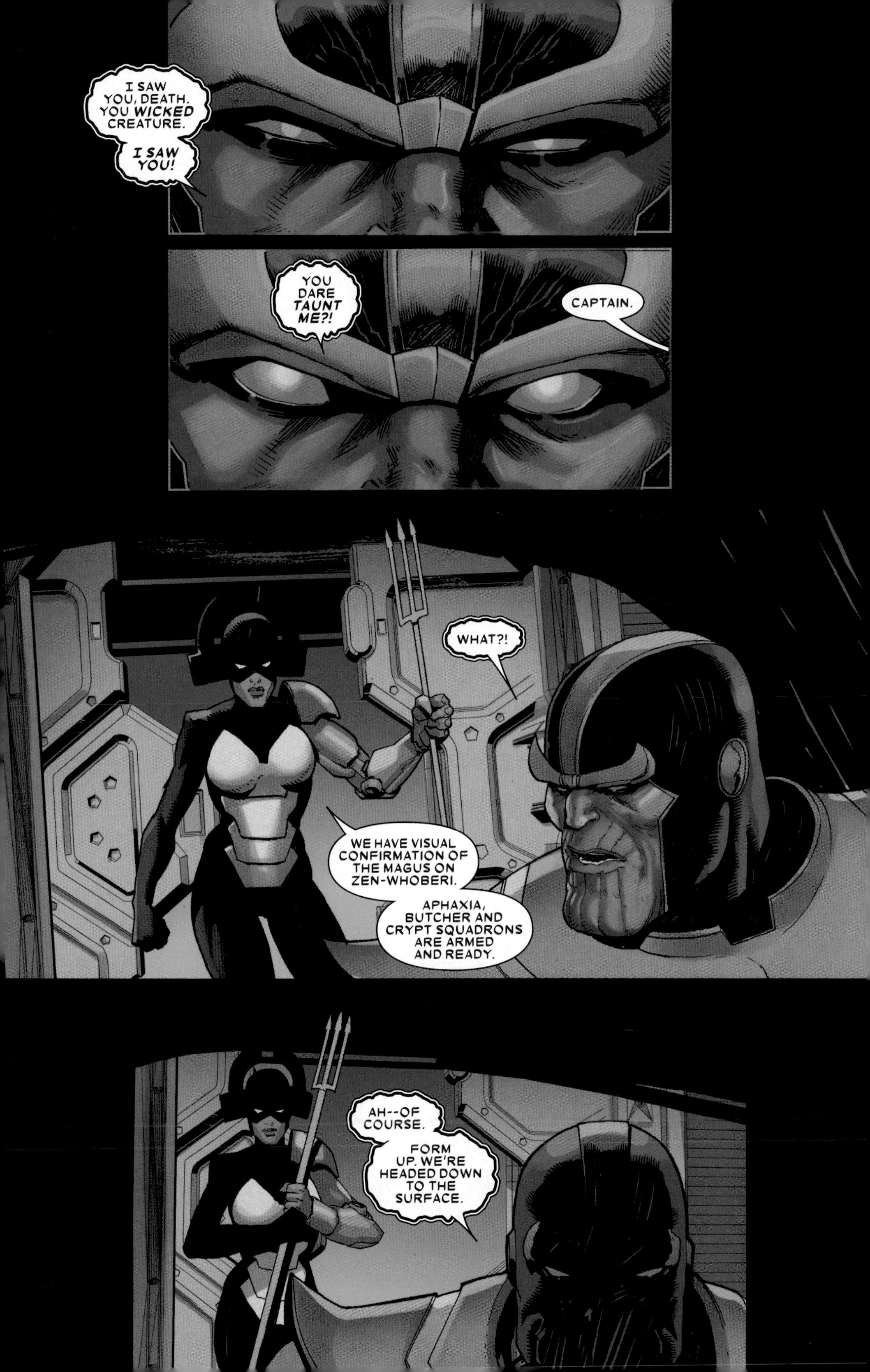
I SAW YOU, DEATH. YOU WICKED CREATURE.
I SAW YOU!
YOU DARE TAUNT ME?!
CAPTAIN.
WHAT?!
WE HAVE VISUAL CONFIRMATION OF THE MAGUS ON ZEN-WHOBERI.
APHAXIA, BUTCHER AND CRYPT SQUADRONS ARE ARMED AND READY.
AH--OF COURSE.
FORM UP. WE'RE HEADED DOWN TO THE SURFACE.

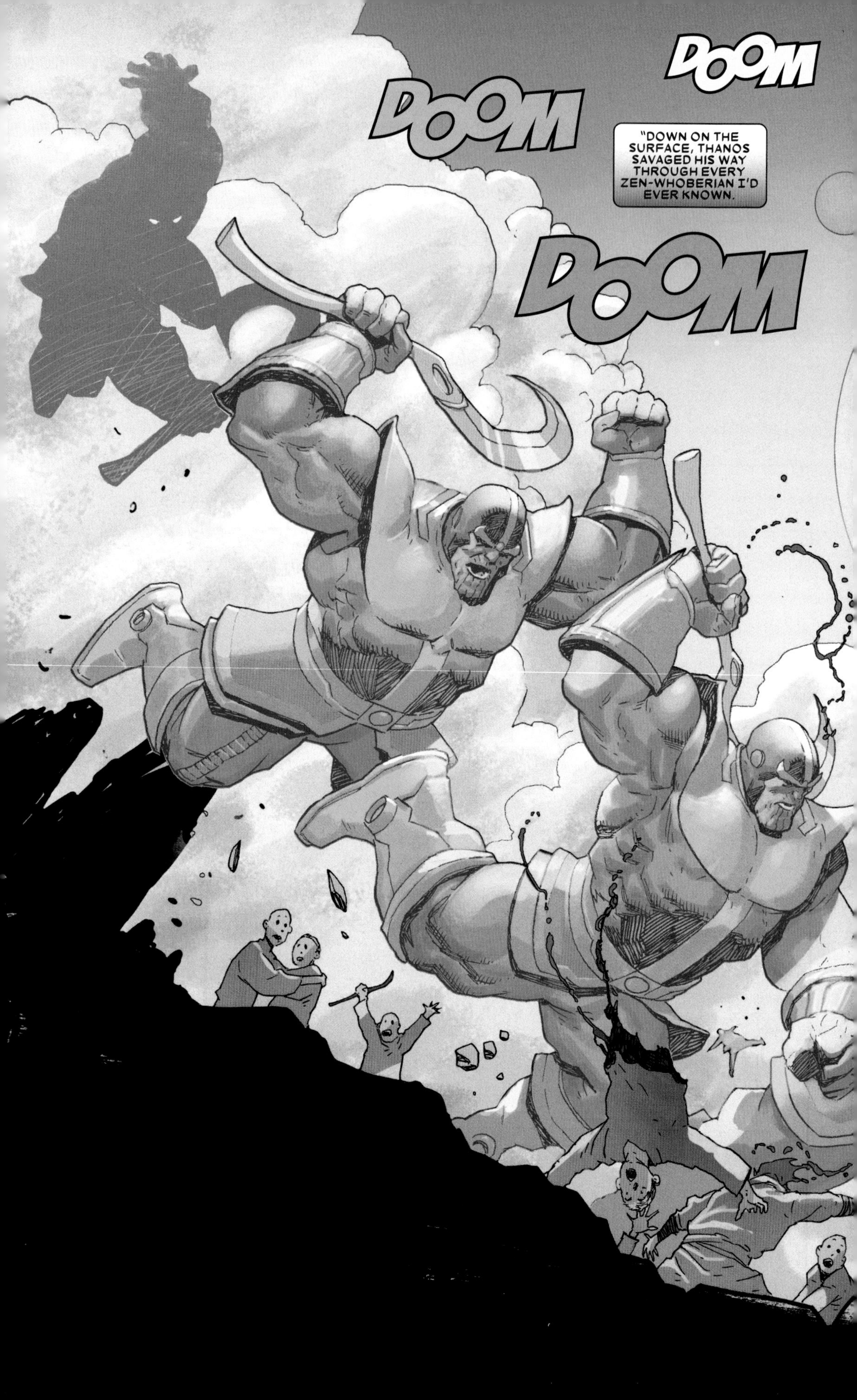
DOOM
DOOM
"DOWN ON THE SURFACE, THANOS SAVAGED HIS WAY THROUGH EVERY ZEN-WHOBERIAN I'D EVER KNOWN.
DOOM

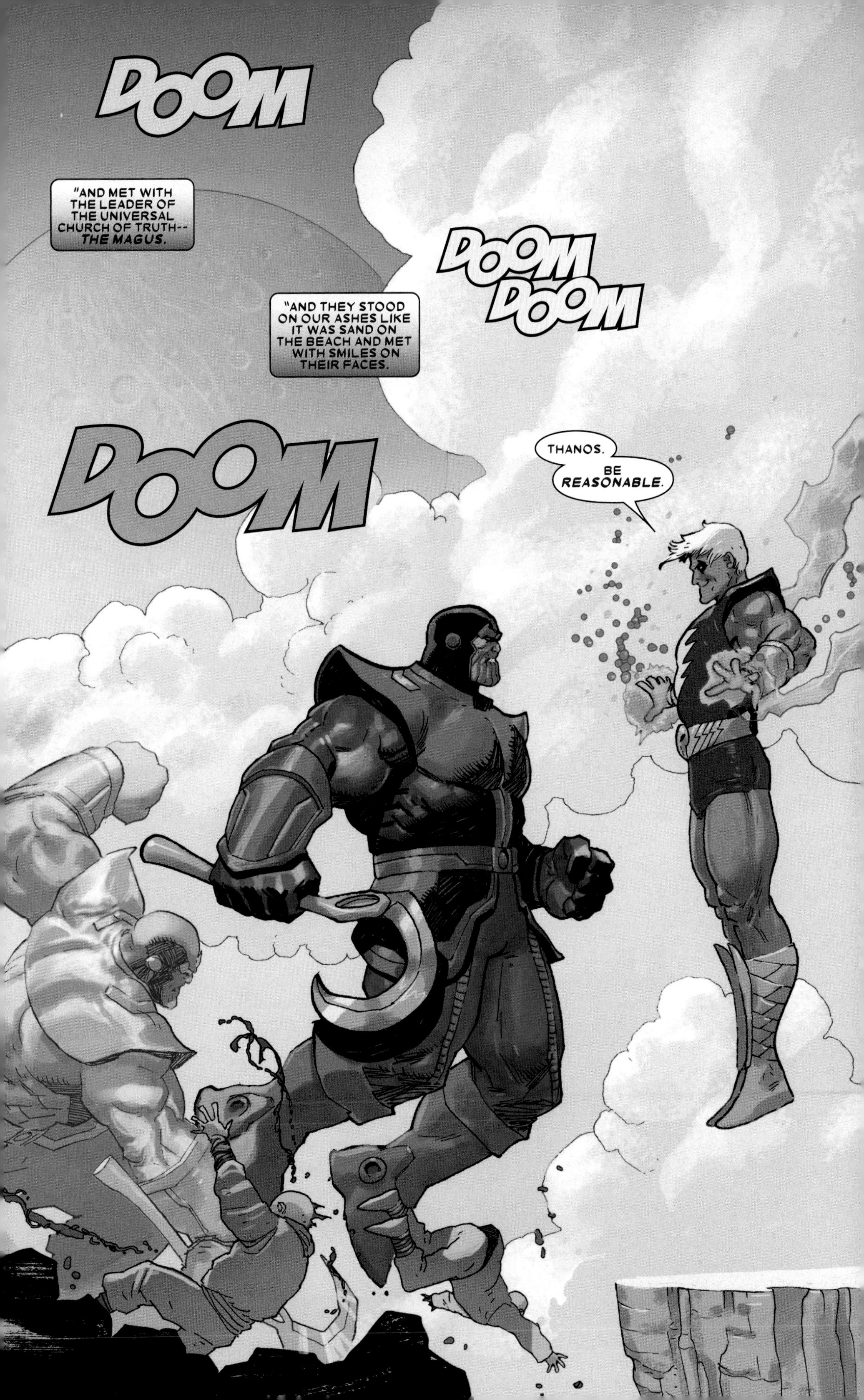
DOOM
"AND MET WITH THE LEADER OF THE UNIVERSAL CHURCH OF TRUTH-- THE MAGUS.
DOOM DOOM
"AND THEY STOOD ON OUR ASHES LIKE IT WAS SAND ON THE BEACH AND MET WITH SMILES ON THEIR FACES.
DOOM
THANOS.
BE REASONABLE.

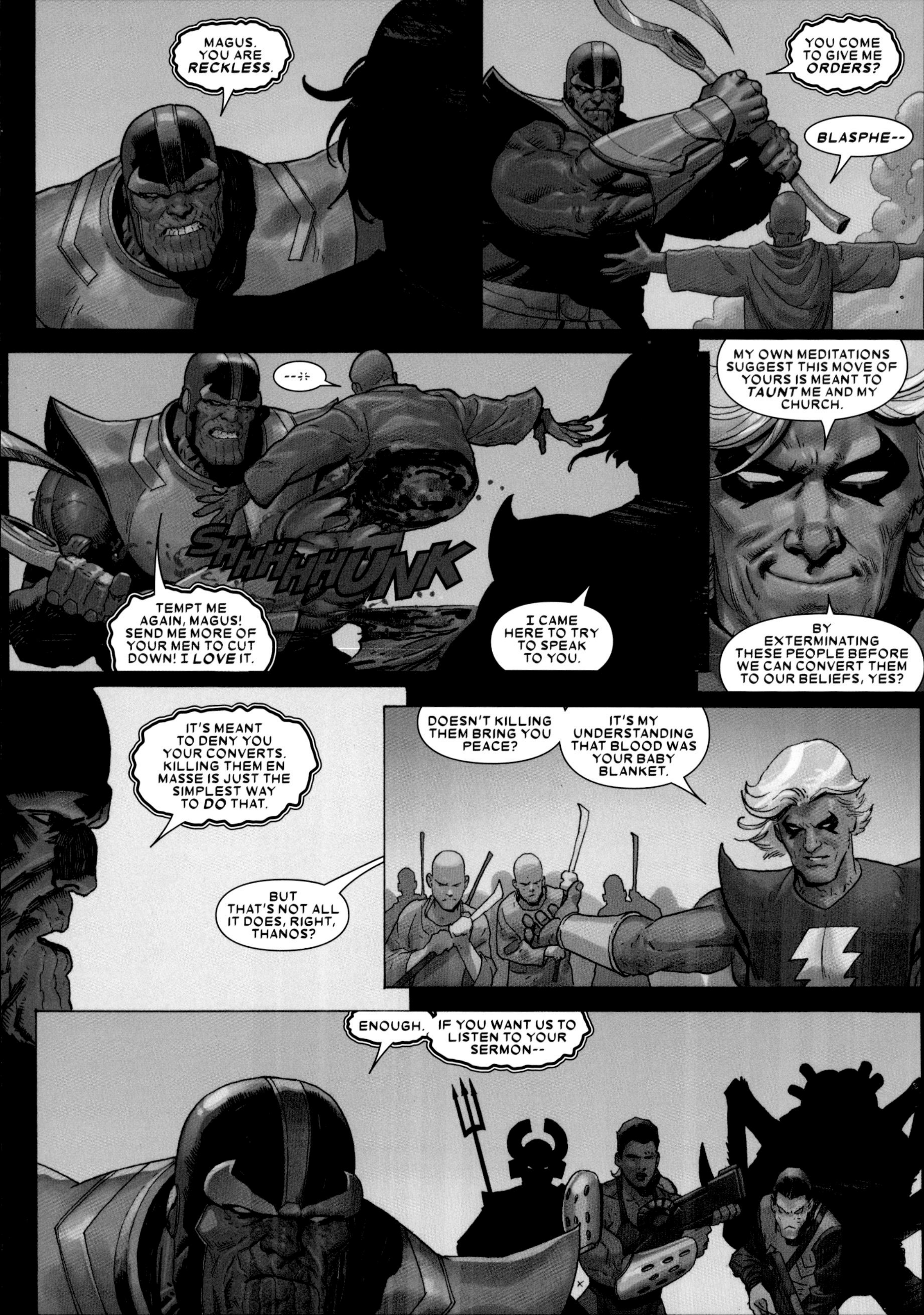
MAGUS. YOU ARE RECKLESS.
YOU COME TO GIVE ME ORDERS?
BLASPHE--
--!
SHHHHHUNK
TEMPT ME AGAIN, MAGUS! SEND ME MORE OF YOUR MEN TO CUT DOWN! I LOVE IT.
I CAME HERE TO TRY TO SPEAK TO YOU.
MY OWN MEDITATIONS SUGGEST THIS MOVE OF YOURS IS MEANT TO TAUNT ME AND MY CHURCH.
BY EXTERMINATING THESE PEOPLE BEFORE WE CAN CONVERT THEM TO OUR BELIEFS, YES?
IT'S MEANT TO DENY YOU YOUR CONVERTS. KILLING THEM EN MASSE IS JUST THE SIMPLEST WAY TO DO THAT.
BUT THAT'S NOT ALL IT DOES, RIGHT, THANOS?
DOESN'T KILLING THEM BRING YOU PEACE?
IT'S MY UNDERSTANDING THAT BLOOD WAS YOUR BABY BLANKET.
ENOUGH.
IF YOU WANT US TO LISTEN TO YOUR SERMON--

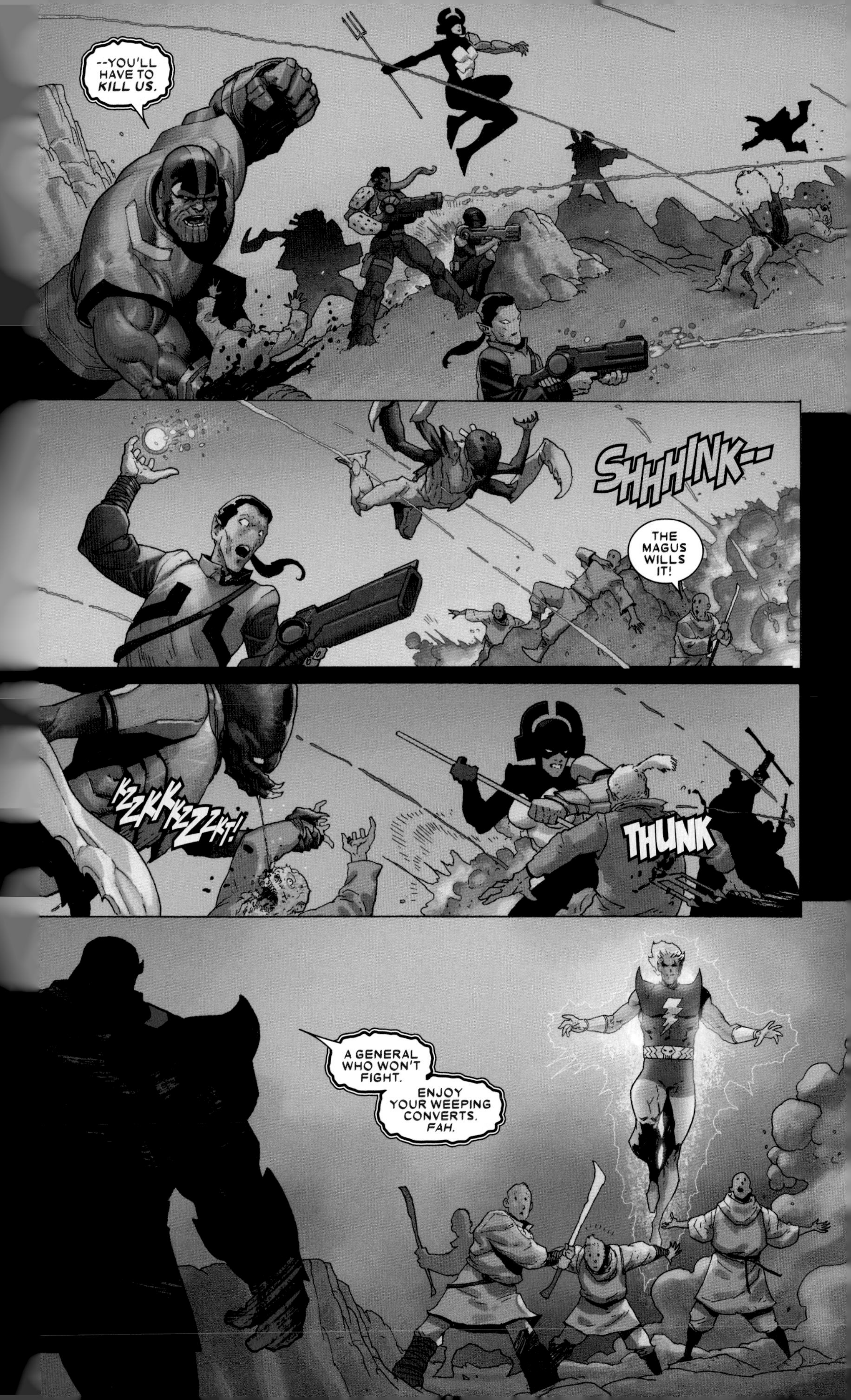
--YOU'LL HAVE TO KILL US.
SHHHINK--
THE MAGUS WILLS IT!
KZZKKKZZZKT!
THUNK
A GENERAL WHO WON'T FIGHT.
ENJOY YOUR WEEPING CONVERTS. FAH.

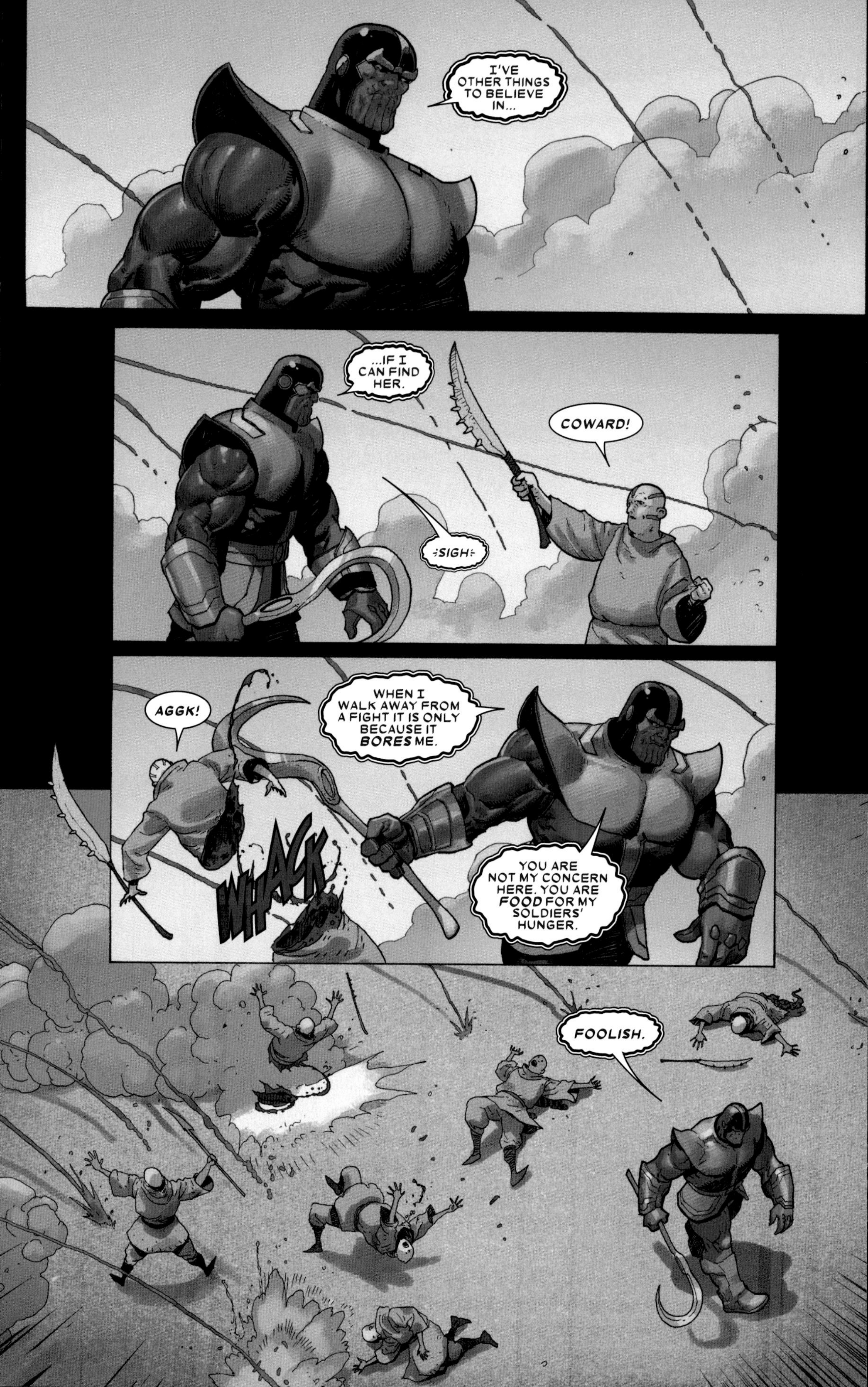
I'VE OTHER THINGS TO BELIEVE IN...
...IF I CAN FIND HER.
COWARD!
SIGH
AGGK!
WHEN I WALK AWAY FROM A FIGHT IT IS ONLY BECAUSE IT BORES ME.
WHACK
YOU ARE NOT MY CONCERN HERE. YOU ARE FOOD FOR MY SOLDIERS' HUNGER.
FOOLISH.

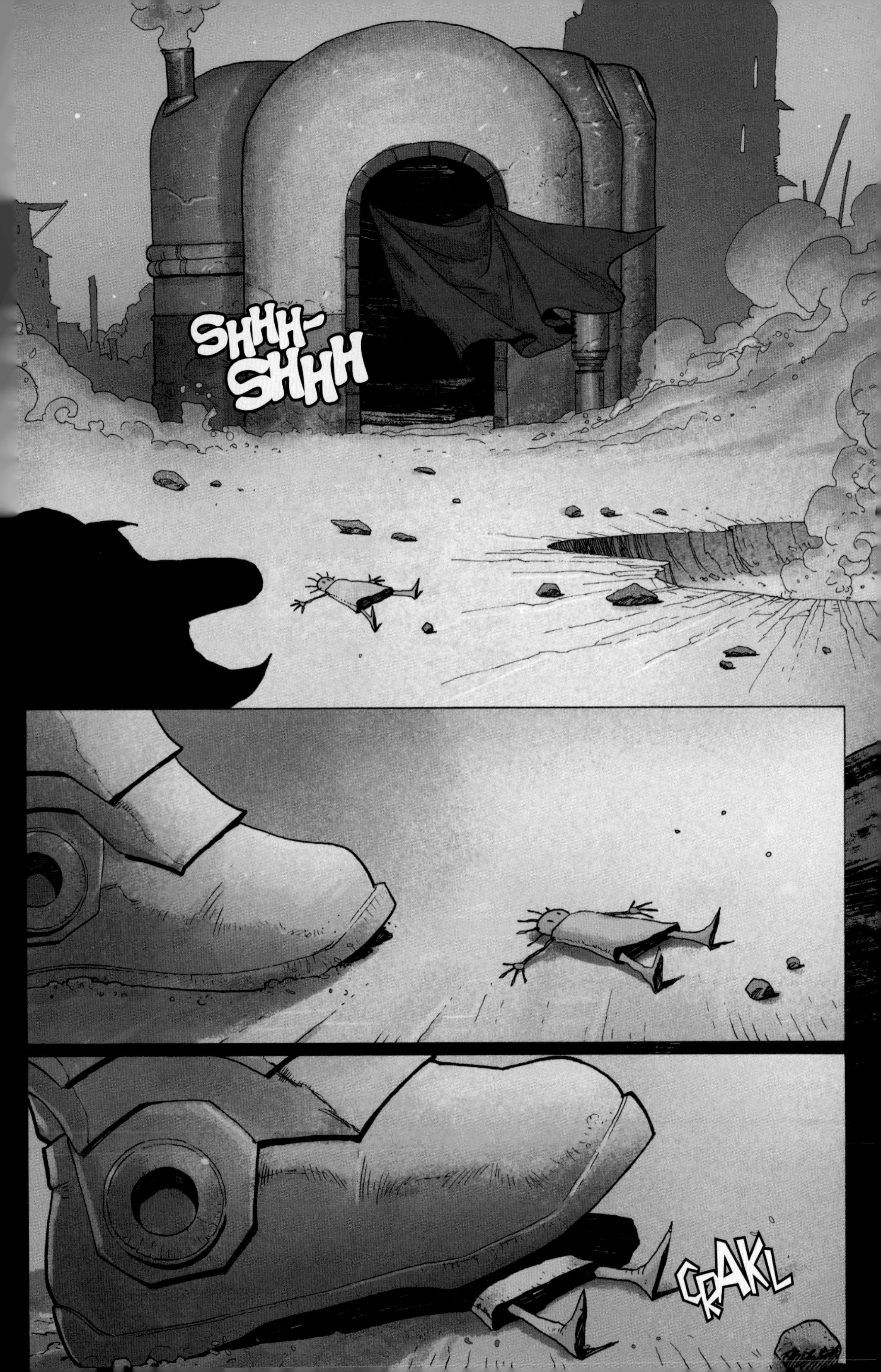
SHHH-SHHH
CRAKL

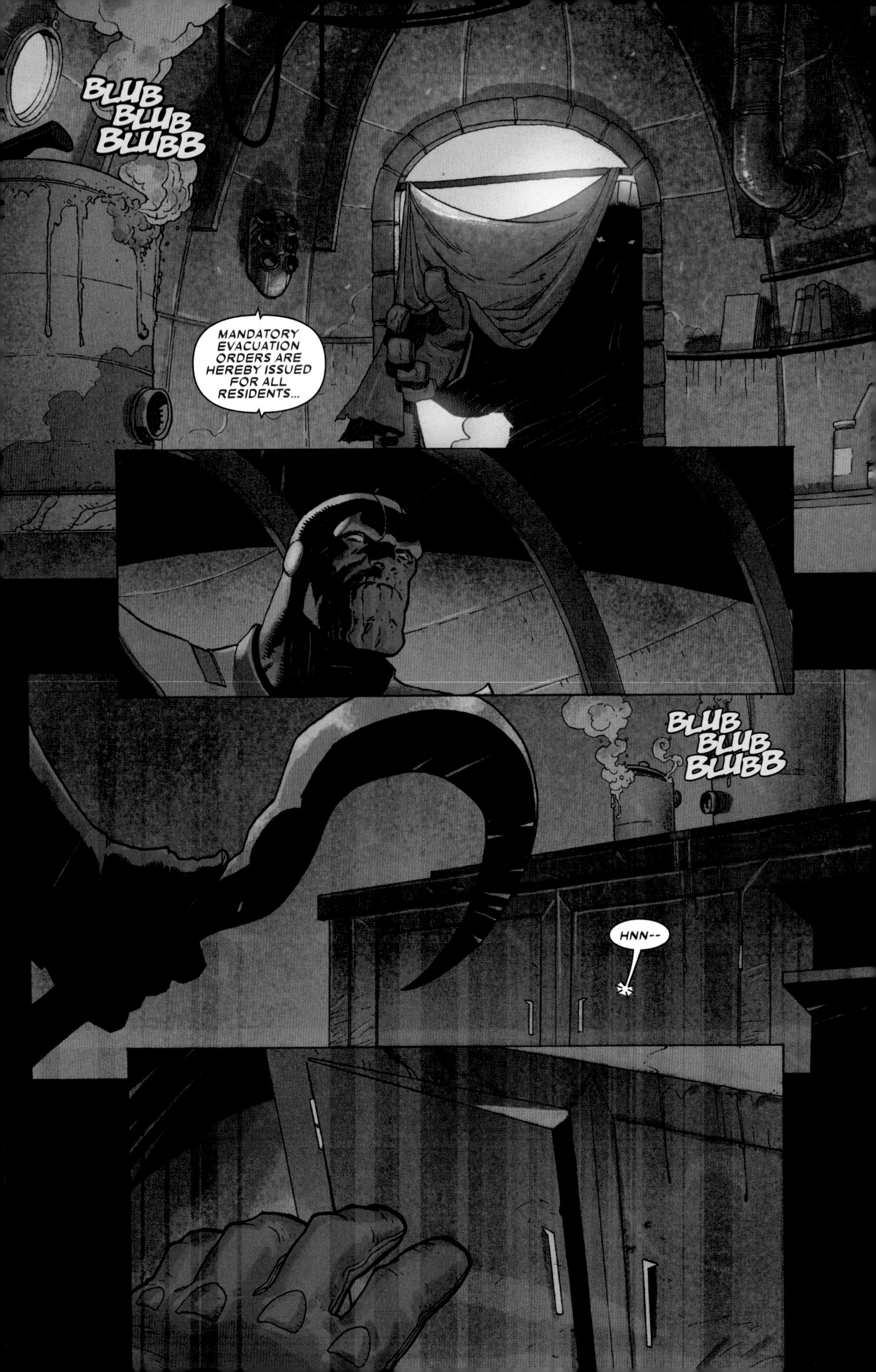
BLUB BLUB BLUBB
MANDATORY EVACUATION ORDERS ARE HEREBY ISSUED FOR ALL RESIDENTS...
BLUB BLUB BLUBB
HNN--

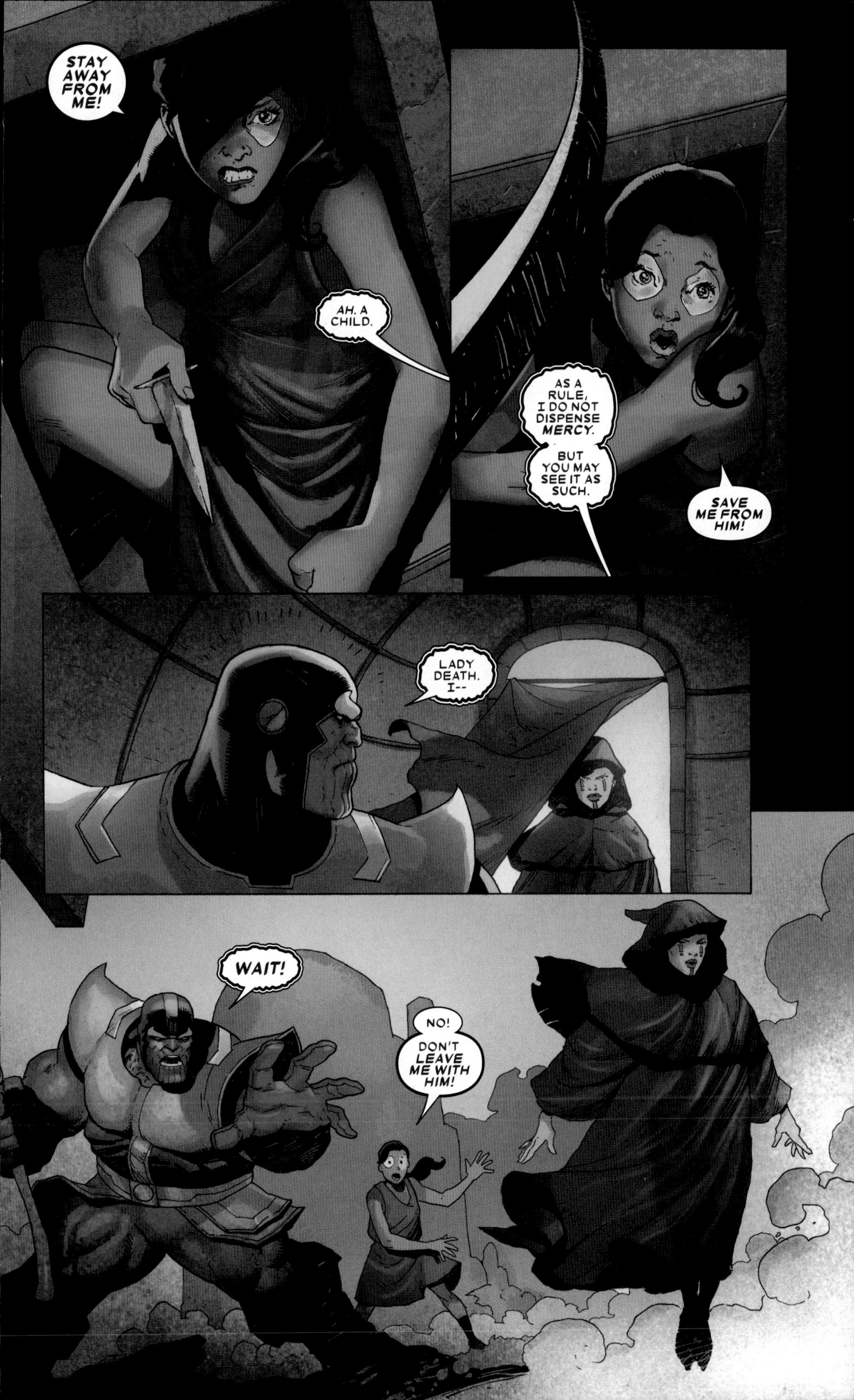
STAY AWAY FROM ME!
AH. A CHILD.
AS A RULE, I DO NOT DISPENSE MERCY.
BUT YOU MAY SEE IT AS SUCH.
SAVE ME FROM HIM!
LADY DEATH. I--
WAIT!
NO!
DON'T LEAVE ME WITH HIM!

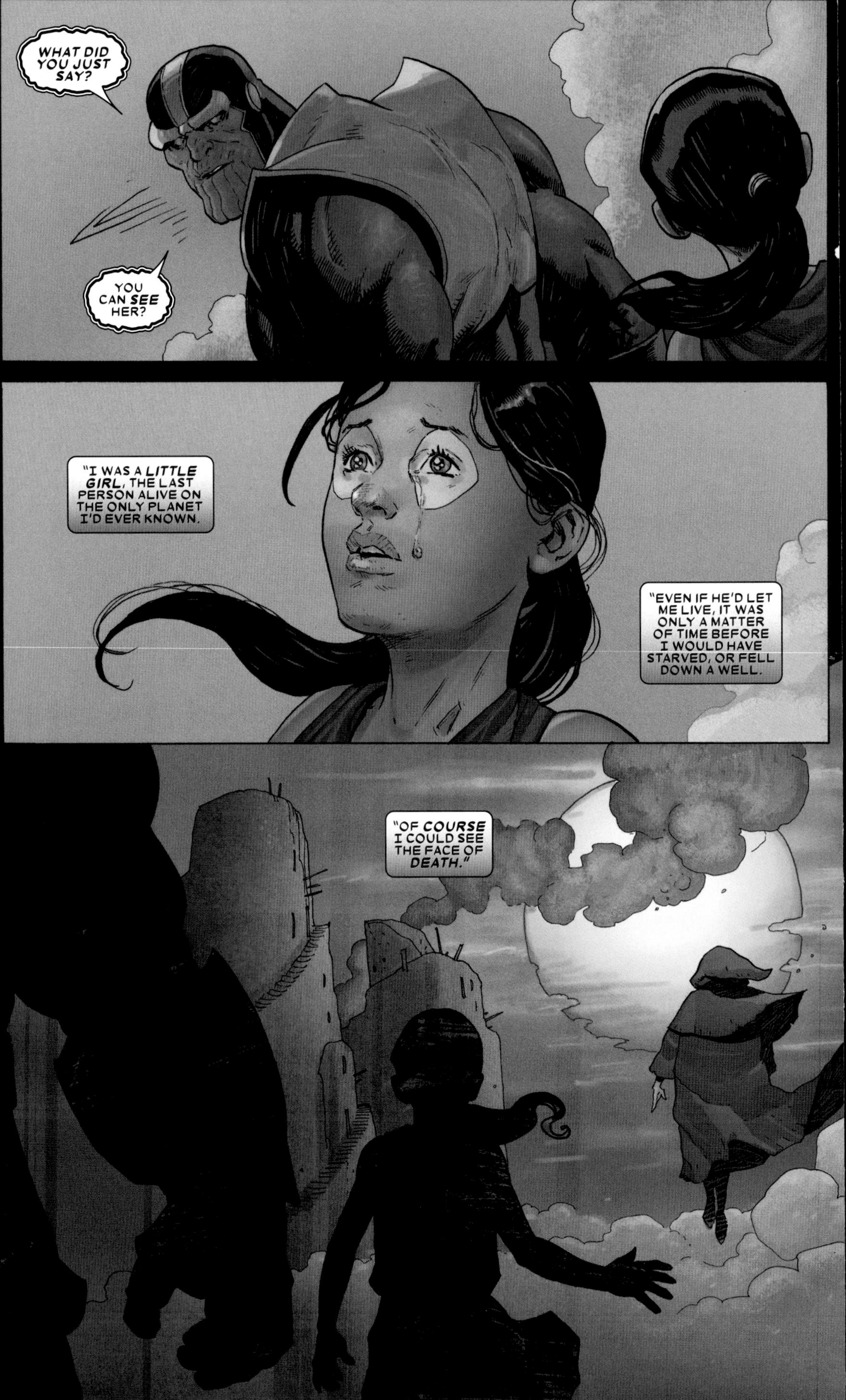
WHAT DID YOU JUST SAY?
YOU CAN SEE HER?
"I WAS A LITTLE GIRL, THE LAST PERSON ALIVE ON THE ONLY PLANET I'D EVER KNOWN.
"EVEN IF HE'D LET ME LIVE, IT WAS ONLY A MATTER OF TIME BEFORE I WOULD HAVE STARVED, OR FELL DOWN A WELL.
"OF COURSE I COULD SEE THE FACE OF DEATH."

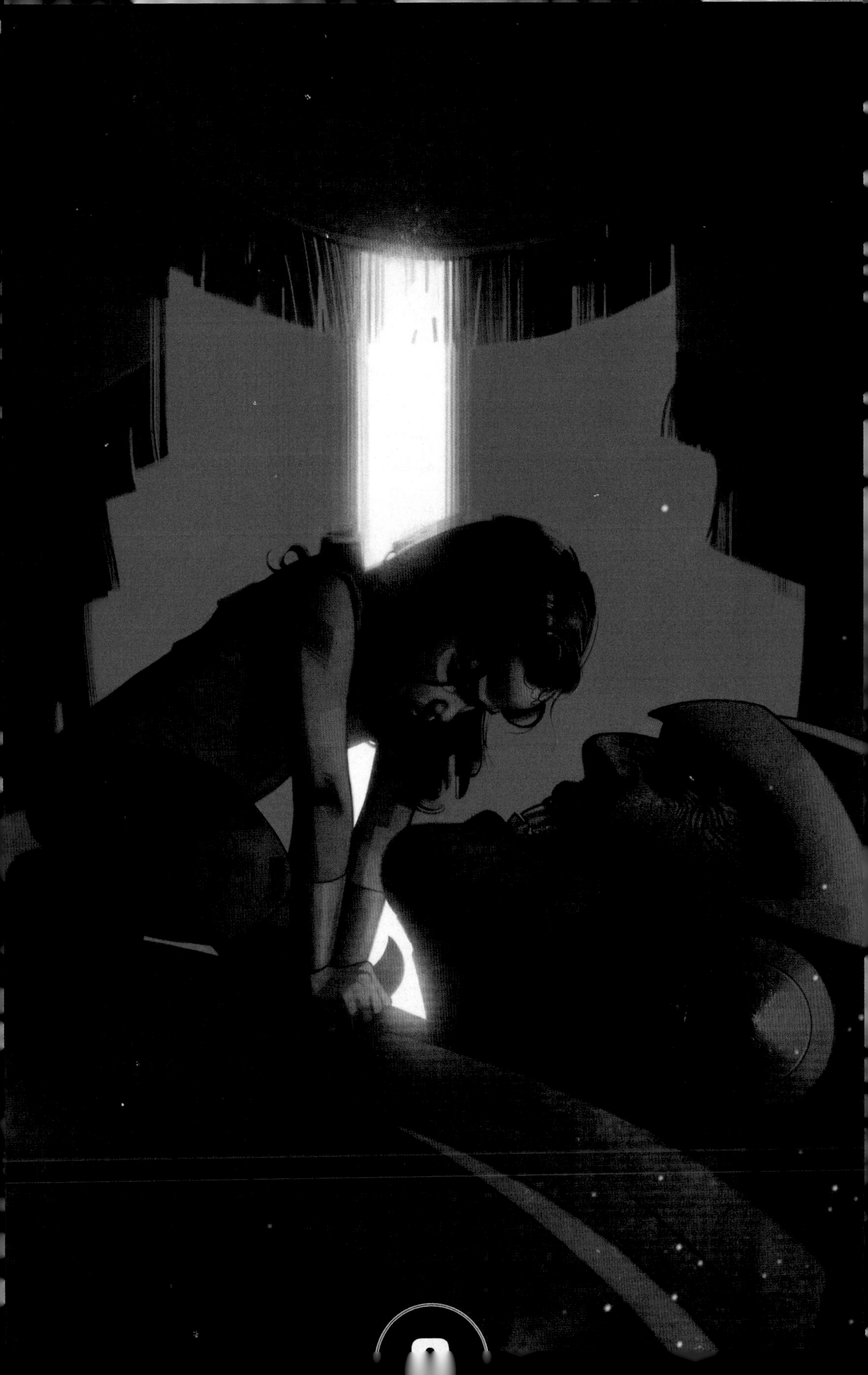

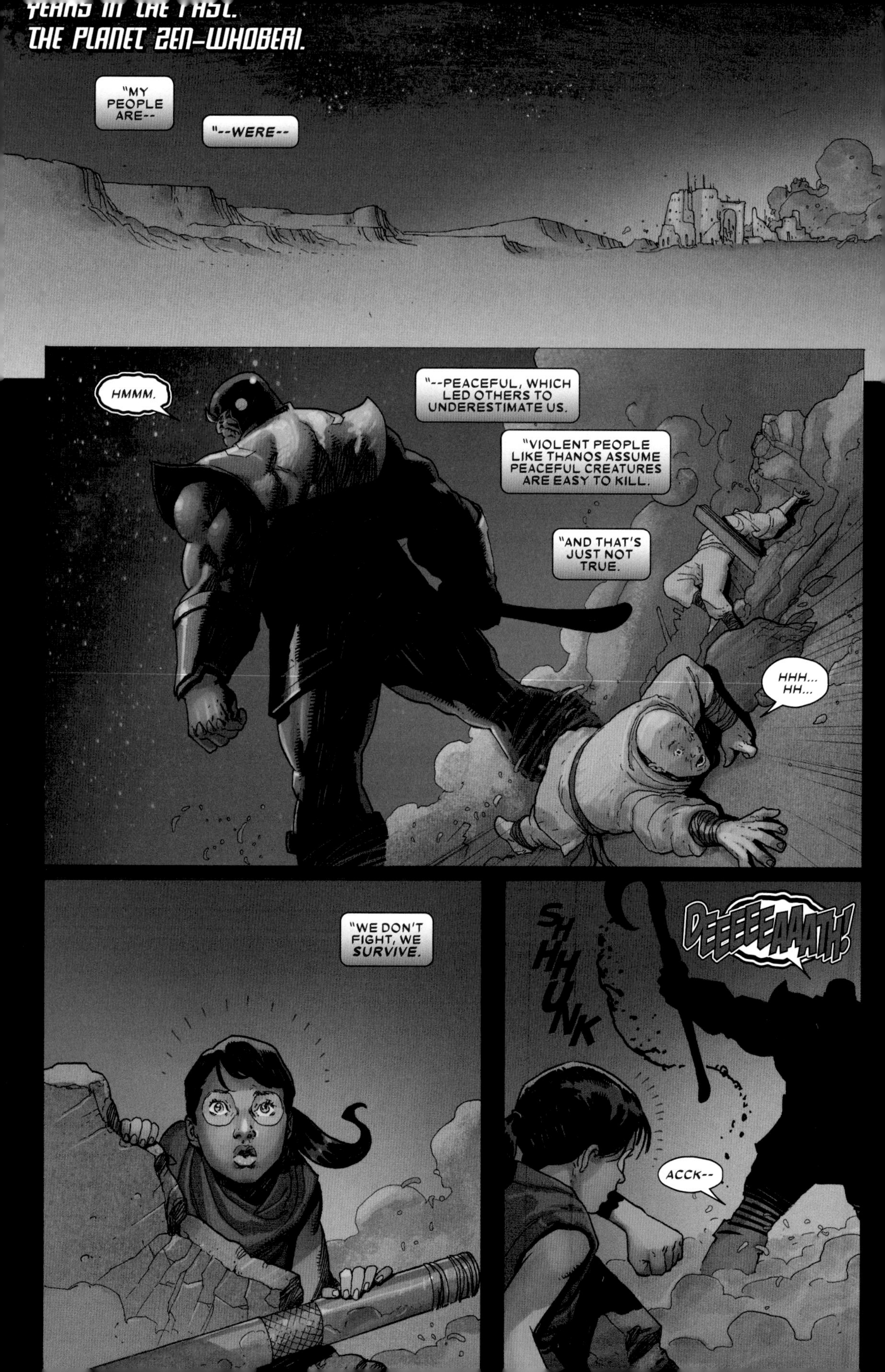
YEARS IN THE PAST.
THE PLANET ZEN-WHOBERI.
"MY PEOPLE ARE--
"--WERE--
HMMM.
"--PEACEFUL, WHICH LED OTHERS TO UNDERESTIMATE US.
"VIOLENT PEOPLE LIKE THANOS ASSUME PEACEFUL CREATURES ARE EASY TO KILL.
"AND THAT'S JUST NOT TRUE.
HHH... HH...
"WE DON'T FIGHT, WE *SURVIVE*.
SHHHUNK
DEEEEEAAATH!
ACCK--

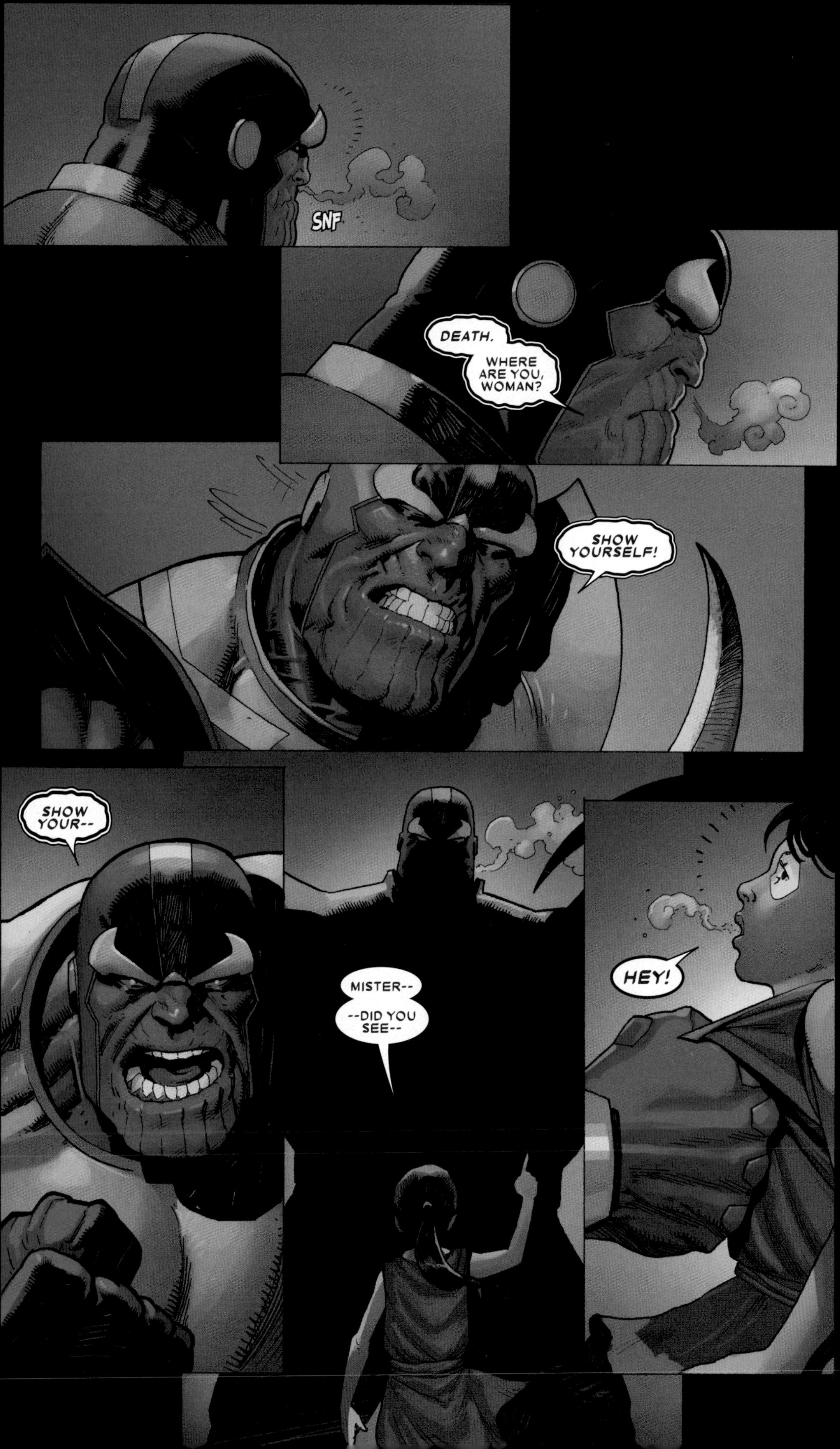
SNF
DEATH.
WHERE ARE YOU, WOMAN?
SHOW YOURSELF!
SHOW YOUR--
MISTER--
--DID YOU SEE--
HEY!

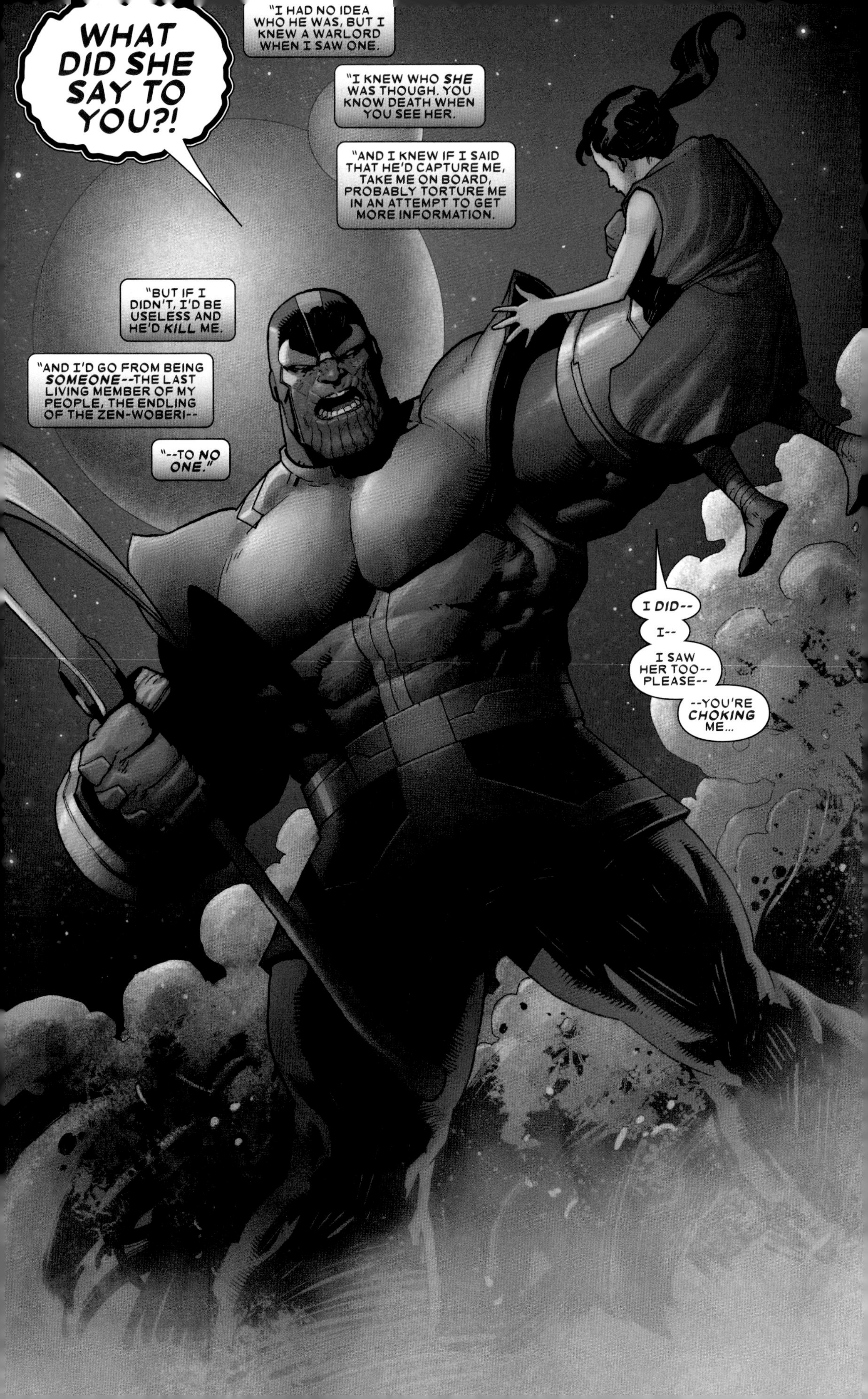
WHAT DID SHE SAY TO YOU?!
"I HAD NO IDEA WHO HE WAS, BUT I KNEW A WARLORD WHEN I SAW ONE.
"I KNEW WHO SHE WAS THOUGH. YOU KNOW DEATH WHEN YOU SEE HER.
"AND I KNEW IF I SAID THAT HE'D CAPTURE ME, TAKE ME ON BOARD, PROBABLY TORTURE ME IN AN ATTEMPT TO GET MORE INFORMATION.
"BUT IF I DIDN'T, I'D BE USELESS AND HE'D KILL ME.
"AND I'D GO FROM BEING SOMEONE--THE LAST LIVING MEMBER OF MY PEOPLE, THE ENDLING OF THE ZEN-WOBERI--
"--TO NO ONE."
I DID--
I--
I SAW HER TOO--
PLEASE--
--YOU'RE CHOKING ME...

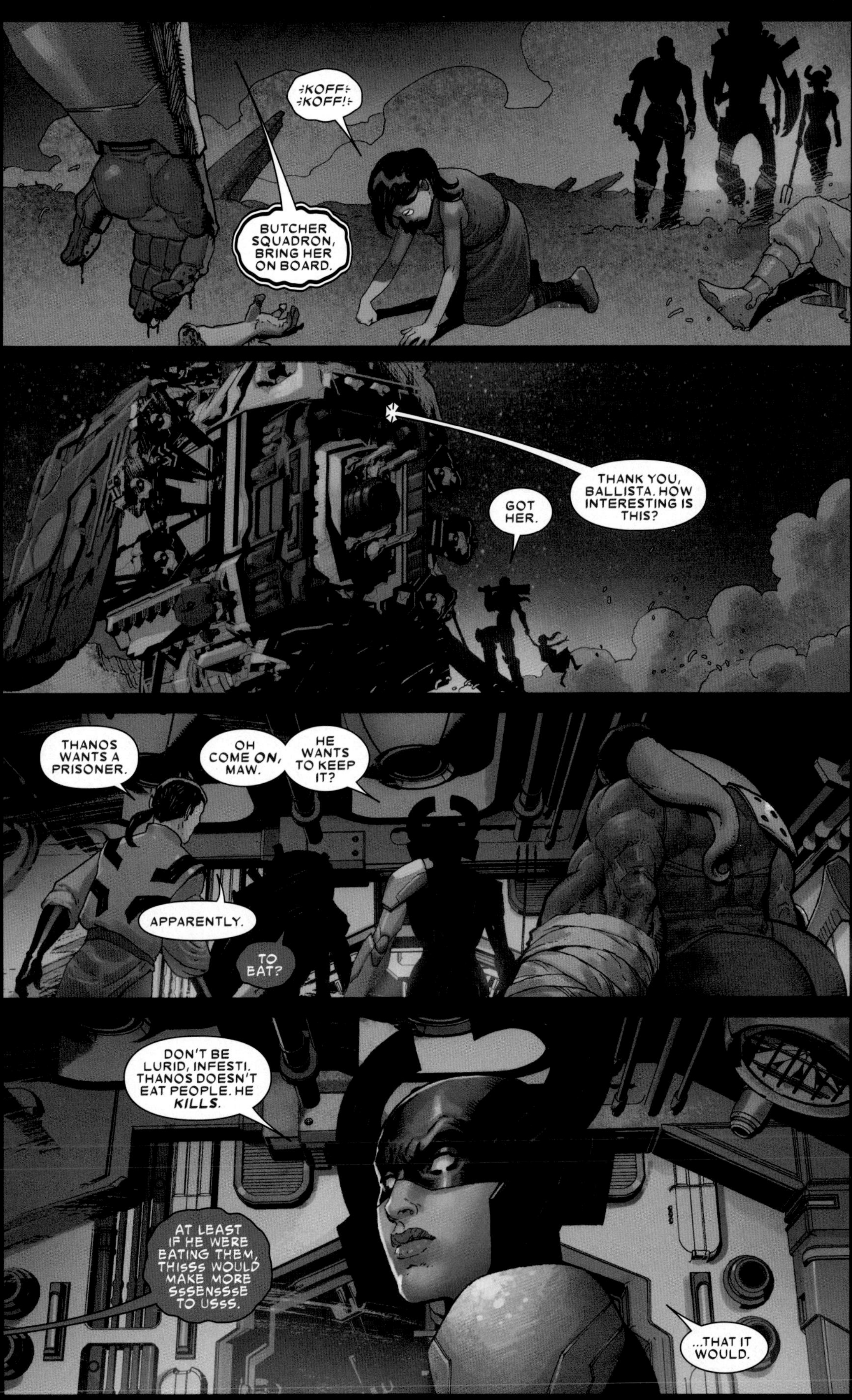

KOFF! KOFF!
BUTCHER SQUADRON, BRING HER ON BOARD.
THANK YOU, BALLISTA. HOW INTERESTING IS THIS?
GOT HER.
THANOS WANTS A PRISONER.
OH COME ON, MAW.
HE WANTS TO KEEP IT?
APPARENTLY.
TO EAT?
DON'T BE LURID, INFESTI. THANOS DOESN'T EAT PEOPLE. HE KILLS.
AT LEAST IF HE WERE EATING THEM, THISSS WOULD MAKE MORE SSSENSSSE TO USSS.
...THAT IT WOULD.

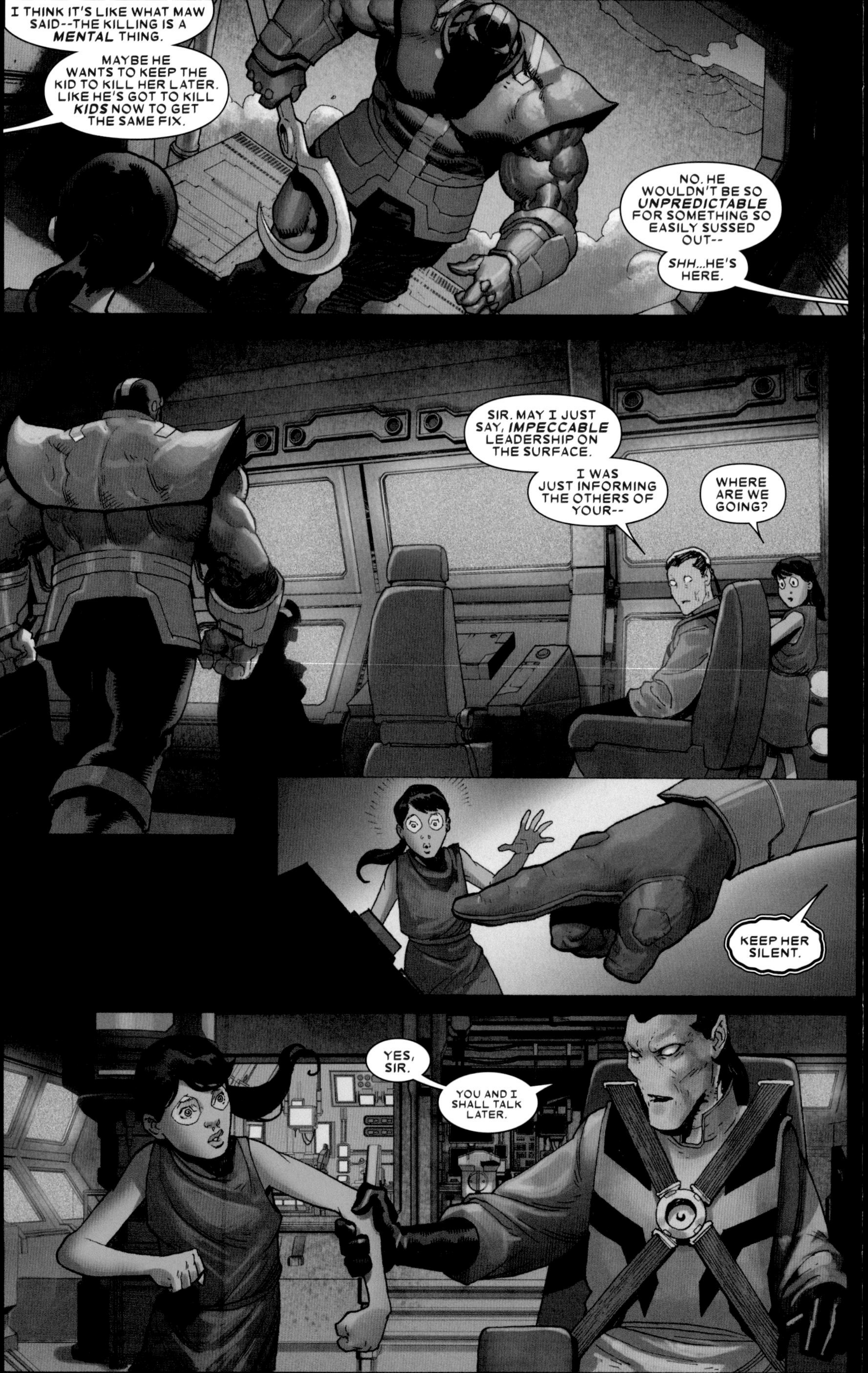
I THINK IT'S LIKE WHAT MAW SAID--THE KILLING IS A MENTAL THING.
MAYBE HE WANTS TO KEEP THE KID TO KILL HER LATER. LIKE HE'S GOT TO KILL KIDS NOW TO GET THE SAME FIX.
NO. HE WOULDN'T BE SO UNPREDICTABLE FOR SOMETHING SO EASILY SUSSED OUT--
SHH...HE'S HERE.
SIR. MAY I JUST SAY, IMPECCABLE LEADERSHIP ON THE SURFACE.
I WAS JUST INFORMING THE OTHERS OF YOUR--
WHERE ARE WE GOING?
KEEP HER SILENT.
YES, SIR.
YOU AND I SHALL TALK LATER.

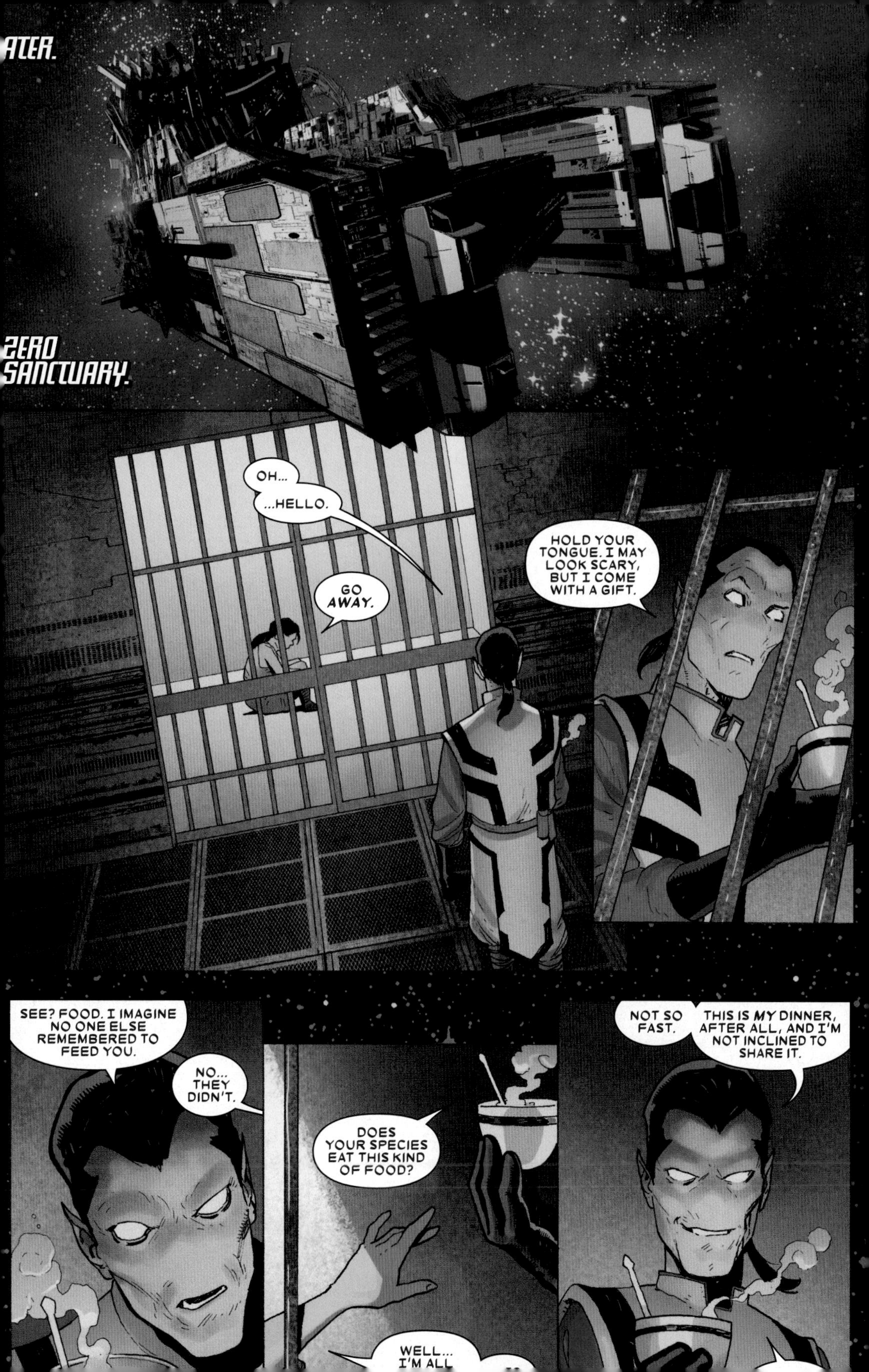

ATER.
ZERO SANCTUARY.
OH...
...HELLO.
GO AWAY.
HOLD YOUR TONGUE. I MAY LOOK SCARY, BUT I COME WITH A GIFT.
SEE? FOOD. I IMAGINE NO ONE ELSE REMEMBERED TO FEED YOU.
NO... THEY DIDN'T.
DOES YOUR SPECIES EAT THIS KIND OF FOOD?
WELL... I'M ALL
NOT SO FAST.
THIS IS MY DINNER, AFTER ALL, AND I'M NOT INCLINED TO SHARE IT.

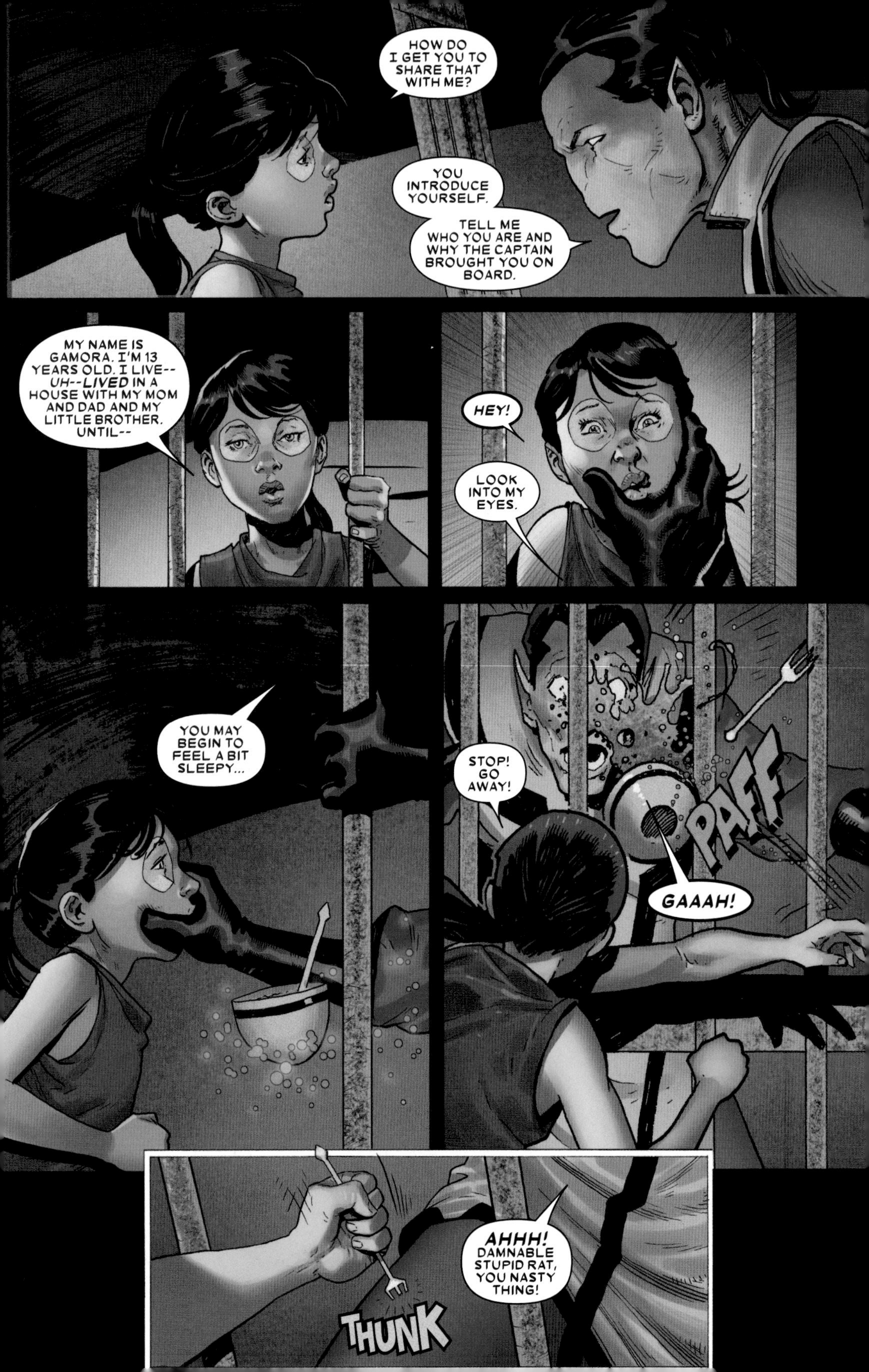
HOW DO I GET YOU TO SHARE THAT WITH ME?
YOU INTRODUCE YOURSELF.
TELL ME WHO YOU ARE AND WHY THE CAPTAIN BROUGHT YOU ON BOARD.
MY NAME IS GAMORA. I'M 13 YEARS OLD. I LIVE-- *UH--LIVED* IN A HOUSE WITH MY MOM AND DAD AND MY LITTLE BROTHER. UNTIL--
HEY!
LOOK INTO MY EYES.
YOU MAY BEGIN TO FEEL A BIT SLEEPY...
STOP! GO AWAY!
PAFF
GAAAH!
AHHH! DAMNABLE STUPID RAT, YOU NASTY THING!
THUNK

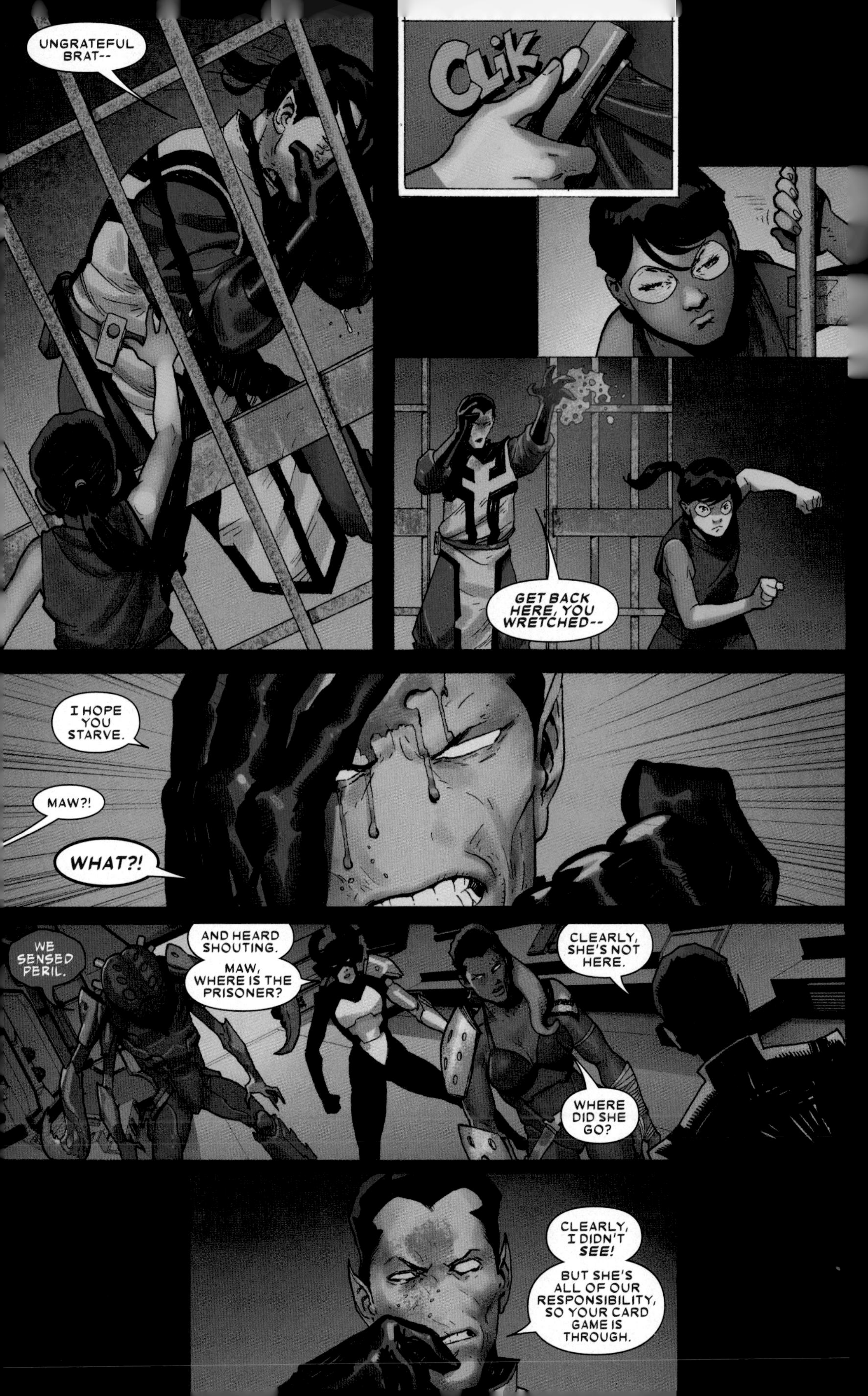
UNGRATEFUL BRAT--
CLIK
GET BACK HERE, YOU WRETCHED--
I HOPE YOU STARVE.
MAW?!
WHAT?!
WE SENSED PERIL.
AND HEARD SHOUTING.
MAW, WHERE IS THE PRISONER?
CLEARLY, SHE'S NOT HERE.
WHERE DID SHE GO?
CLEARLY, I DIDN'T SEE!
BUT SHE'S ALL OF OUR RESPONSIBILITY, SO YOUR CARD GAME IS THROUGH.

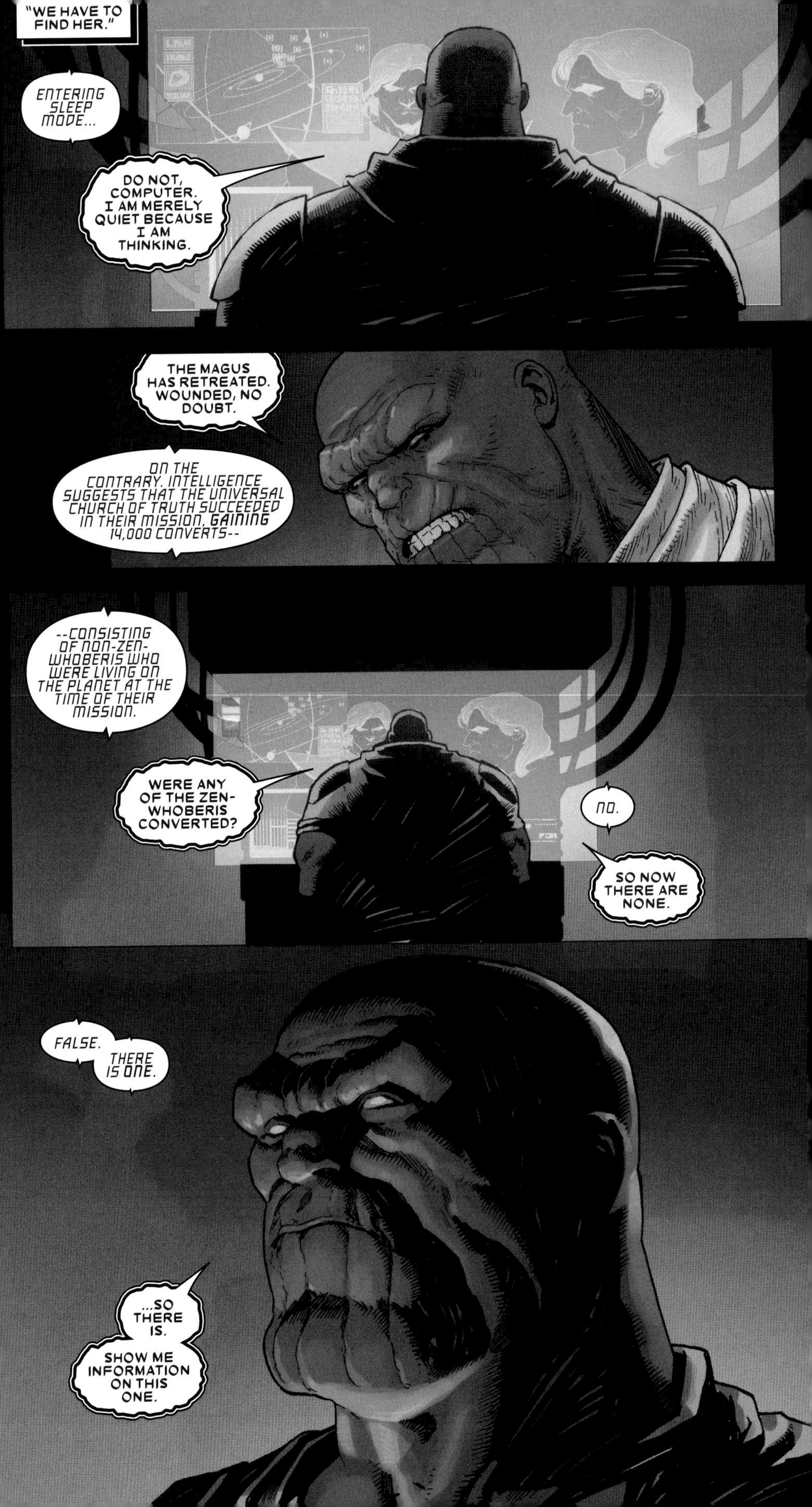
"WE HAVE TO FIND HER."
ENTERING SLEEP MODE...
DO NOT, COMPUTER. I AM MERELY QUIET BECAUSE I AM THINKING.
THE MAGUS HAS RETREATED. WOUNDED, NO DOUBT.
ON THE CONTRARY. INTELLIGENCE SUGGESTS THAT THE UNIVERSAL CHURCH OF TRUTH SUCCEEDED IN THEIR MISSION, GAINING 14,000 CONVERTS--
--CONSISTING OF NON-ZEN-WHOBERIS WHO WERE LIVING ON THE PLANET AT THE TIME OF THEIR MISSION.
WERE ANY OF THE ZEN-WHOBERIS CONVERTED?
NO.
SO NOW THERE ARE NONE.
FALSE.
THERE IS ONE.
...SO THERE IS.
SHOW ME INFORMATION ON THIS ONE.

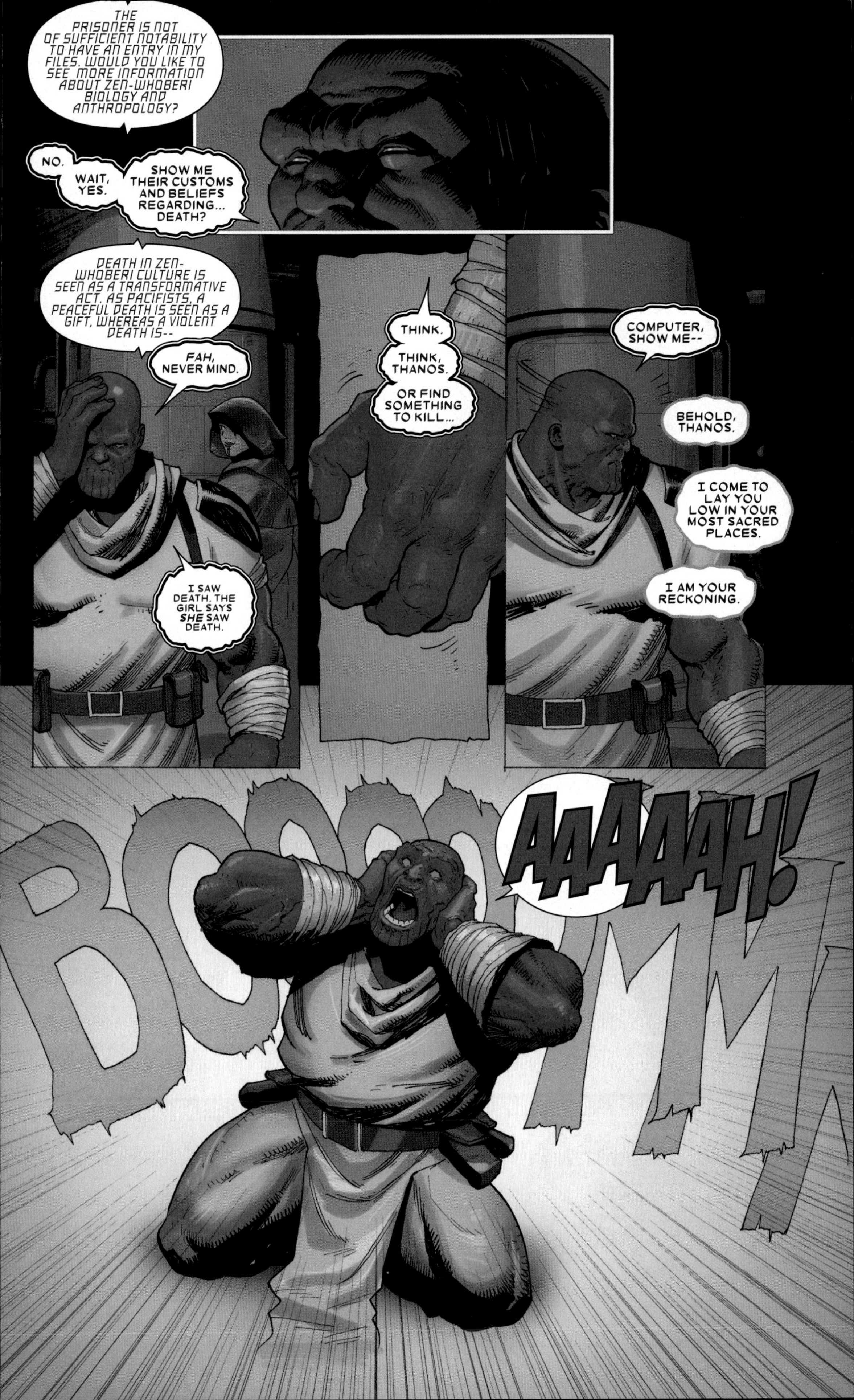
THE PRISONER IS NOT OF SUFFICIENT NOTABILITY TO HAVE AN ENTRY IN MY FILES. WOULD YOU LIKE TO SEE MORE INFORMATION ABOUT ZEN-WHOBERI BIOLOGY AND ANTHROPOLOGY?
NO.
WAIT, YES.
SHOW ME THEIR CUSTOMS AND BELIEFS REGARDING... DEATH?
DEATH IN ZEN-WHOBERI CULTURE IS SEEN AS A TRANSFORMATIVE ACT. AS PACIFISTS, A PEACEFUL DEATH IS SEEN AS A GIFT, WHEREAS A VIOLENT DEATH IS--
FAH, NEVER MIND.
I SAW DEATH. THE GIRL SAYS *SHE* SAW DEATH.
THINK.
THINK, THANOS.
OR FIND SOMETHING TO KILL...
COMPUTER, SHOW ME--
BEHOLD, THANOS.
I COME TO LAY YOU LOW IN YOUR MOST SACRED PLACES.
I AM YOUR RECKONING.
AAAAAH!

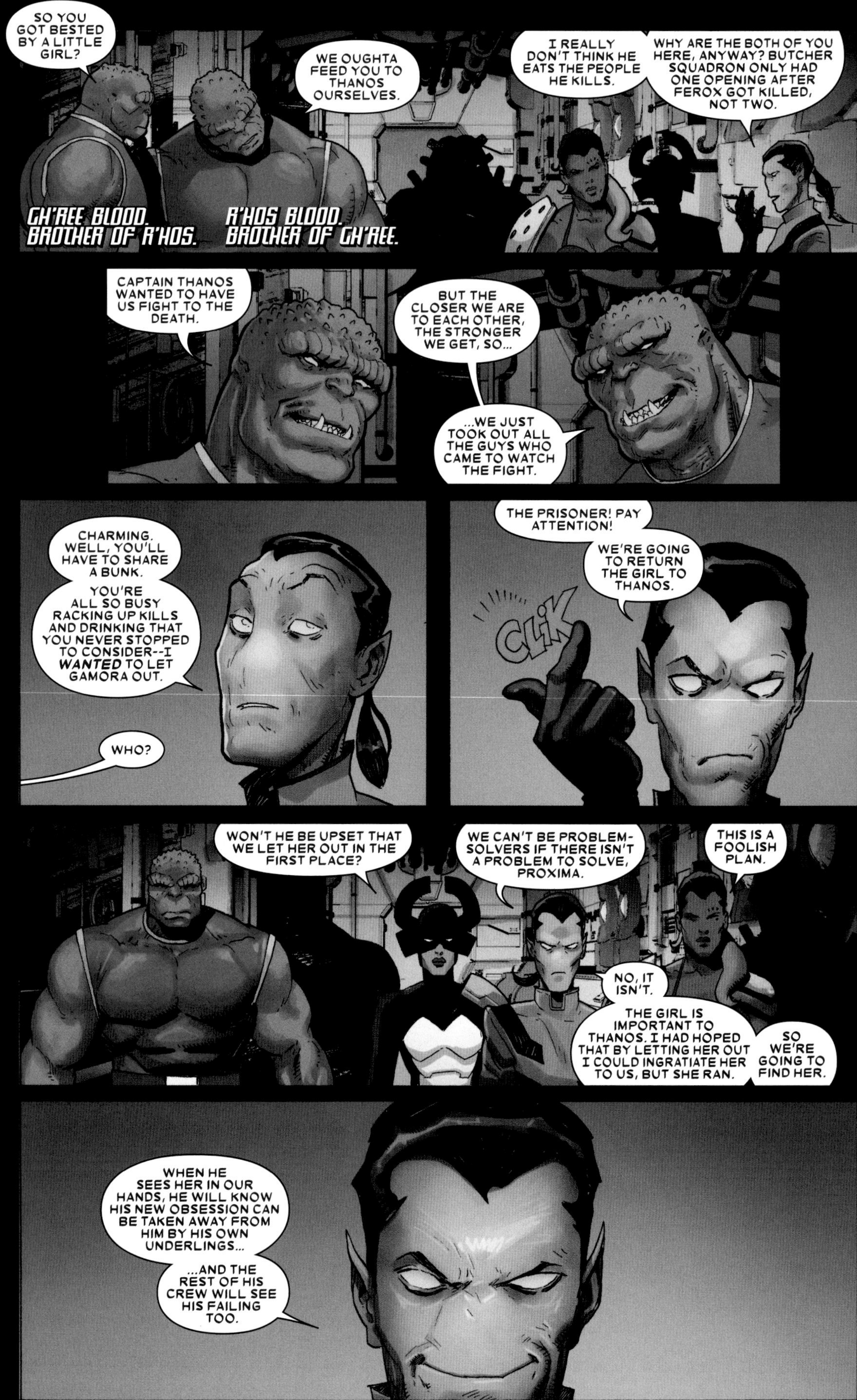
SO YOU GOT BESTED BY A LITTLE GIRL?
WE OUGHTA FEED YOU TO THANOS OURSELVES.
GH'REE BLOOD. BROTHER OF R'HOS.
R'HOS BLOOD. BROTHER OF GH'REE.
I REALLY DON'T THINK HE EATS THE PEOPLE HE KILLS.
WHY ARE THE BOTH OF YOU HERE, ANYWAY? BUTCHER SQUADRON ONLY HAD ONE OPENING AFTER FEROX GOT KILLED, NOT TWO.
CAPTAIN THANOS WANTED TO HAVE US FIGHT TO THE DEATH.
BUT THE CLOSER WE ARE TO EACH OTHER, THE STRONGER WE GET, SO...
...WE JUST TOOK OUT ALL THE GUYS WHO CAME TO WATCH THE FIGHT.
CHARMING. WELL, YOU'LL HAVE TO SHARE A BUNK.
YOU'RE ALL SO BUSY RACKING UP KILLS AND DRINKING THAT YOU NEVER STOPPED TO CONSIDER--I *WANTED* TO LET GAMORA OUT.
WHO?
THE PRISONER! PAY ATTENTION!
CLIK
WE'RE GOING TO RETURN THE GIRL TO THANOS.
WON'T HE BE UPSET THAT WE LET HER OUT IN THE FIRST PLACE?
WE CAN'T BE PROBLEM-SOLVERS IF THERE ISN'T A PROBLEM TO SOLVE, PROXIMA.
THIS IS A FOOLISH PLAN.
NO, IT ISN'T.
THE GIRL IS IMPORTANT TO THANOS. I HAD HOPED THAT BY LETTING HER OUT I COULD INGRATIATE HER TO US, BUT SHE RAN.
SO WE'RE GOING TO FIND HER.
WHEN HE SEES HER IN OUR HANDS, HE WILL KNOW HIS NEW OBSESSION CAN BE TAKEN AWAY FROM HIM BY HIS OWN UNDERLINGS...
...AND THE REST OF HIS CREW WILL SEE HIS FAILING TOO.

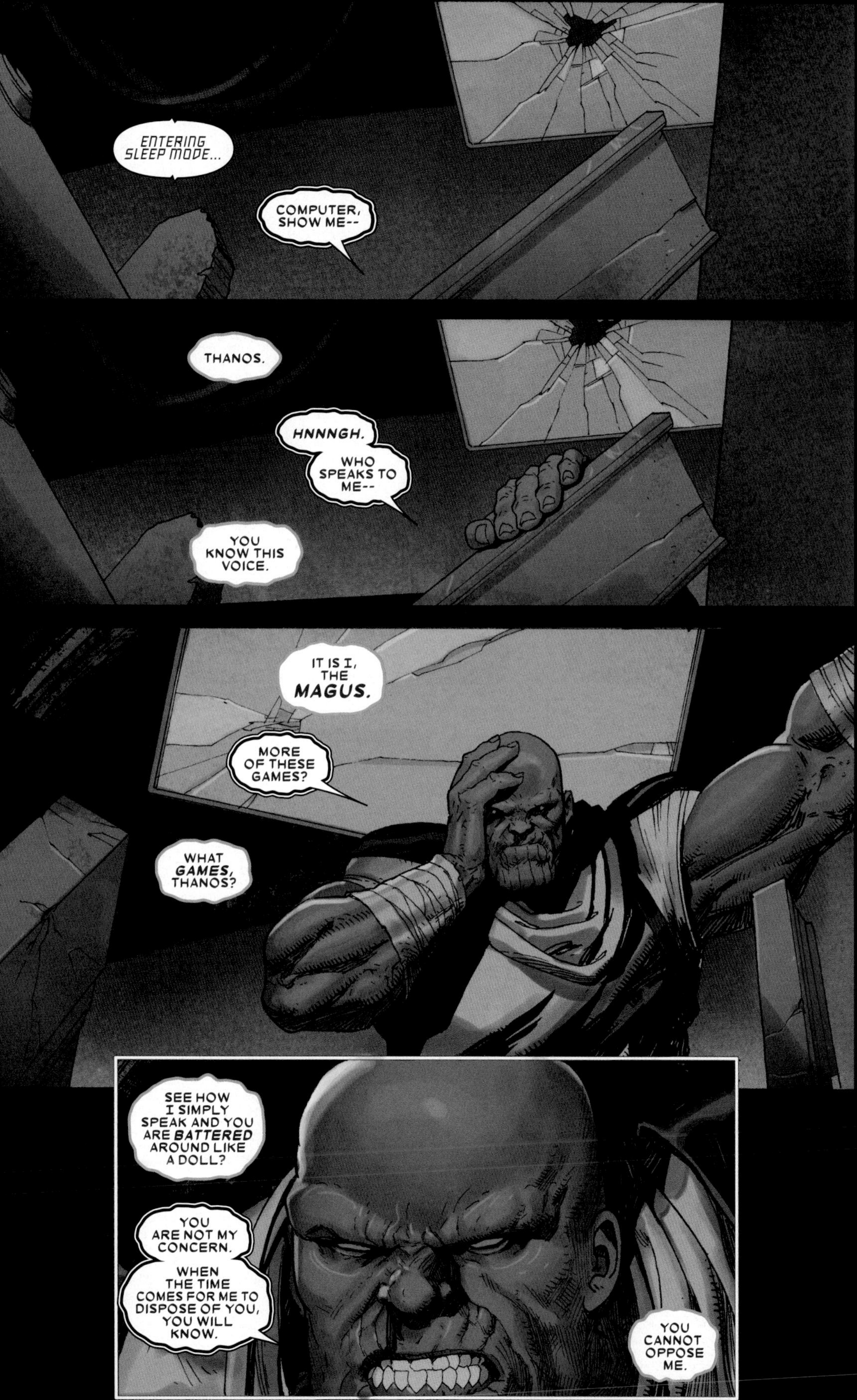
ENTERING SLEEP MODE...
COMPUTER, SHOW ME--
THANOS.
HNNNGH.
WHO SPEAKS TO ME--
YOU KNOW THIS VOICE.
IT IS I, THE MAGUS.
MORE OF THESE GAMES?
WHAT GAMES, THANOS?
SEE HOW I SIMPLY SPEAK AND YOU ARE BATTERED AROUND LIKE A DOLL?
YOU ARE NOT MY CONCERN.
WHEN THE TIME COMES FOR ME TO DISPOSE OF YOU, YOU WILL KNOW.
YOU CANNOT OPPOSE ME.

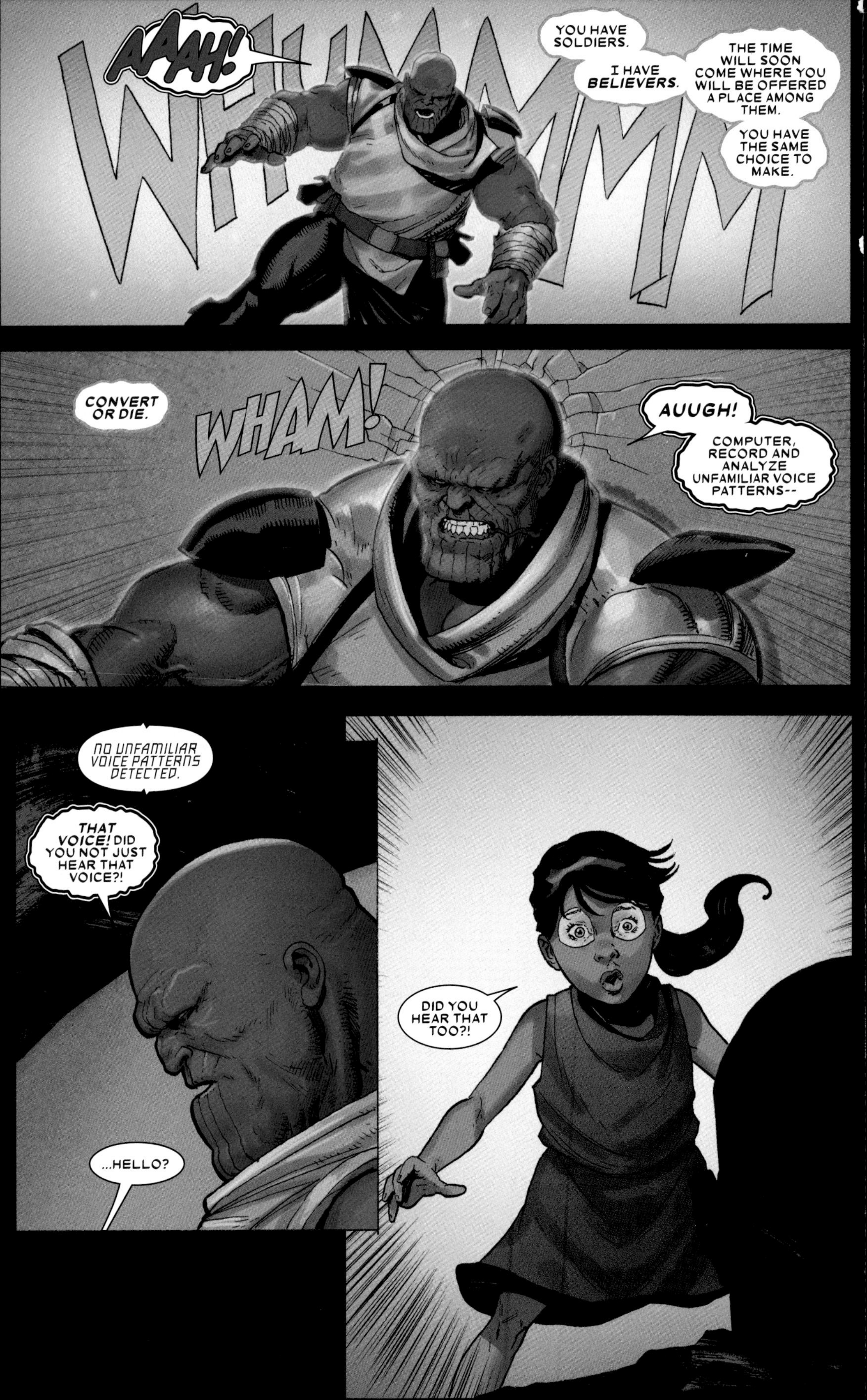
AAAH!
WHHUMMMM
YOU HAVE SOLDIERS.
I HAVE BELIEVERS.
THE TIME WILL SOON COME WHERE YOU WILL BE OFFERED A PLACE AMONG THEM.
YOU HAVE THE SAME CHOICE TO MAKE.
CONVERT OR DIE.
WHAM!
AUUGH!
COMPUTER, RECORD AND ANALYZE UNFAMILIAR VOICE PATTERNS--
NO UNFAMILIAR VOICE PATTERNS DETECTED.
THAT VOICE! DID YOU NOT JUST HEAR THAT VOICE?!
...HELLO?
DID YOU HEAR THAT TOO?!

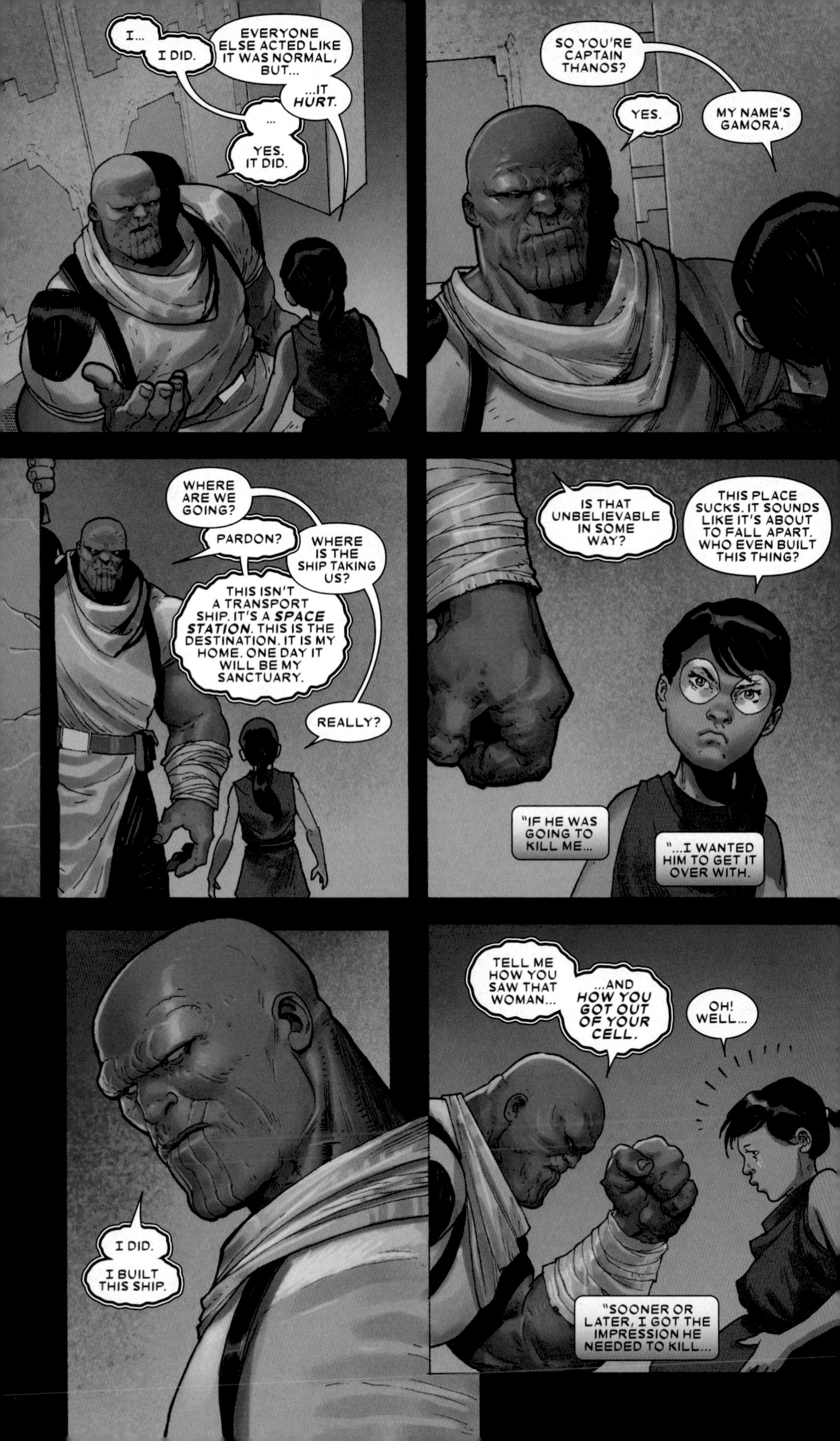
I...
I DID.
EVERYONE ELSE ACTED LIKE IT WAS NORMAL, BUT...
...IT HURT.
...
YES. IT DID.
SO YOU'RE CAPTAIN THANOS?
YES.
MY NAME'S GAMORA.
WHERE ARE WE GOING?
PARDON?
WHERE IS THE SHIP TAKING US?
THIS ISN'T A TRANSPORT SHIP. IT'S A SPACE STATION. THIS IS THE DESTINATION. IT IS MY HOME. ONE DAY IT WILL BE MY SANCTUARY.
REALLY?
IS THAT UNBELIEVABLE IN SOME WAY?
THIS PLACE SUCKS. IT SOUNDS LIKE IT'S ABOUT TO FALL APART. WHO EVEN BUILT THIS THING?
"IF HE WAS GOING TO KILL ME...
"...I WANTED HIM TO GET IT OVER WITH.
I DID.
I BUILT THIS SHIP.
TELL ME HOW YOU SAW THAT WOMAN...
...AND HOW YOU GOT OUT OF YOUR CELL.
OH! WELL...
"SOONER OR LATER, I GOT THE IMPRESSION HE NEEDED TO KILL...

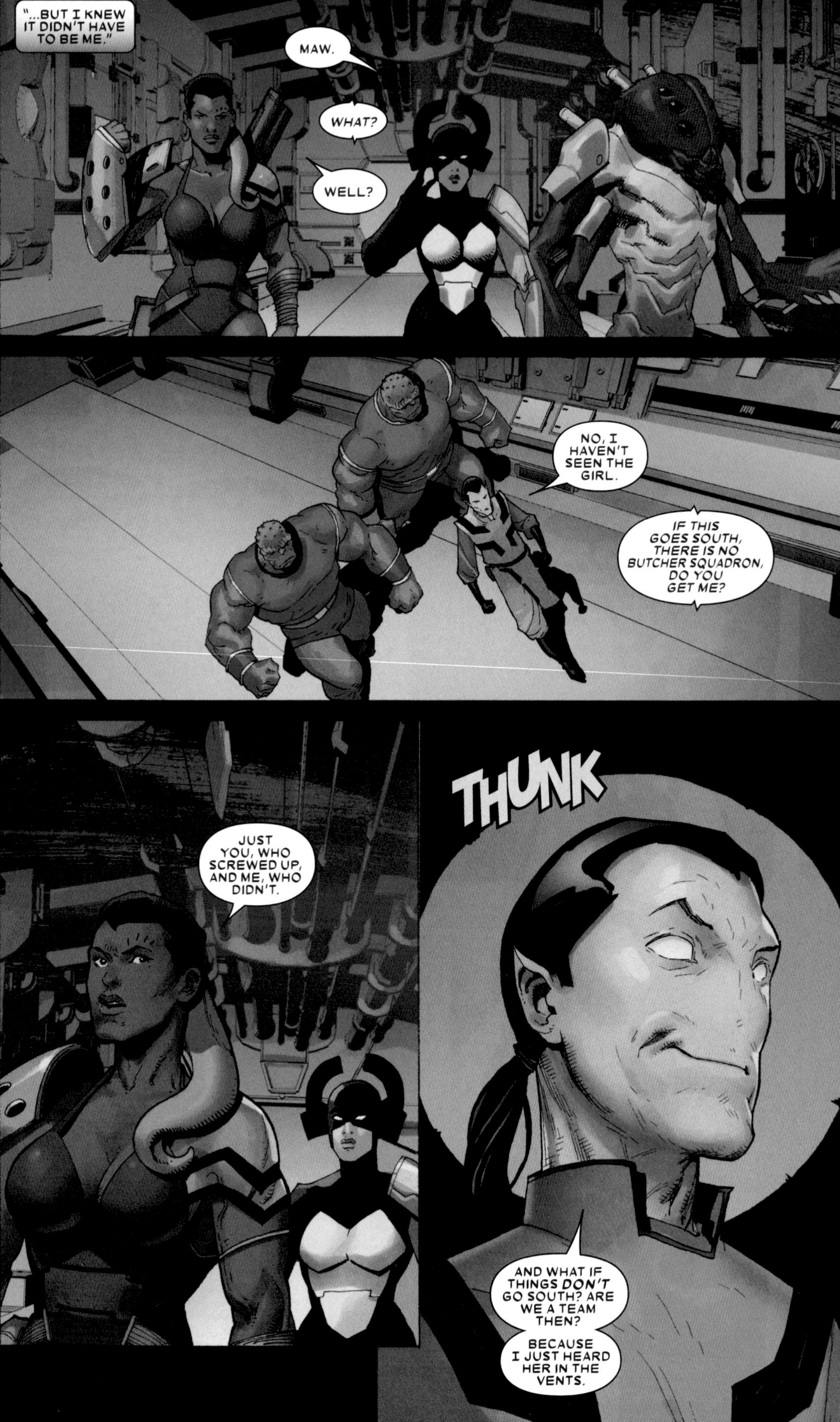
"...BUT I KNEW IT DIDN'T HAVE TO BE ME."
MAW.
WHAT?
WELL?
NO, I HAVEN'T SEEN THE GIRL.
IF THIS GOES SOUTH, THERE IS NO BUTCHER SQUADRON, DO YOU GET ME?
JUST YOU, WHO SCREWED UP, AND ME, WHO DIDN'T.
THUNK
AND WHAT IF THINGS DON'T GO SOUTH? ARE WE A TEAM THEN?
BECAUSE I JUST HEARD HER IN THE VENTS.

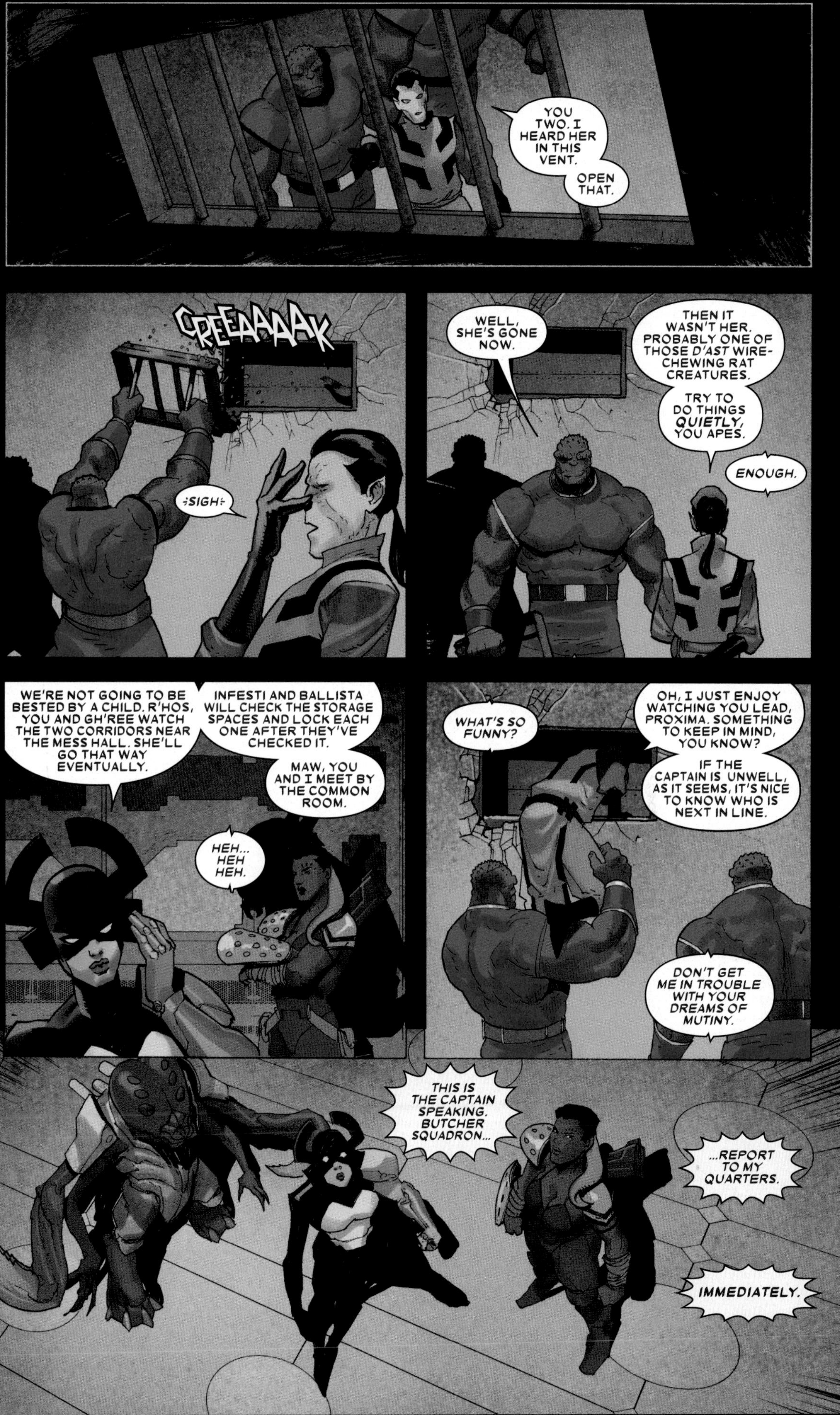
YOU TWO. I HEARD HER IN THIS VENT.
OPEN THAT.
CREEAAAAK
-SIGH-
WELL, SHE'S GONE NOW.
THEN IT WASN'T HER. PROBABLY ONE OF THOSE D'AST WIRE-CHEWING RAT CREATURES.
TRY TO DO THINGS QUIETLY, YOU APES.
ENOUGH.
WE'RE NOT GOING TO BE BESTED BY A CHILD. R'HOS, YOU AND GH'REE WATCH THE TWO CORRIDORS NEAR THE MESS HALL. SHE'LL GO THAT WAY EVENTUALLY.
INFESTI AND BALLISTA WILL CHECK THE STORAGE SPACES AND LOCK EACH ONE AFTER THEY'VE CHECKED IT.
MAW, YOU AND I MEET BY THE COMMON ROOM.
HEH... HEH HEH.
WHAT'S SO FUNNY?
OH, I JUST ENJOY WATCHING YOU LEAD, PROXIMA. SOMETHING TO KEEP IN MIND, YOU KNOW?
IF THE CAPTAIN IS UNWELL, AS IT SEEMS, IT'S NICE TO KNOW WHO IS NEXT IN LINE.
DON'T GET ME IN TROUBLE WITH YOUR DREAMS OF MUTINY.
THIS IS THE CAPTAIN SPEAKING. BUTCHER SQUADRON...
...REPORT TO MY QUARTERS.
IMMEDIATELY.

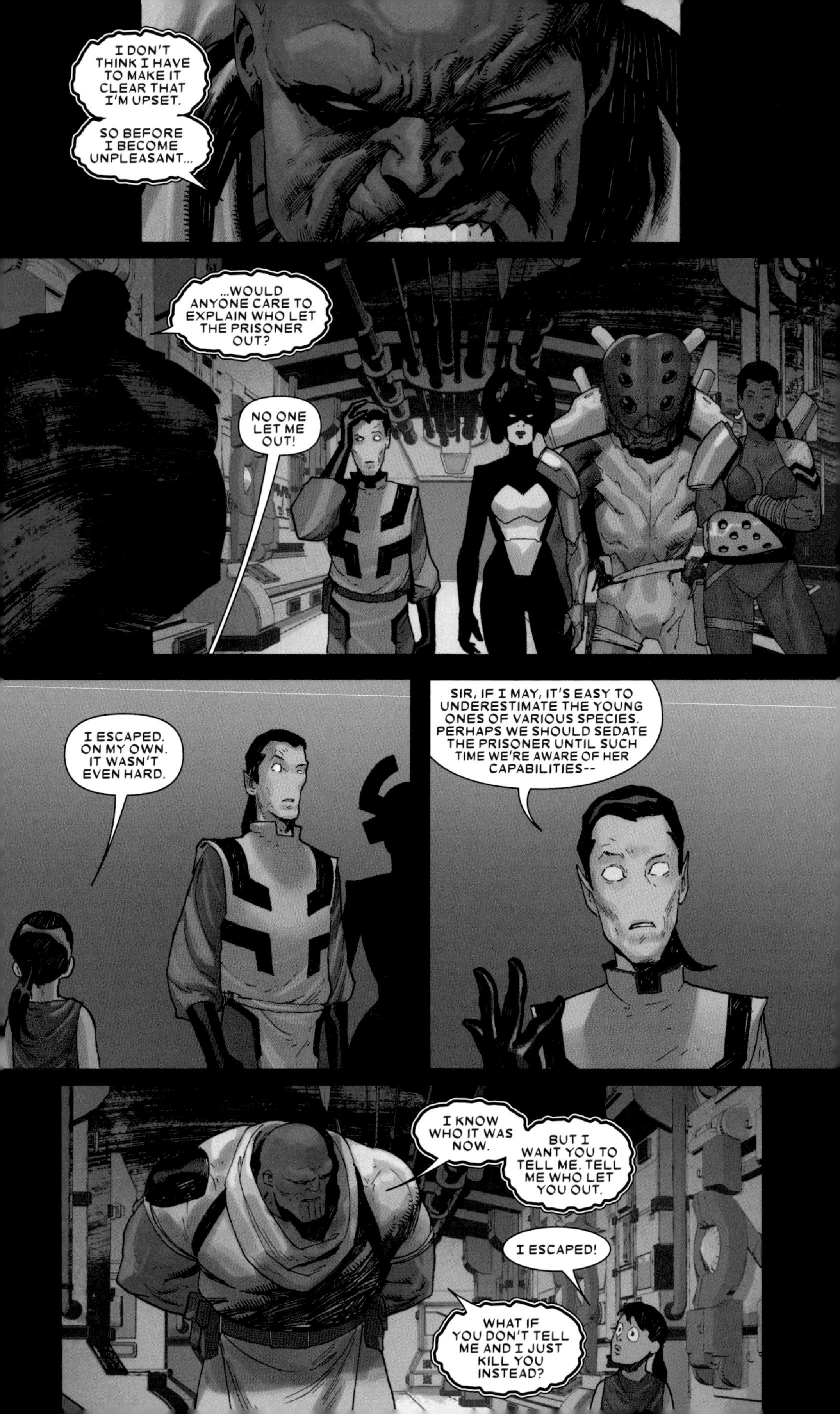
I DON'T THINK I HAVE TO MAKE IT CLEAR THAT I'M UPSET.
SO BEFORE I BECOME UNPLEASANT...
...WOULD ANYONE CARE TO EXPLAIN WHO LET THE PRISONER OUT?
NO ONE LET ME OUT!
I ESCAPED. ON MY OWN. IT WASN'T EVEN HARD.
SIR, IF I MAY, IT'S EASY TO UNDERESTIMATE THE YOUNG ONES OF VARIOUS SPECIES. PERHAPS WE SHOULD SEDATE THE PRISONER UNTIL SUCH TIME WE'RE AWARE OF HER CAPABILITIES--
I KNOW WHO IT WAS NOW.
BUT I WANT YOU TO TELL ME. TELL ME WHO LET YOU OUT.
I ESCAPED!
WHAT IF YOU DON'T TELL ME AND I JUST KILL YOU INSTEAD?

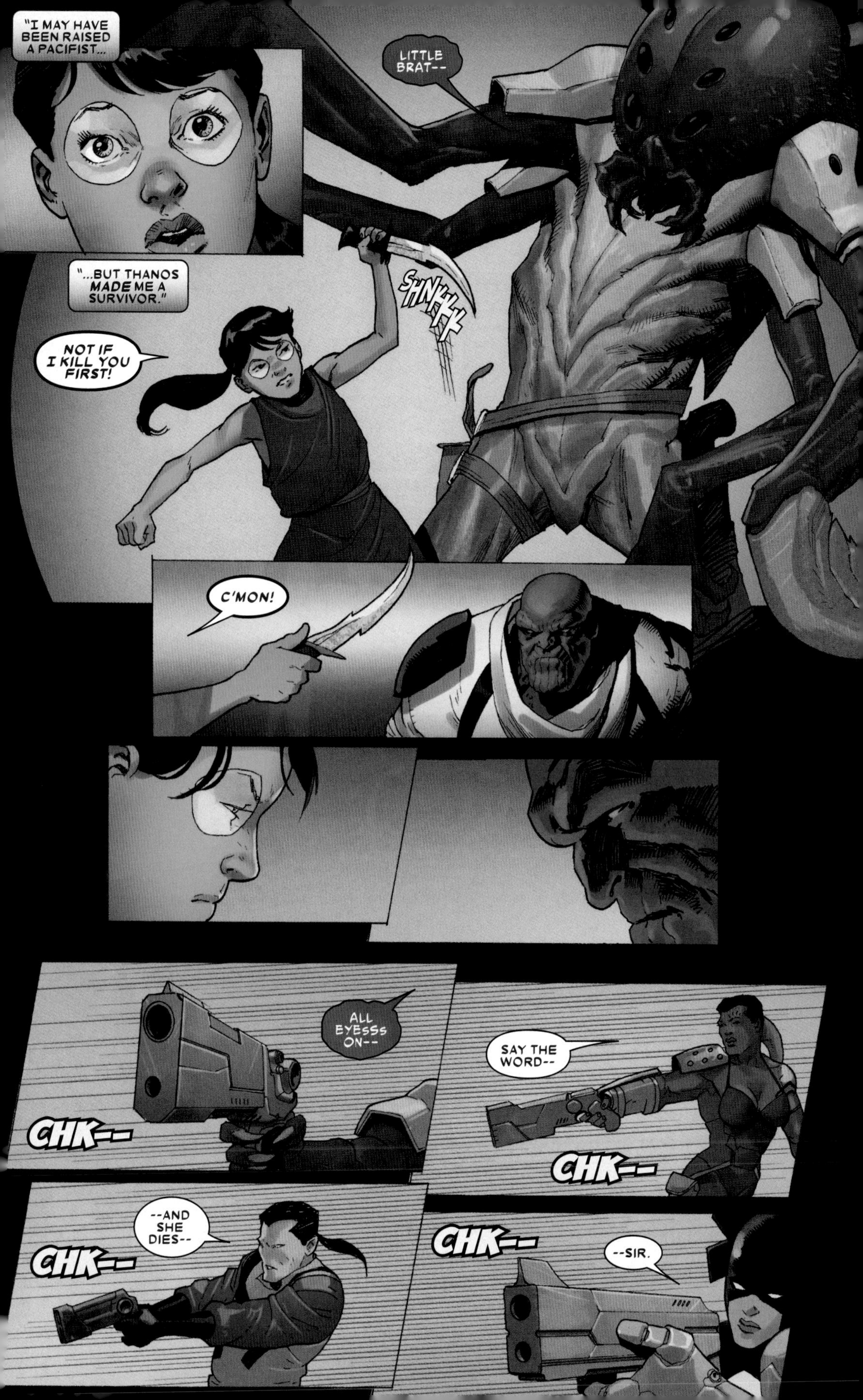
"I MAY HAVE BEEN RAISED A PACIFIST...
LITTLE BRAT--
"...BUT THANOS *MADE* ME A SURVIVOR."
SHNKKK
NOT IF I KILL YOU FIRST!
C'MON!
ALL EYESSS ON--
CHK--
SAY THE WORD--
CHK--
--AND SHE DIES--
CHK--
CHK--
--SIR.

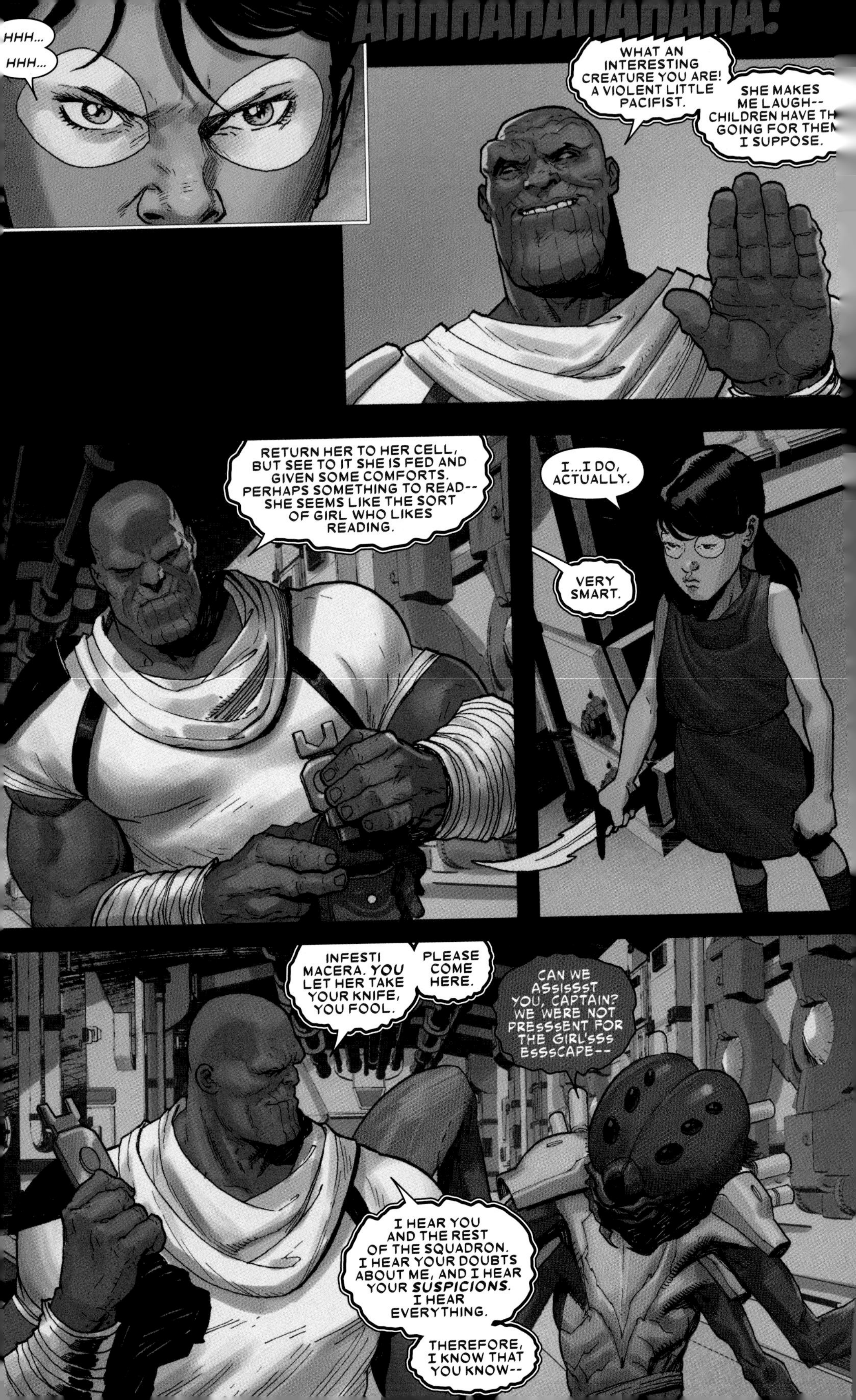

HHH... HHH...
WHAT AN INTERESTING CREATURE YOU ARE! A VIOLENT LITTLE PACIFIST.
SHE MAKES ME LAUGH-- CHILDREN HAVE TH GOING FOR THEM I SUPPOSE.
RETURN HER TO HER CELL, BUT SEE TO IT SHE IS FED AND GIVEN SOME COMFORTS. PERHAPS SOMETHING TO READ-- SHE SEEMS LIKE THE SORT OF GIRL WHO LIKES READING.
I...I DO, ACTUALLY.
VERY SMART.
INFESTI MACERA. *YOU* LET HER TAKE YOUR KNIFE, YOU FOOL.
PLEASE COME HERE.
CAN WE ASSISSST YOU, CAPTAIN? WE WERE NOT PRESSSENT FOR THE GIRL'SSS ESSSCAPE--
I HEAR YOU AND THE REST OF THE SQUADRON. I HEAR YOUR DOUBTS ABOUT ME, AND I HEAR YOUR ***SUSPICIONS***. I HEAR EVERYTHING.
THEREFORE, I KNOW THAT YOU KNOW--

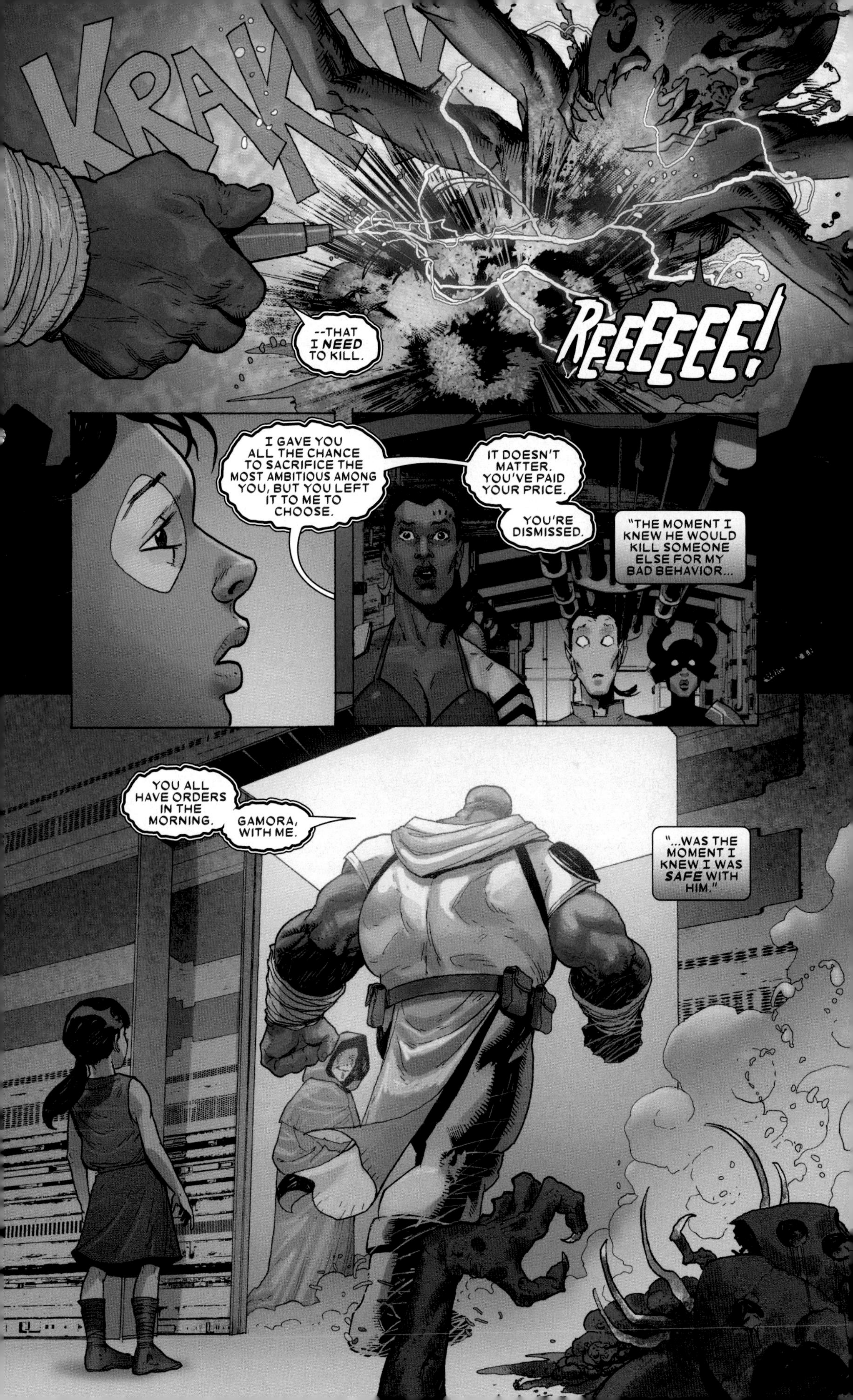
KRAKK
--THAT I *NEED* TO KILL.
REEEEEEE!
I GAVE YOU ALL THE CHANCE TO SACRIFICE THE MOST AMBITIOUS AMONG YOU, BUT YOU LEFT IT TO ME TO CHOOSE.
IT DOESN'T MATTER. YOU'VE PAID YOUR PRICE.
YOU'RE DISMISSED.
"THE MOMENT I KNEW HE WOULD KILL SOMEONE ELSE FOR MY BAD BEHAVIOR...
YOU ALL HAVE ORDERS IN THE MORNING.
GAMORA, WITH ME.
"...WAS THE MOMENT I KNEW I WAS *SAFE* WITH HIM."

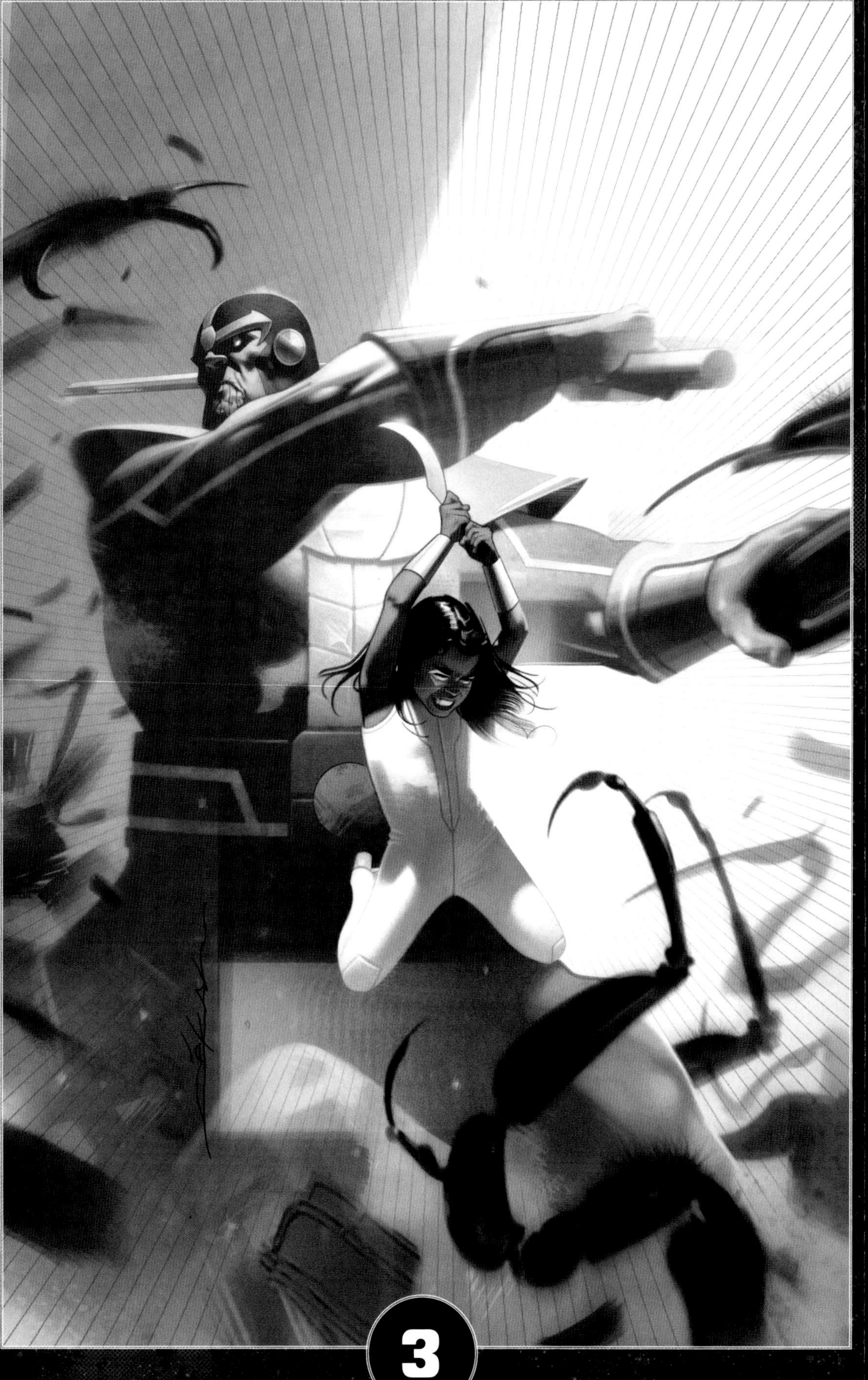
3

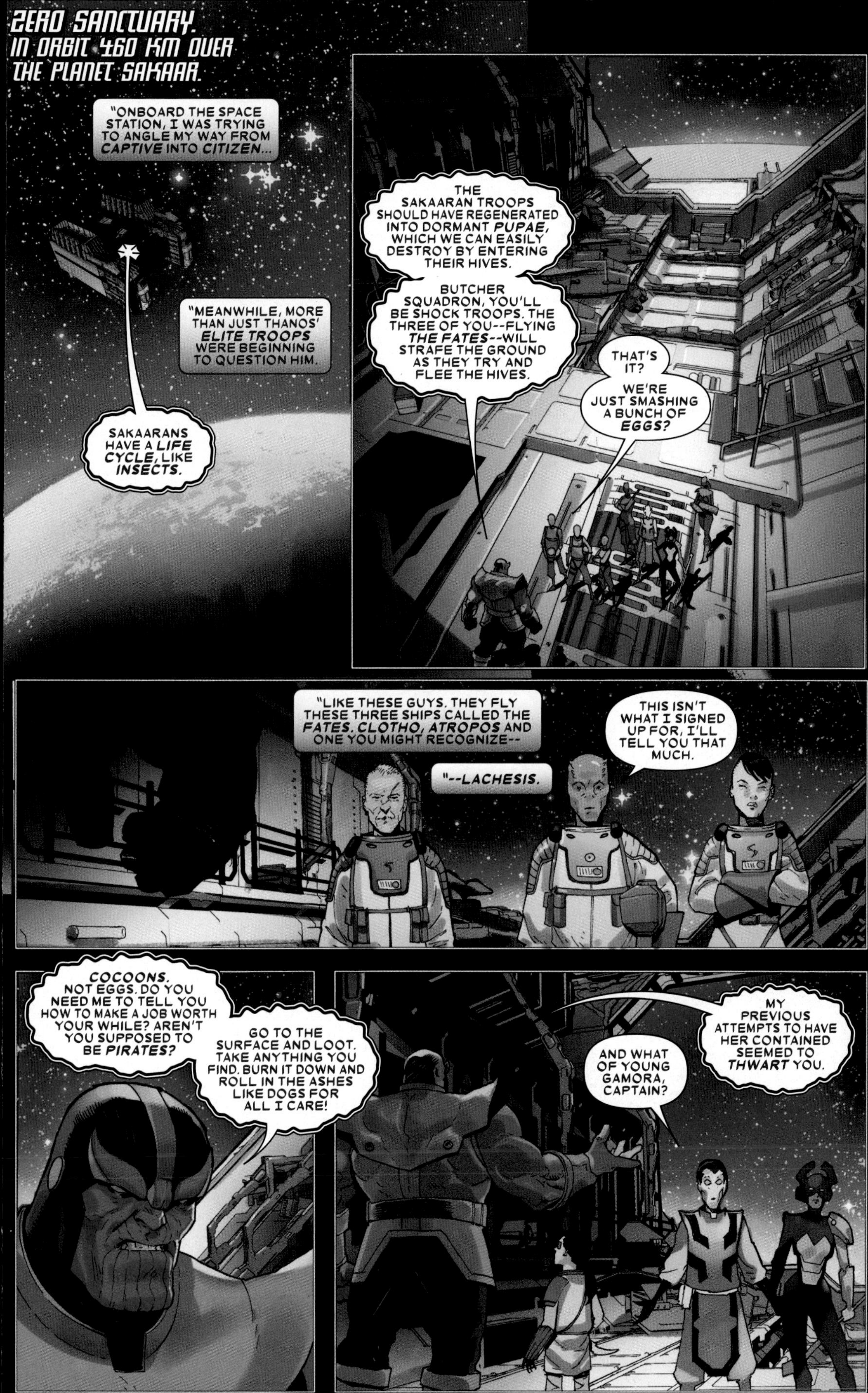
ZERO SANCTUARY. IN ORBIT 460 KM OVER THE PLANET SAKAAR.
"ONBOARD THE SPACE STATION, I WAS TRYING TO ANGLE MY WAY FROM CAPTIVE INTO CITIZEN...
"MEANWHILE, MORE THAN JUST THANOS' ELITE TROOPS WERE BEGINNING TO QUESTION HIM.
SAKAARANS HAVE A LIFE CYCLE, LIKE INSECTS.
THE SAKAARAN TROOPS SHOULD HAVE REGENERATED INTO DORMANT PUPAE, WHICH WE CAN EASILY DESTROY BY ENTERING THEIR HIVES.
BUTCHER SQUADRON, YOU'LL BE SHOCK TROOPS. THE THREE OF YOU--FLYING THE FATES--WILL STRAFE THE GROUND AS THEY TRY AND FLEE THE HIVES.
THAT'S IT?
WE'RE JUST SMASHING A BUNCH OF EGGS?
"LIKE THESE GUYS. THEY FLY THESE THREE SHIPS CALLED THE FATES. CLOTHO, ATROPOS AND ONE YOU MIGHT RECOGNIZE--
"--LACHESIS.
THIS ISN'T WHAT I SIGNED UP FOR, I'LL TELL YOU THAT MUCH.
COCOONS. NOT EGGS. DO YOU NEED ME TO TELL YOU HOW TO MAKE A JOB WORTH YOUR WHILE? AREN'T YOU SUPPOSED TO BE PIRATES?
GO TO THE SURFACE AND LOOT. TAKE ANYTHING YOU FIND. BURN IT DOWN AND ROLL IN THE ASHES LIKE DOGS FOR ALL I CARE!
AND WHAT OF YOUNG GAMORA, CAPTAIN?
MY PREVIOUS ATTEMPTS TO HAVE HER CONTAINED SEEMED TO THWART YOU.

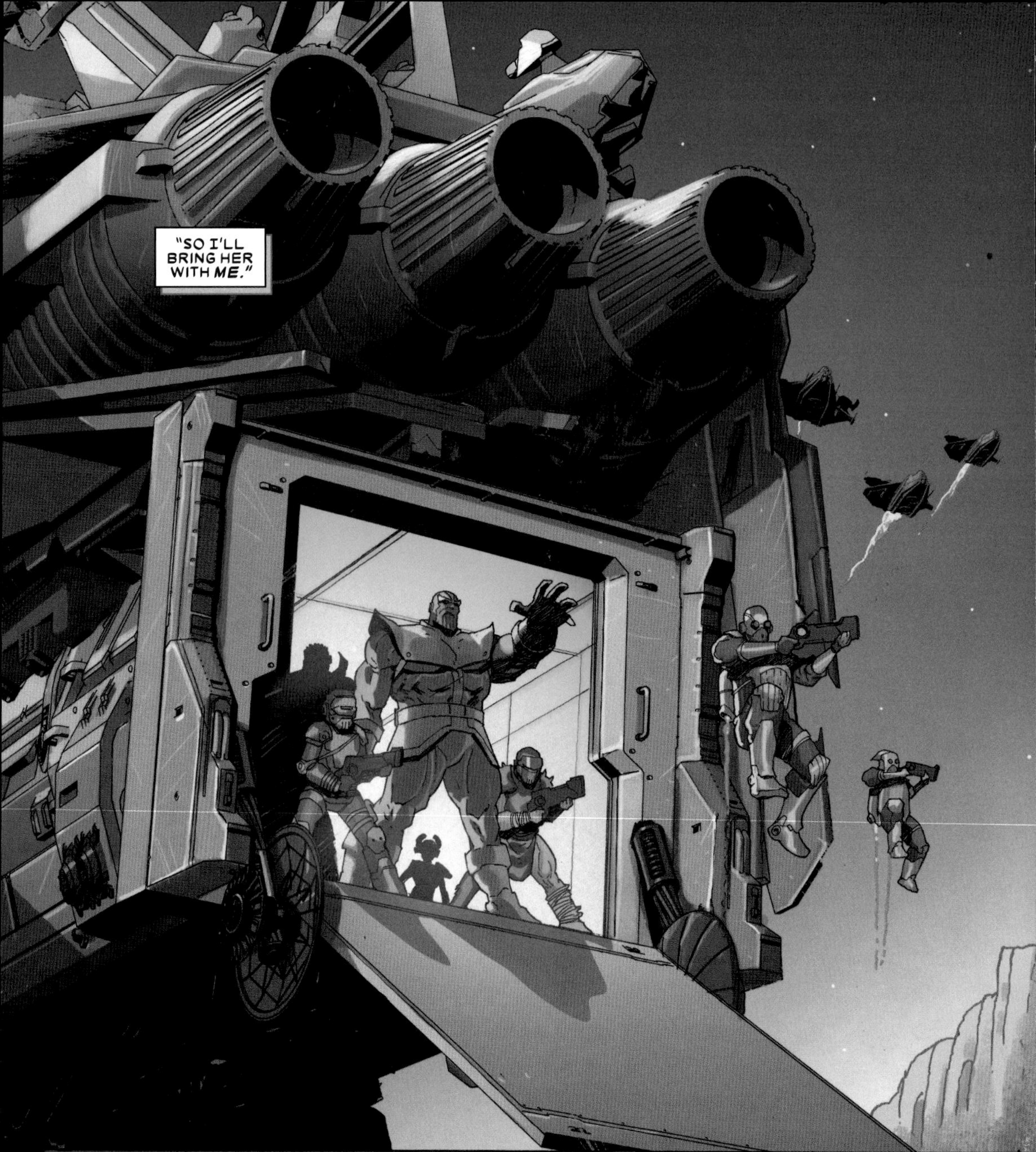
"SO I'LL BRING HER WITH *ME.*"

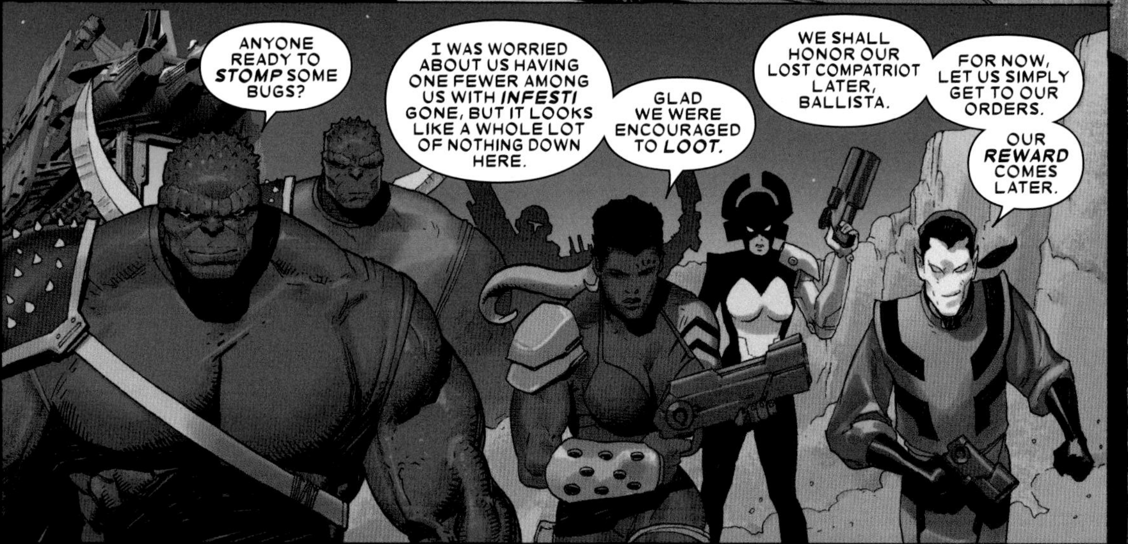
ANYONE READY TO *STOMP* SOME BUGS?
I WAS WORRIED ABOUT US HAVING ONE FEWER AMONG US WITH *INFESTI* GONE, BUT IT LOOKS LIKE A WHOLE LOT OF NOTHING DOWN HERE.
GLAD WE WERE ENCOURAGED TO *LOOT.*
WE SHALL HONOR OUR LOST COMPATRIOT LATER, BALLISTA.
FOR NOW, LET US SIMPLY GET TO OUR ORDERS.
OUR *REWARD* COMES LATER.

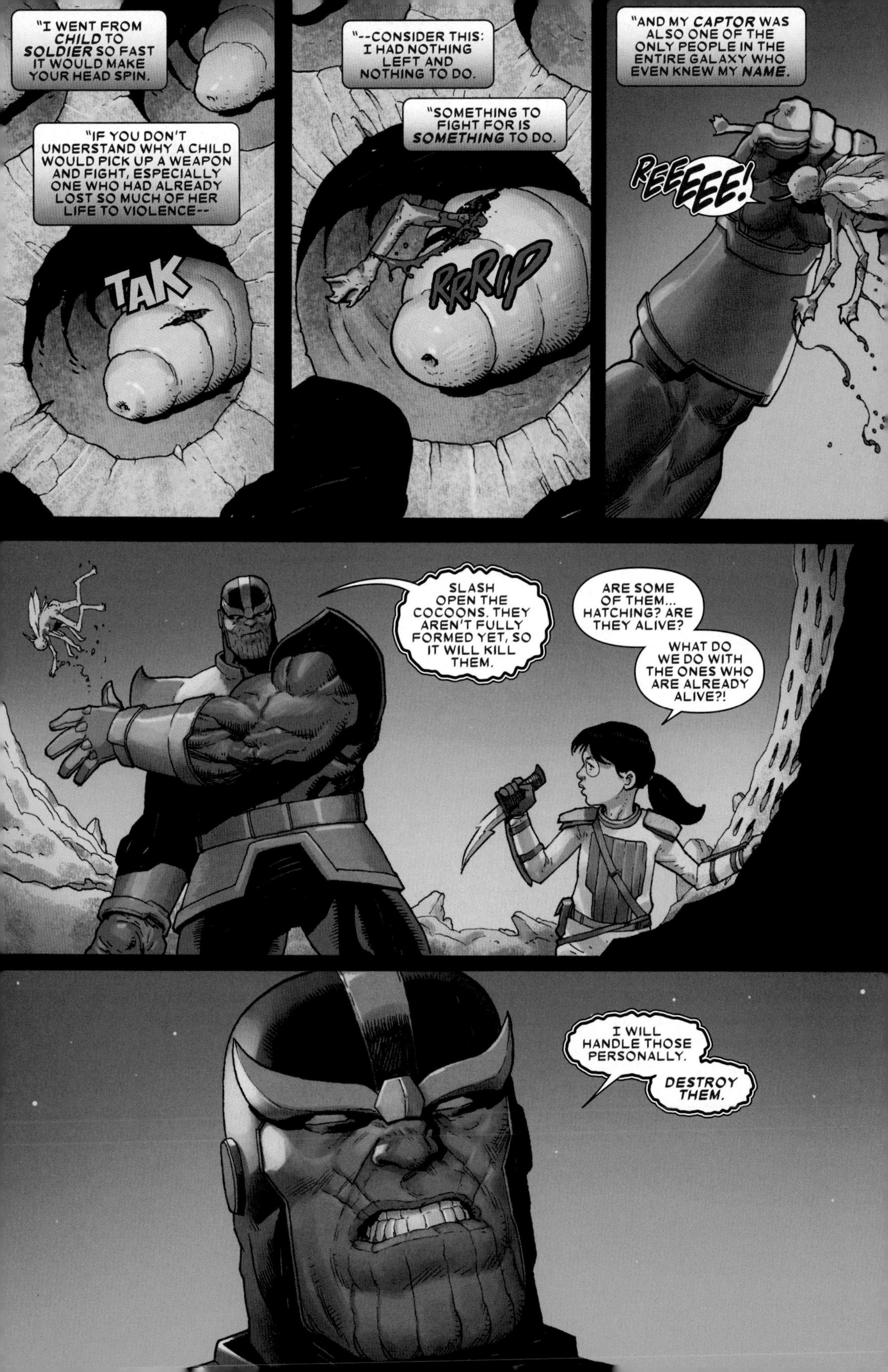
"I WENT FROM CHILD TO SOLDIER SO FAST IT WOULD MAKE YOUR HEAD SPIN.
"IF YOU DON'T UNDERSTAND WHY A CHILD WOULD PICK UP A WEAPON AND FIGHT, ESPECIALLY ONE WHO HAD ALREADY LOST SO MUCH OF HER LIFE TO VIOLENCE--
TAK
"--CONSIDER THIS: I HAD NOTHING LEFT AND NOTHING TO DO.
"SOMETHING TO FIGHT FOR IS SOMETHING TO DO.
RRRIP
"AND MY CAPTOR WAS ALSO ONE OF THE ONLY PEOPLE IN THE ENTIRE GALAXY WHO EVEN KNEW MY NAME.
REEEEEE!
SLASH OPEN THE COCOONS. THEY AREN'T FULLY FORMED YET, SO IT WILL KILL THEM.
ARE SOME OF THEM... HATCHING? ARE THEY ALIVE?
WHAT DO WE DO WITH THE ONES WHO ARE ALREADY ALIVE?!
I WILL HANDLE THOSE PERSONALLY.
DESTROY THEM.

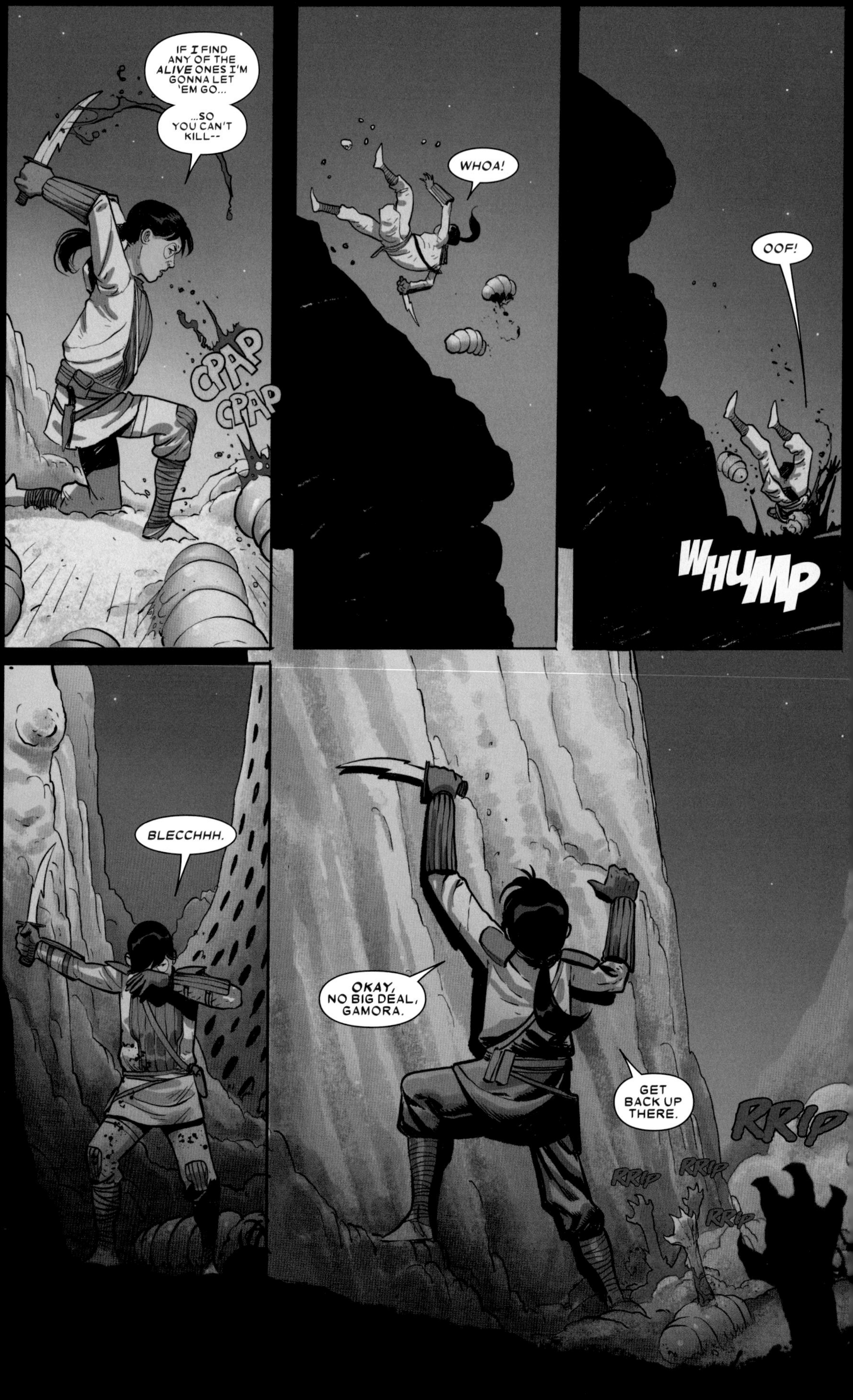
IF I FIND ANY OF THE ALIVE ONES I'M GONNA LET 'EM GO...
...SO YOU CAN'T KILL--
CPAP
CPAP
WHOA!
OOF!
WHUMP
BLECCHHH.
OKAY, NO BIG DEAL, GAMORA.
GET BACK UP THERE.
RRIP
RRIP
RRIP
RRIP

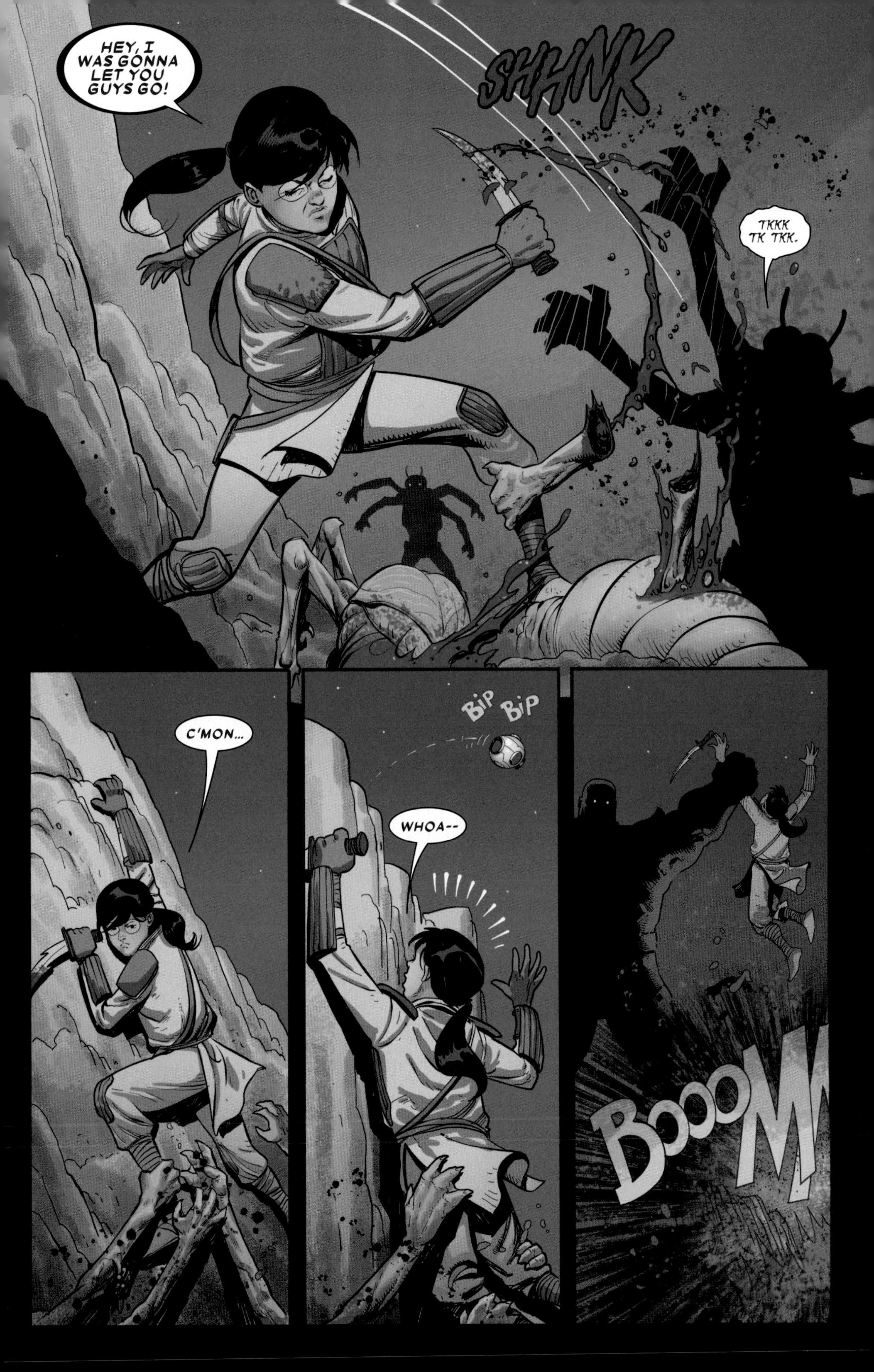
HEY, I WAS GONNA LET YOU GUYS GO!
SHHINK
TKKK TK TKK.
C'MON...
BIP BIP
WHOA--
BOOOM

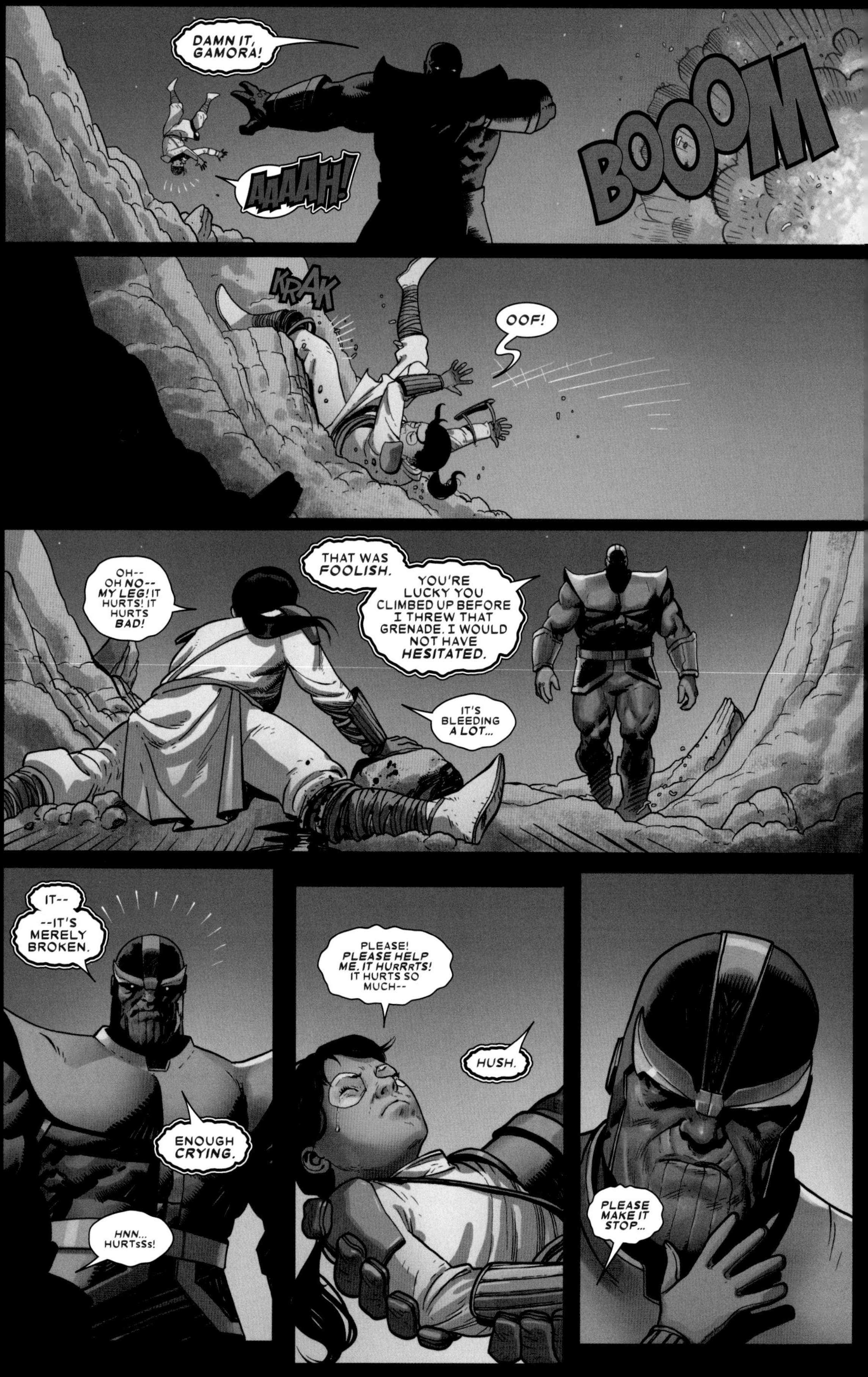

DAMN IT, GAMORA!
AAAAH!
BOOOM
KRAK
OOF!
OH-- OH NO-- MY LEG! IT HURTS! IT HURTS BAD!
THAT WAS FOOLISH.
YOU'RE LUCKY YOU CLIMBED UP BEFORE I THREW THAT GRENADE. I WOULD NOT HAVE HESITATED.
IT'S BLEEDING A LOT...
IT--
--IT'S MERELY BROKEN.
ENOUGH CRYING.
HNN... HURTsSs!
PLEASE! PLEASE HELP ME. IT HURRrTS! IT HURTS SO MUCH--
HUSH.
PLEASE MAKE IT STOP...

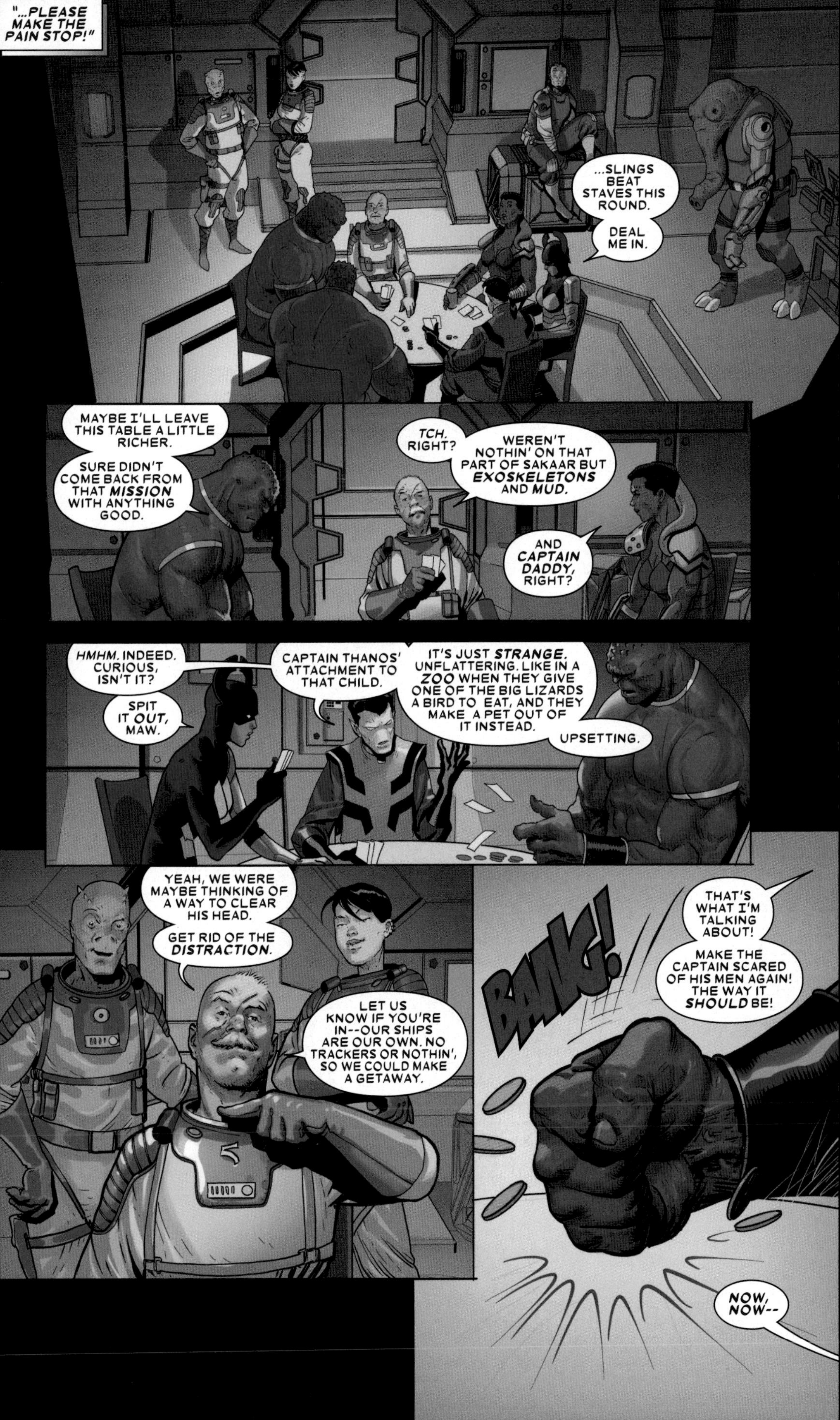
"...PLEASE MAKE THE PAIN STOP!"
...SLINGS BEAT STAVES THIS ROUND.
DEAL ME IN.
MAYBE I'LL LEAVE THIS TABLE A LITTLE RICHER.
SURE DIDN'T COME BACK FROM THAT *MISSION* WITH ANYTHING GOOD.
TCH. RIGHT?
WEREN'T NOTHIN' ON THAT PART OF SAKAAR BUT *EXOSKELETONS* AND *MUD.*
AND *CAPTAIN DADDY,* RIGHT?
HMHM. INDEED. CURIOUS, ISN'T IT?
SPIT IT *OUT,* MAW.
CAPTAIN THANOS' ATTACHMENT TO THAT CHILD.
IT'S JUST *STRANGE.* UNFLATTERING. LIKE IN A *ZOO* WHEN THEY GIVE ONE OF THE BIG LIZARDS A BIRD TO EAT, AND THEY MAKE A PET OUT OF IT INSTEAD.
UPSETTING.
YEAH, WE WERE MAYBE THINKING OF A WAY TO CLEAR HIS HEAD.
GET RID OF THE *DISTRACTION.*
LET US KNOW IF YOU'RE IN--OUR SHIPS ARE OUR OWN. NO TRACKERS OR NOTHIN', SO WE COULD MAKE A GETAWAY.
BANG!
THAT'S WHAT I'M TALKING ABOUT!
MAKE THE CAPTAIN SCARED OF HIS MEN AGAIN! THE WAY IT *SHOULD* BE!
NOW, NOW--

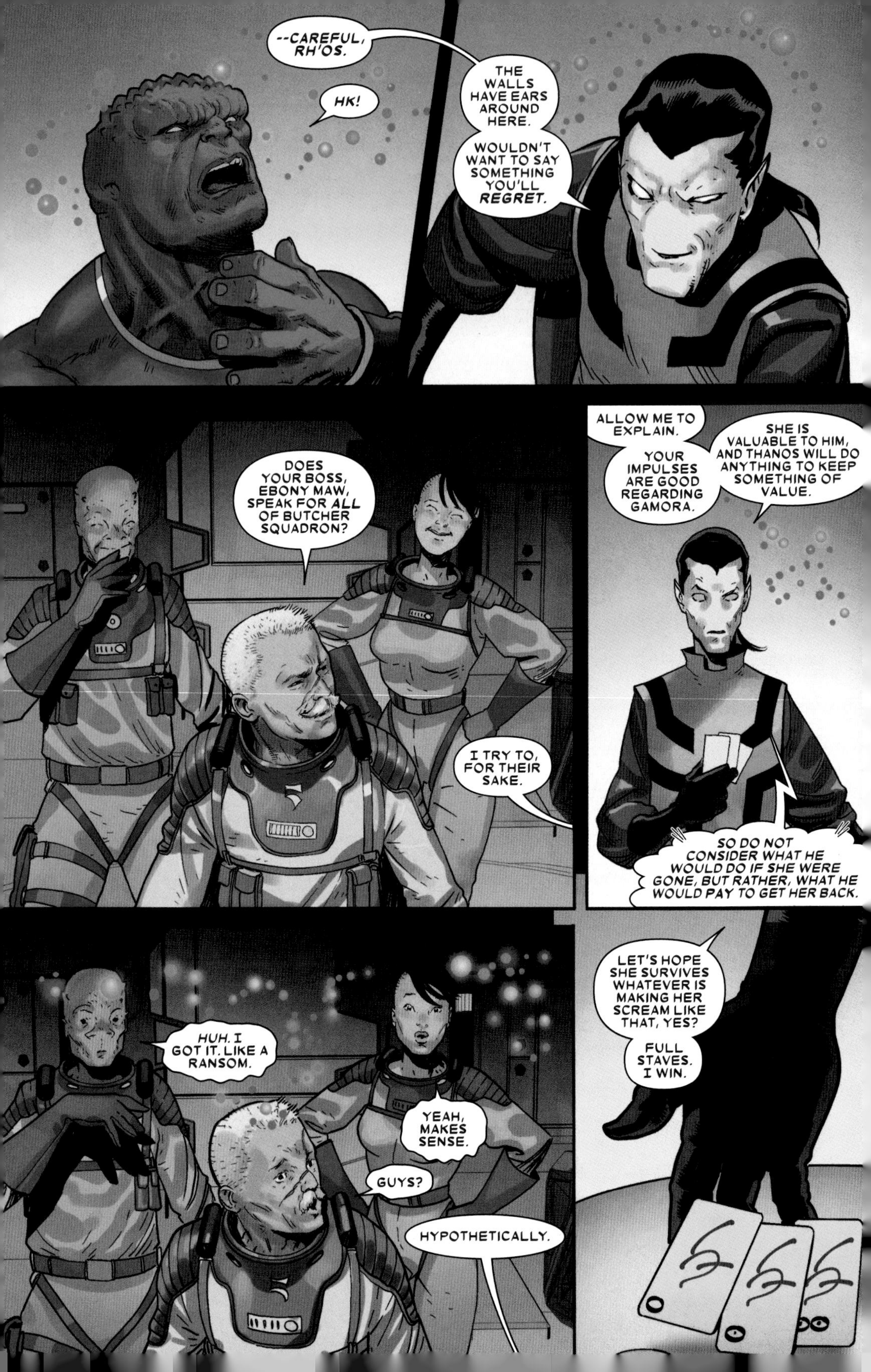
--CAREFUL, RH'OS.
HK!
THE WALLS HAVE EARS AROUND HERE.
WOULDN'T WANT TO SAY SOMETHING YOU'LL *REGRET*.
DOES YOUR BOSS, EBONY MAW, SPEAK FOR *ALL* OF BUTCHER SQUADRON?
I TRY TO, FOR THEIR SAKE.
ALLOW ME TO EXPLAIN.
YOUR IMPULSES ARE GOOD REGARDING GAMORA.
SHE IS VALUABLE TO HIM, AND THANOS WILL DO ANYTHING TO KEEP SOMETHING OF VALUE.
SO DO NOT CONSIDER WHAT HE WOULD DO IF SHE WERE GONE, BUT RATHER, WHAT HE WOULD PAY TO GET HER BACK.
HUH. I GOT IT. LIKE A RANSOM.
YEAH, MAKES SENSE.
GUYS?
HYPOTHETICALLY.
LET'S HOPE SHE SURVIVES WHATEVER IS MAKING HER SCREAM LIKE THAT, YES?
FULL STAVES. I WIN.

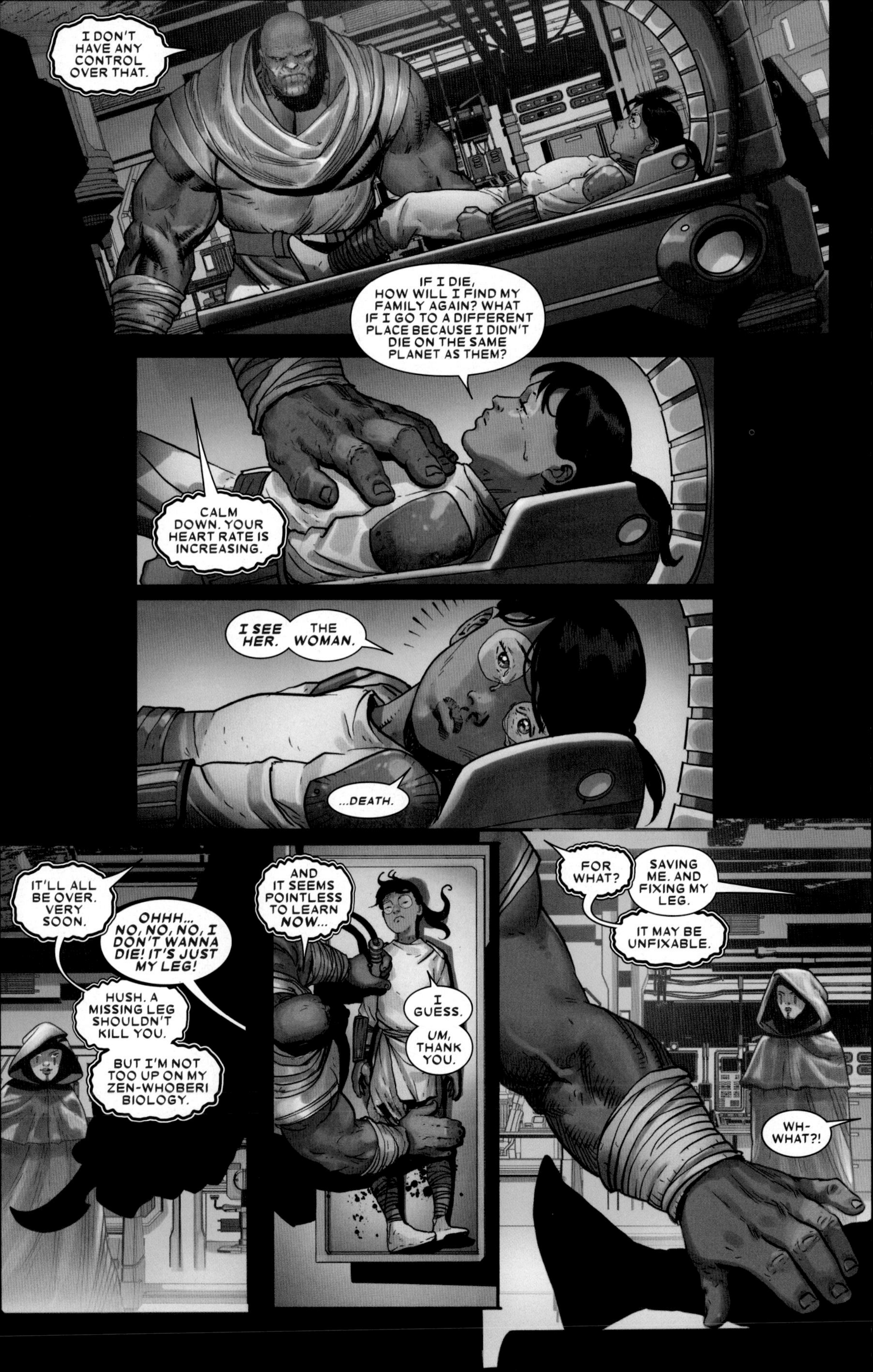
I DON'T HAVE ANY CONTROL OVER THAT.
IF I DIE, HOW WILL I FIND MY FAMILY AGAIN? WHAT IF I GO TO A DIFFERENT PLACE BECAUSE I DIDN'T DIE ON THE SAME PLANET AS THEM?
CALM DOWN. YOUR HEART RATE IS INCREASING.
I SEE HER. *THE WOMAN.*
...DEATH.
IT'LL ALL BE OVER. VERY SOON.
OHHH... NO, NO, NO, I DON'T WANNA DIE! IT'S JUST MY LEG!
HUSH. A MISSING LEG SHOULDN'T KILL YOU.
BUT I'M NOT TOO UP ON MY ZEN-WHOBERI BIOLOGY.
AND IT SEEMS POINTLESS TO LEARN *NOW*...
I GUESS.
UM, THANK YOU.
FOR WHAT?
SAVING ME. AND FIXING MY LEG.
IT MAY BE UNFIXABLE.
WH-WHAT?!

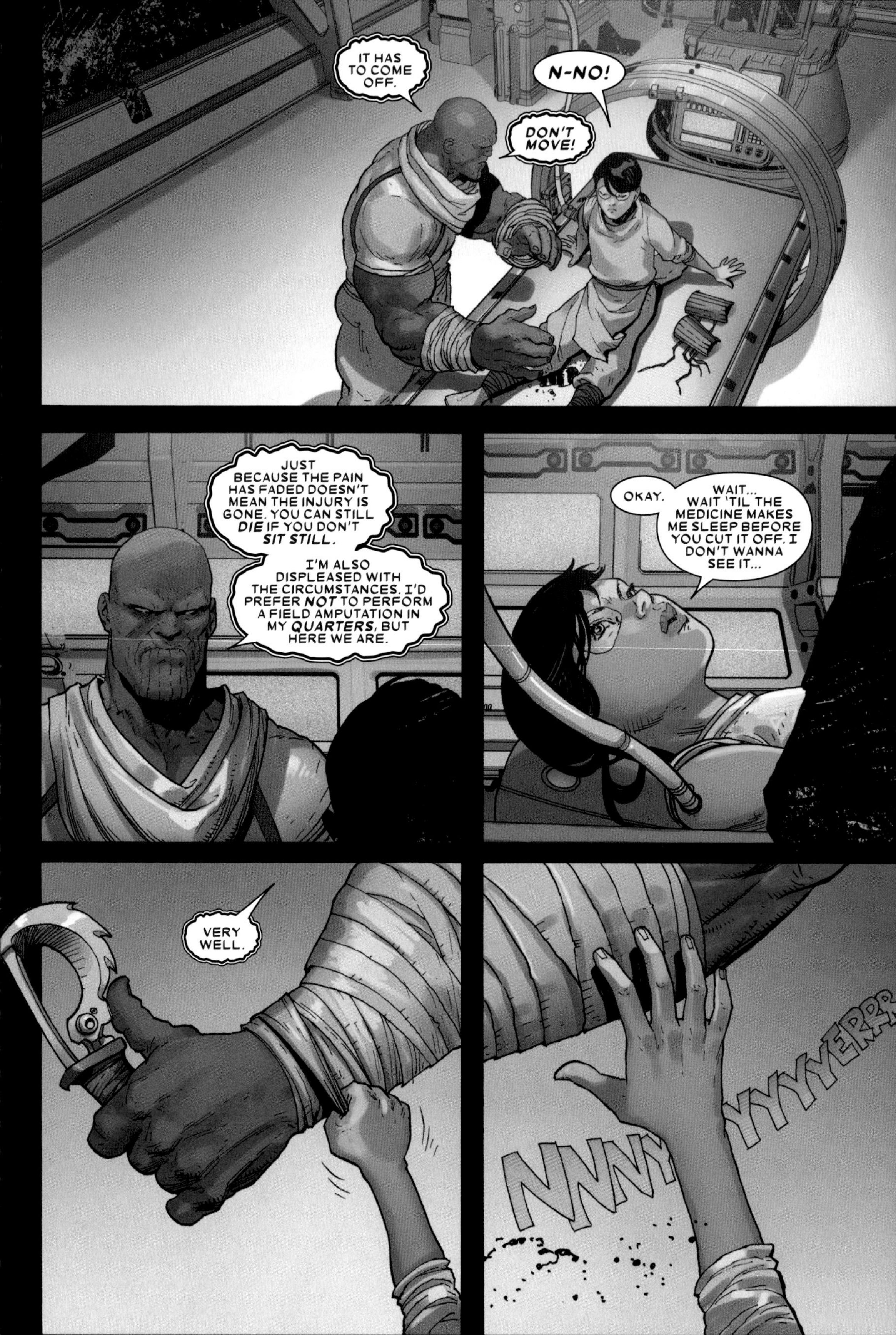
IT HAS TO COME OFF.
N-NO!
DON'T MOVE!
JUST BECAUSE THE PAIN HAS FADED DOESN'T MEAN THE INJURY IS GONE. YOU CAN STILL DIE IF YOU DON'T SIT STILL.
I'M ALSO DISPLEASED WITH THE CIRCUMSTANCES. I'D PREFER NOT TO PERFORM A FIELD AMPUTATION IN MY QUARTERS, BUT HERE WE ARE.
OKAY.
WAIT... WAIT 'TIL THE MEDICINE MAKES ME SLEEP BEFORE YOU CUT IT OFF. I DON'T WANNA SEE IT...
VERY WELL.
NNNYYYYERRR

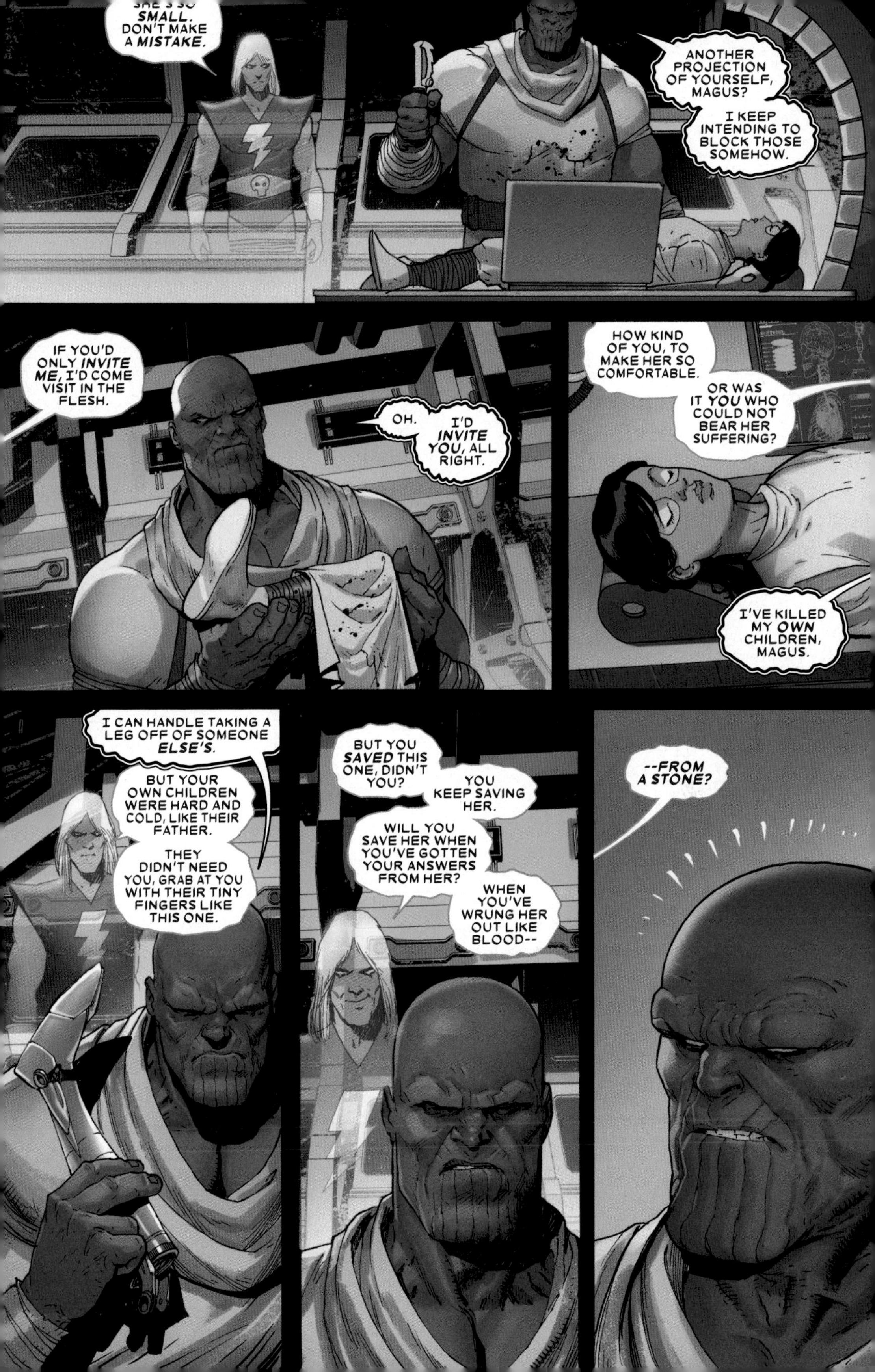
SHE'S SO SMALL. DON'T MAKE A MISTAKE.
ANOTHER PROJECTION OF YOURSELF, MAGUS?
I KEEP INTENDING TO BLOCK THOSE SOMEHOW.
IF YOU'D ONLY INVITE ME, I'D COME VISIT IN THE FLESH.
OH.
I'D INVITE YOU, ALL RIGHT.
HOW KIND OF YOU, TO MAKE HER SO COMFORTABLE.
OR WAS IT YOU WHO COULD NOT BEAR HER SUFFERING?
I'VE KILLED MY OWN CHILDREN, MAGUS.
I CAN HANDLE TAKING A LEG OFF OF SOMEONE ELSE'S.
BUT YOUR OWN CHILDREN WERE HARD AND COLD, LIKE THEIR FATHER.
THEY DIDN'T NEED YOU, GRAB AT YOU WITH THEIR TINY FINGERS LIKE THIS ONE.
BUT YOU SAVED THIS ONE, DIDN'T YOU?
YOU KEEP SAVING HER.
WILL YOU SAVE HER WHEN YOU'VE GOTTEN YOUR ANSWERS FROM HER?
WHEN YOU'VE WRUNG HER OUT LIKE BLOOD--
--FROM A STONE?

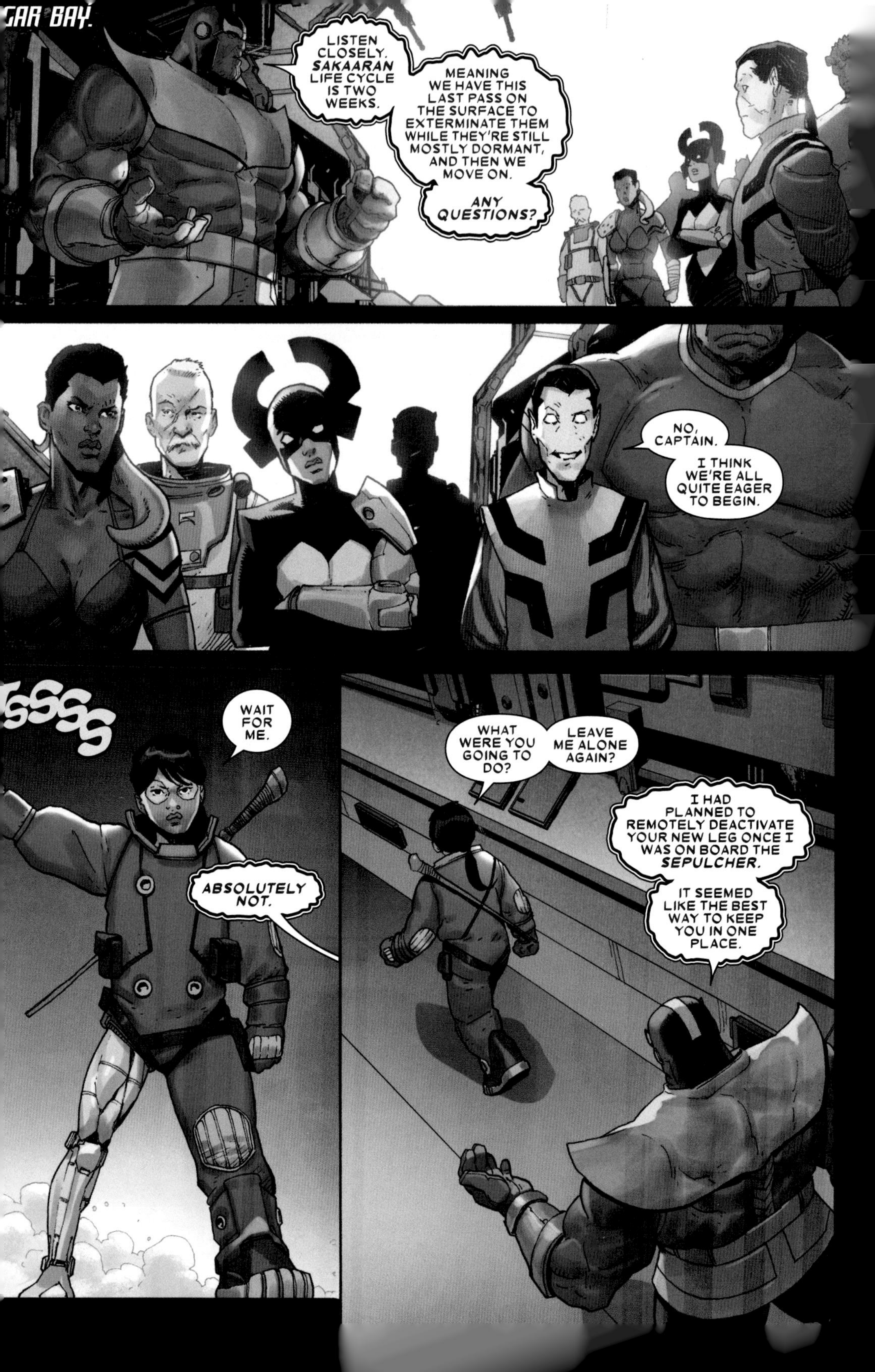
GAR BAY.
LISTEN CLOSELY. SAKAARAN LIFE CYCLE IS TWO WEEKS.
MEANING WE HAVE THIS LAST PASS ON THE SURFACE TO EXTERMINATE THEM WHILE THEY'RE STILL MOSTLY DORMANT, AND THEN WE MOVE ON.
ANY QUESTIONS?
NO, CAPTAIN.
I THINK WE'RE ALL QUITE EAGER TO BEGIN.
TSSSS
WAIT FOR ME.
ABSOLUTELY NOT.
WHAT WERE YOU GOING TO DO?
LEAVE ME ALONE AGAIN?
I HAD PLANNED TO REMOTELY DEACTIVATE YOUR NEW LEG ONCE I WAS ON BOARD THE SEPULCHER.
IT SEEMED LIKE THE BEST WAY TO KEEP YOU IN ONE PLACE.

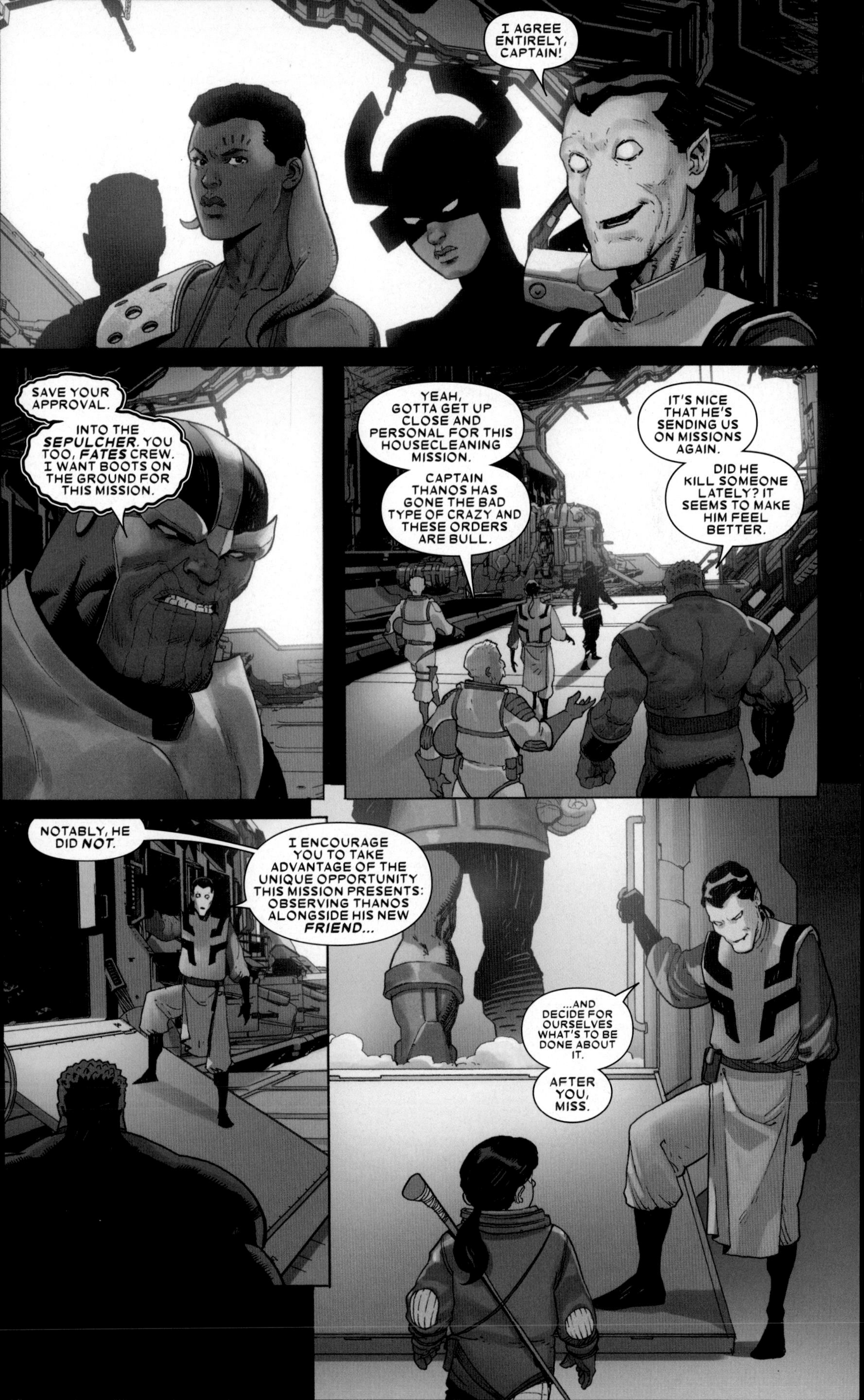
I AGREE ENTIRELY, CAPTAIN!
SAVE YOUR APPROVAL.
INTO THE *SEPULCHER*. YOU TOO, *FATES* CREW. I WANT BOOTS ON THE GROUND FOR THIS MISSION.
YEAH, GOTTA GET UP CLOSE AND PERSONAL FOR THIS HOUSECLEANING MISSION.
CAPTAIN THANOS HAS GONE THE BAD TYPE OF CRAZY AND THESE ORDERS ARE BULL.
IT'S NICE THAT HE'S SENDING US ON MISSIONS AGAIN.
DID HE KILL SOMEONE LATELY? IT SEEMS TO MAKE HIM FEEL BETTER.
NOTABLY, HE DID *NOT*.
I ENCOURAGE YOU TO TAKE ADVANTAGE OF THE UNIQUE OPPORTUNITY THIS MISSION PRESENTS: OBSERVING THANOS ALONGSIDE HIS NEW *FRIEND*...
...AND DECIDE FOR OURSELVES WHAT'S TO BE DONE ABOUT IT.
AFTER YOU, MISS.

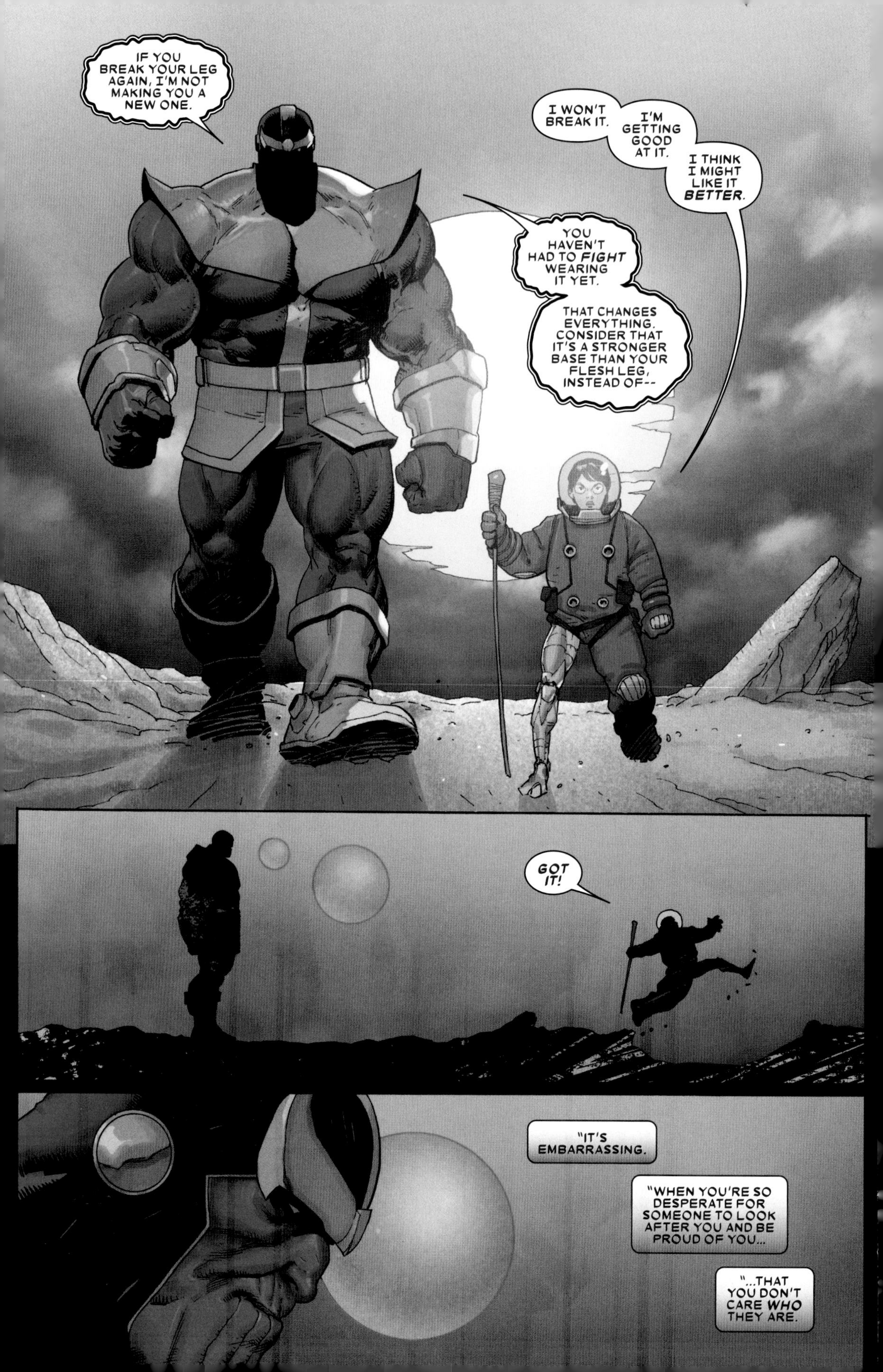
IF YOU BREAK YOUR LEG AGAIN, I'M NOT MAKING YOU A NEW ONE.
I WON'T BREAK IT.
I'M GETTING GOOD AT IT.
I THINK I MIGHT LIKE IT *BETTER*.
YOU HAVEN'T HAD TO *FIGHT* WEARING IT YET.
THAT CHANGES EVERYTHING. CONSIDER THAT IT'S A STRONGER BASE THAN YOUR FLESH LEG, INSTEAD OF--
GOT IT!
"IT'S EMBARRASSING.
"WHEN YOU'RE SO DESPERATE FOR SOMEONE TO LOOK AFTER YOU AND BE PROUD OF YOU...
"...THAT YOU DON'T CARE *WHO* THEY ARE.

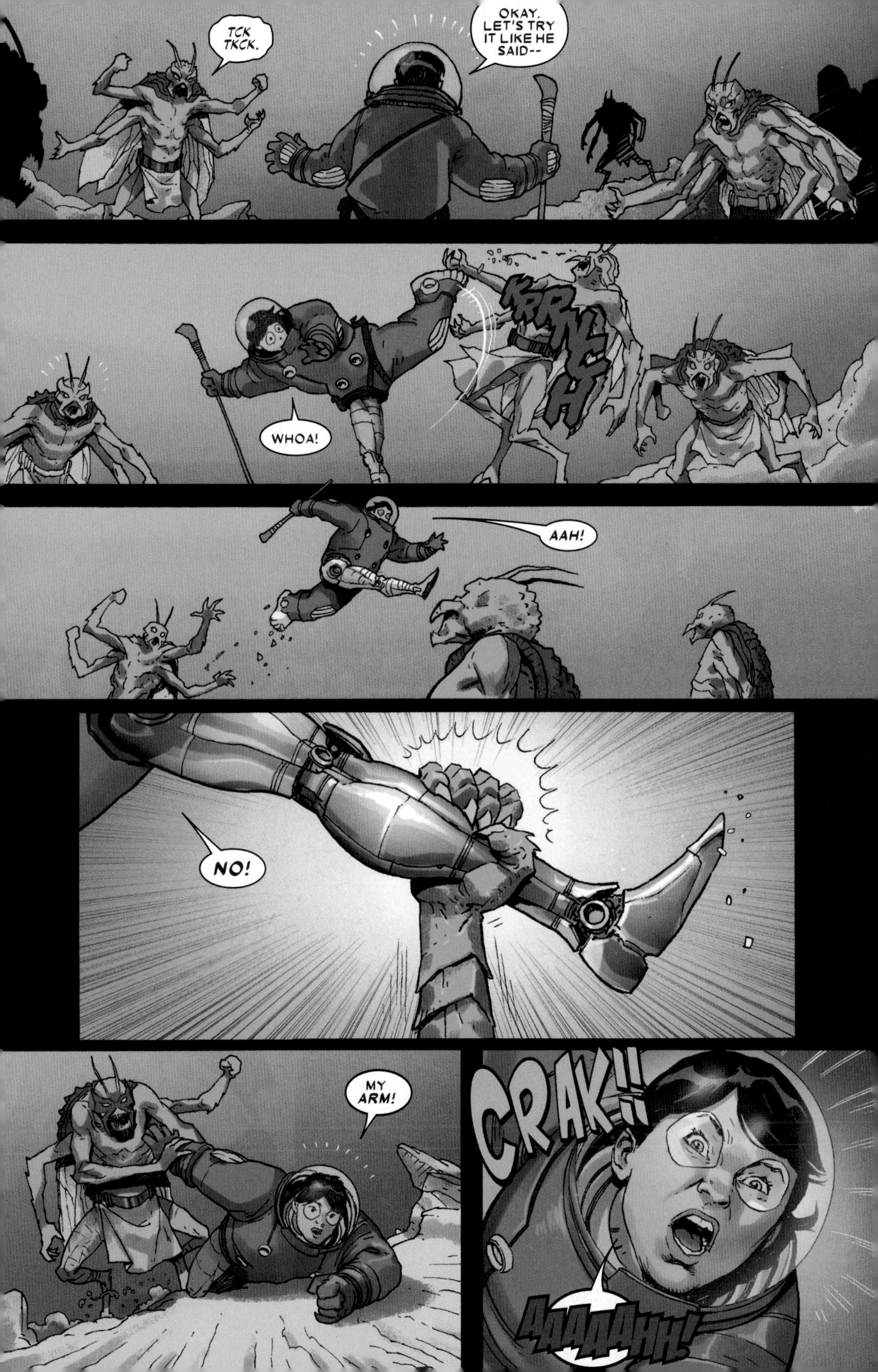

TCK TKCK.
OKAY. LET'S TRY IT LIKE HE SAID--
KRRNCH
WHOA!
AAH!
NO!
MY ARM!
CRAK!!
AAAAAHH!

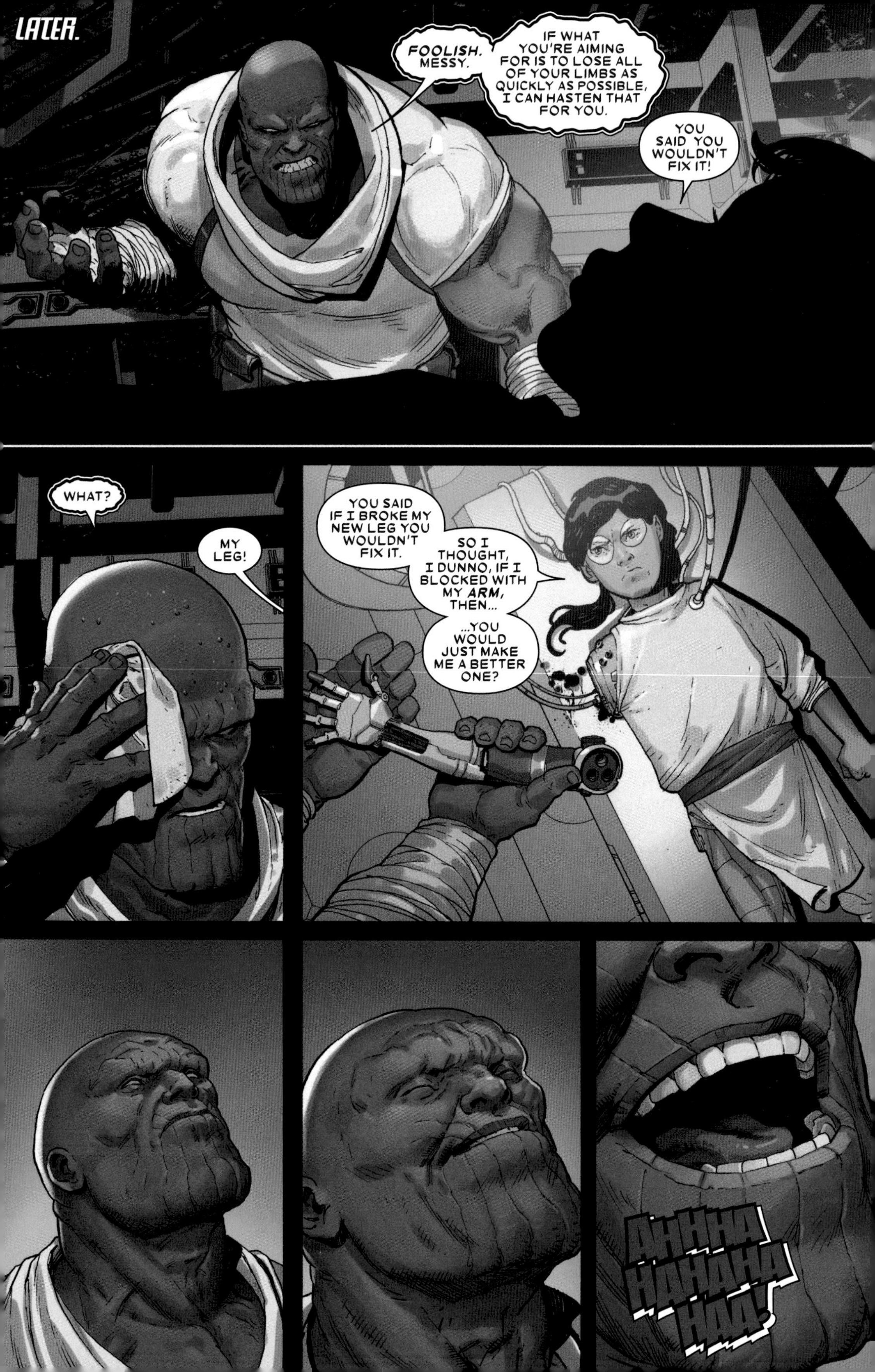
LATER.
FOOLISH. MESSY.
IF WHAT YOU'RE AIMING FOR IS TO LOSE ALL OF YOUR LIMBS AS QUICKLY AS POSSIBLE, I CAN HASTEN THAT FOR YOU.
YOU SAID YOU WOULDN'T FIX IT!
WHAT?
MY LEG!
YOU SAID IF I BROKE MY NEW LEG YOU WOULDN'T FIX IT.
SO I THOUGHT, I DUNNO, IF I BLOCKED WITH MY ARM, THEN...
...YOU WOULD JUST MAKE ME A BETTER ONE?
AHHHA HAHAHA HAA!

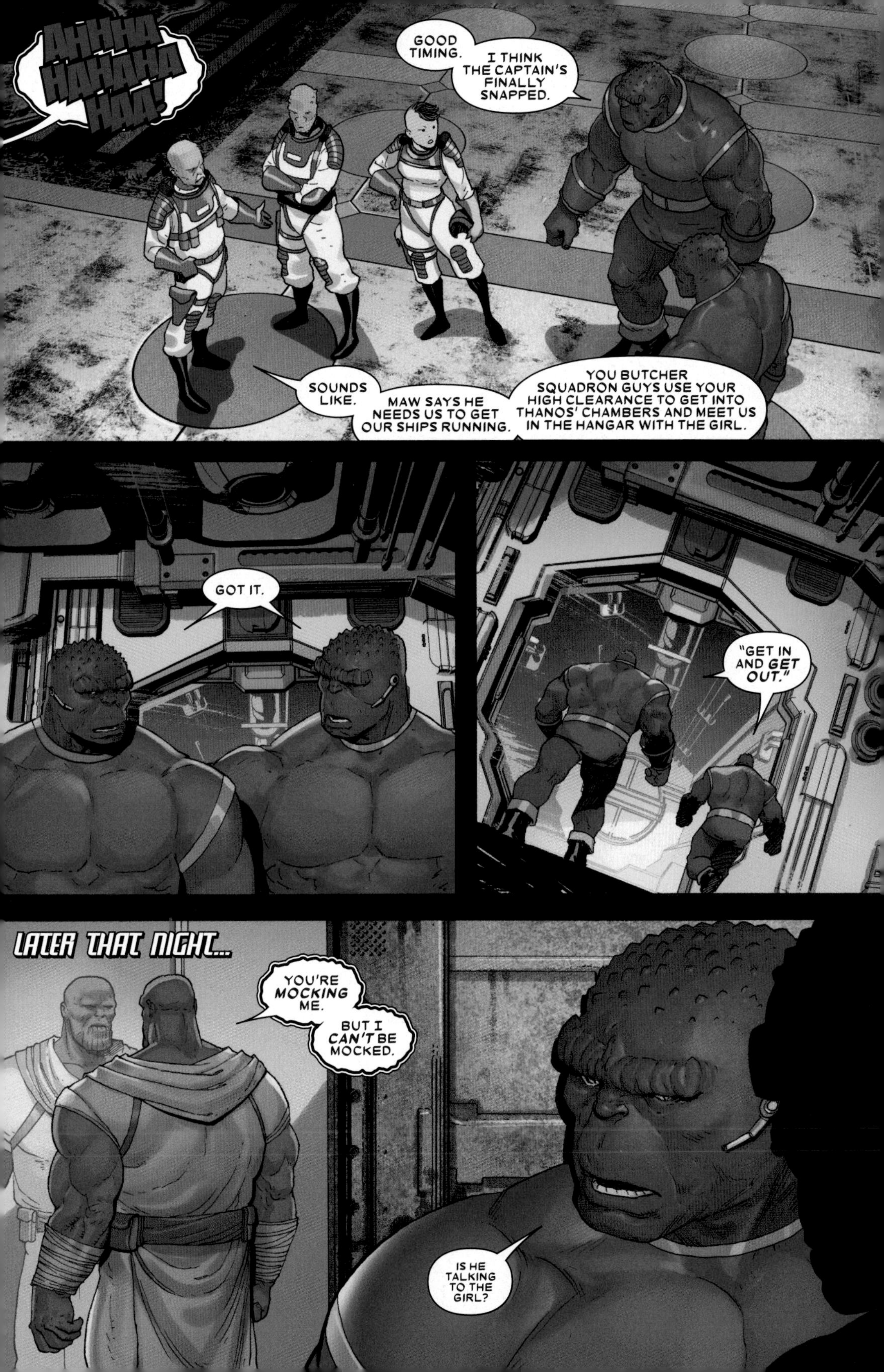

AHHHA HAHAHA HAA!
GOOD TIMING.
I THINK THE CAPTAIN'S FINALLY SNAPPED.
SOUNDS LIKE.
MAW SAYS HE NEEDS US TO GET OUR SHIPS RUNNING.
YOU BUTCHER SQUADRON GUYS USE YOUR HIGH CLEARANCE TO GET INTO THANOS' CHAMBERS AND MEET US IN THE HANGAR WITH THE GIRL.
GOT IT.
"GET IN AND GET OUT."
LATER THAT NIGHT...
YOU'RE MOCKING ME.
BUT I CAN'T BE MOCKED.
IS HE TALKING TO THE GIRL?

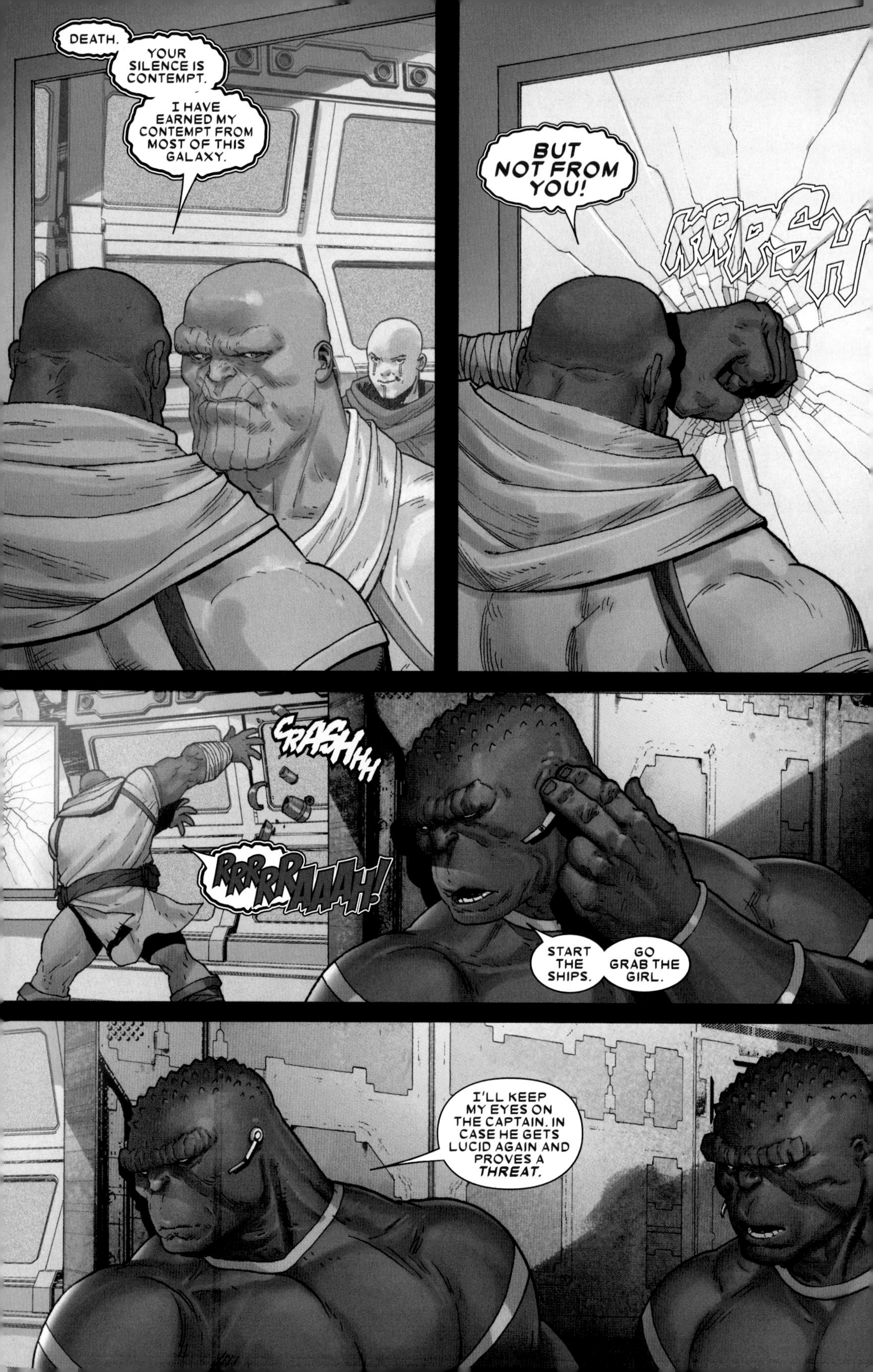
DEATH.
YOUR SILENCE IS CONTEMPT.
I HAVE EARNED MY CONTEMPT FROM MOST OF THIS GALAXY.
BUT NOT FROM YOU!
KRRSH
CRASHHH
RRRRRRAAAAH!
START THE SHIPS.
GO GRAB THE GIRL.
I'LL KEEP MY EYES ON THE CAPTAIN, IN CASE HE GETS LUCID AGAIN AND PROVES A *THREAT.*

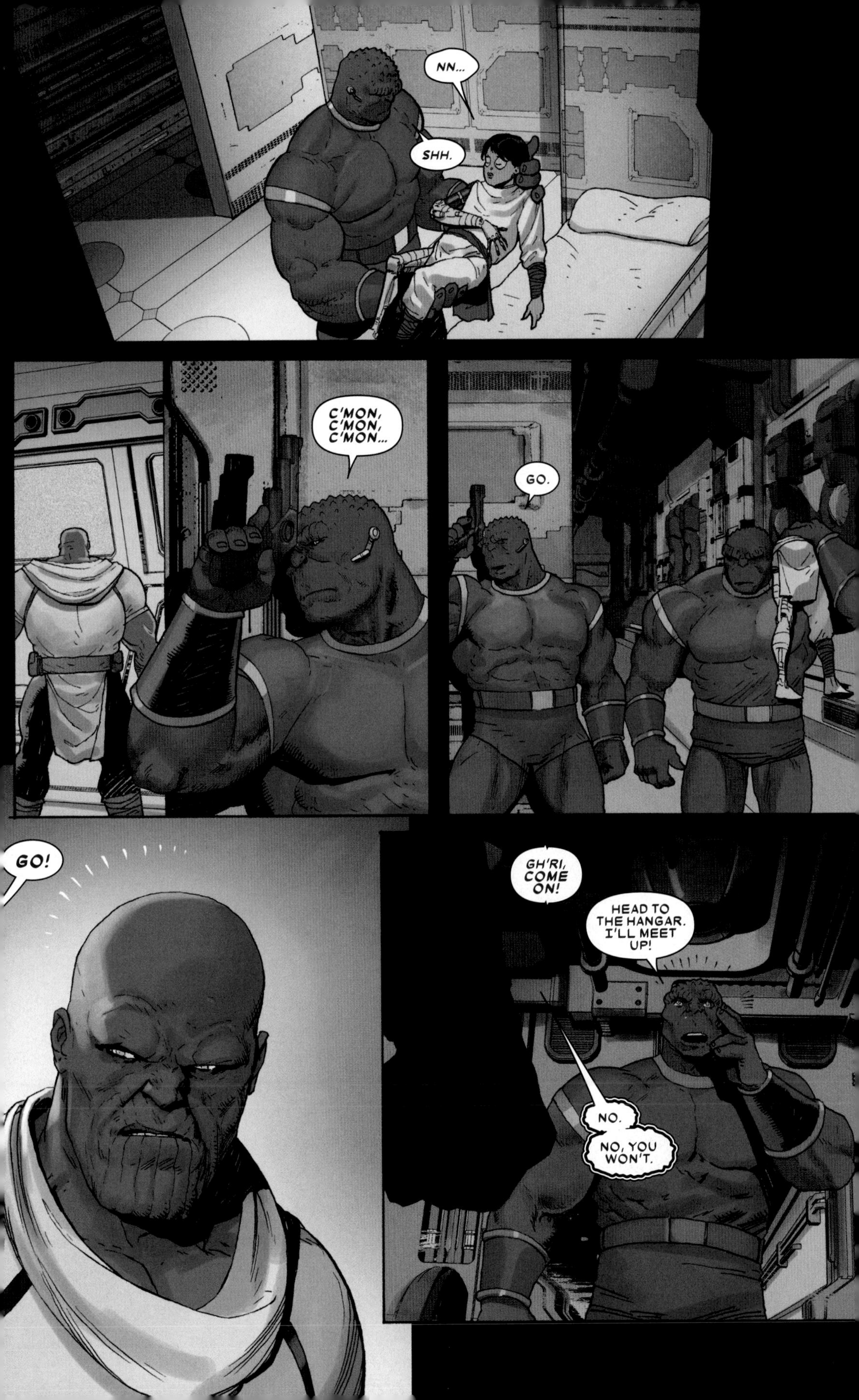
NN...
SHH.
C'MON, C'MON, C'MON...
GO.
GO!
GH'RI, COME ON!
HEAD TO THE HANGAR. I'LL MEET UP!
NO.
NO, YOU WON'T.

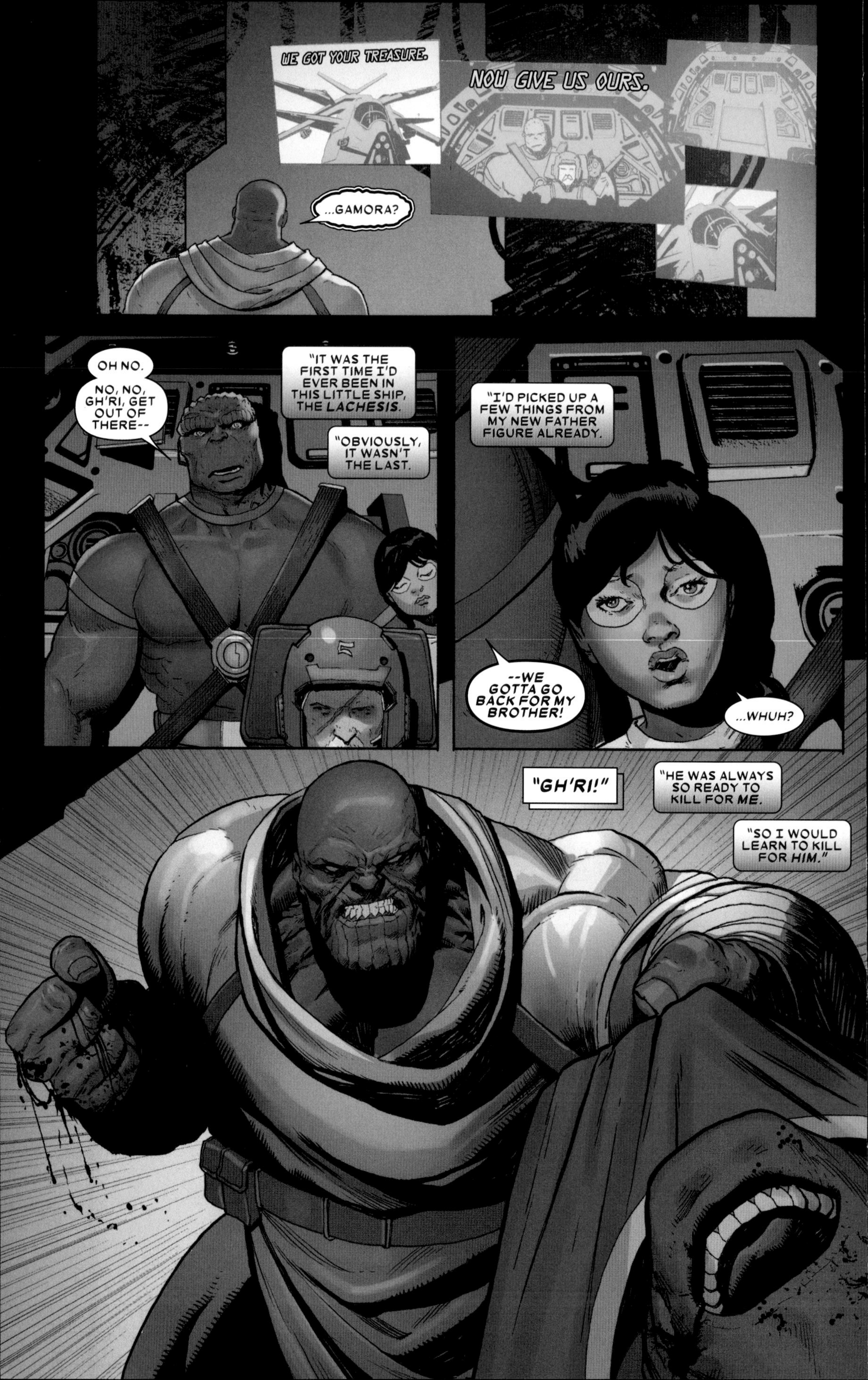

WE GOT YOUR TREASURE.
NOW GIVE US OURS.
...GAMORA?
OH NO.
NO, NO, GH'RI, GET OUT OF THERE--
"IT WAS THE FIRST TIME I'D EVER BEEN IN THIS LITTLE SHIP, THE *LACHESIS*.
"OBVIOUSLY, IT WASN'T THE LAST.
"I'D PICKED UP A FEW THINGS FROM MY NEW FATHER FIGURE ALREADY.
--WE GOTTA GO BACK FOR MY BROTHER!
...WHUH?
"GH'RI!"
"HE WAS ALWAYS SO READY TO KILL FOR *ME*.
"SO I WOULD LEARN TO KILL FOR *HIM*."

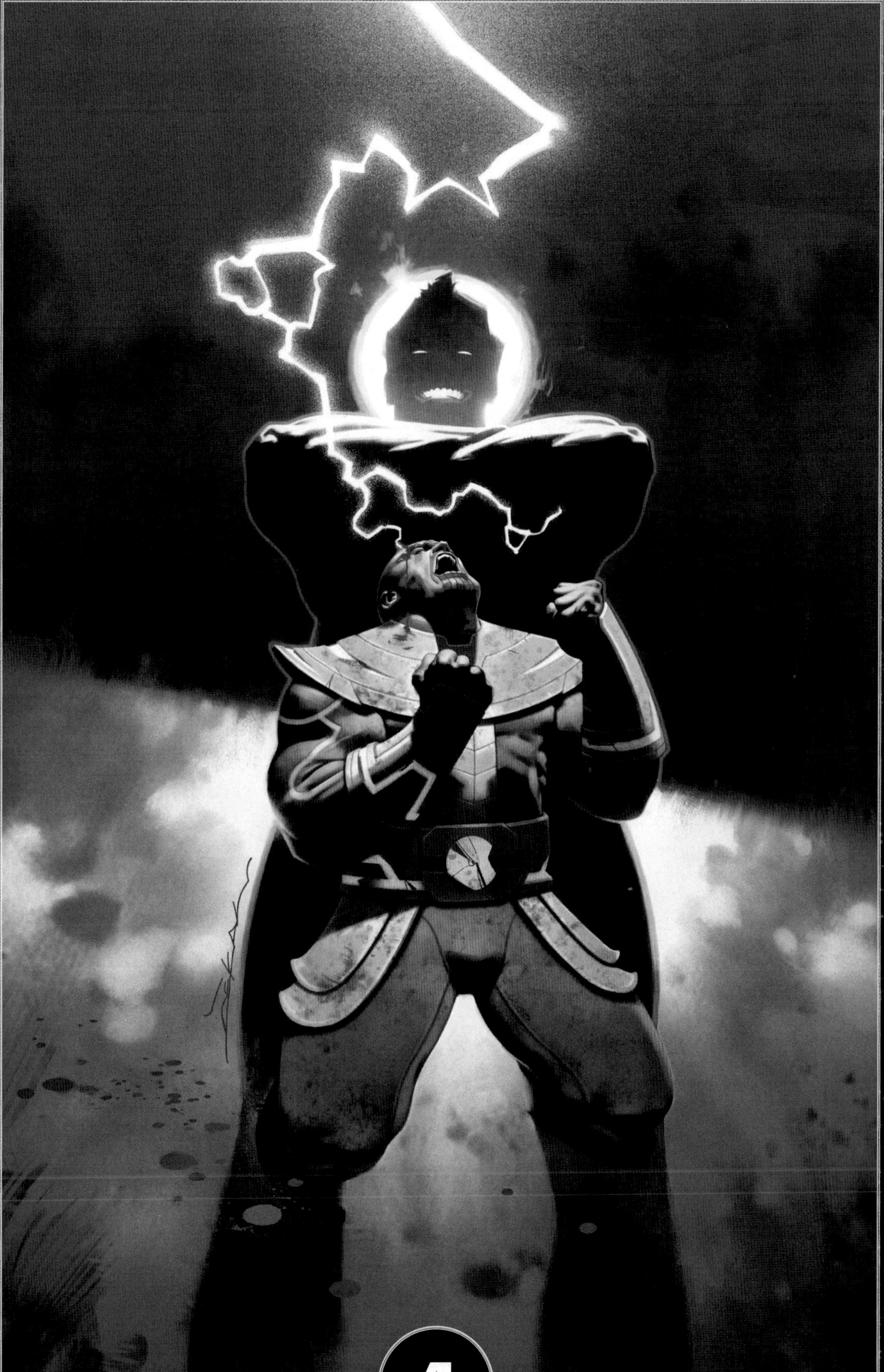

4

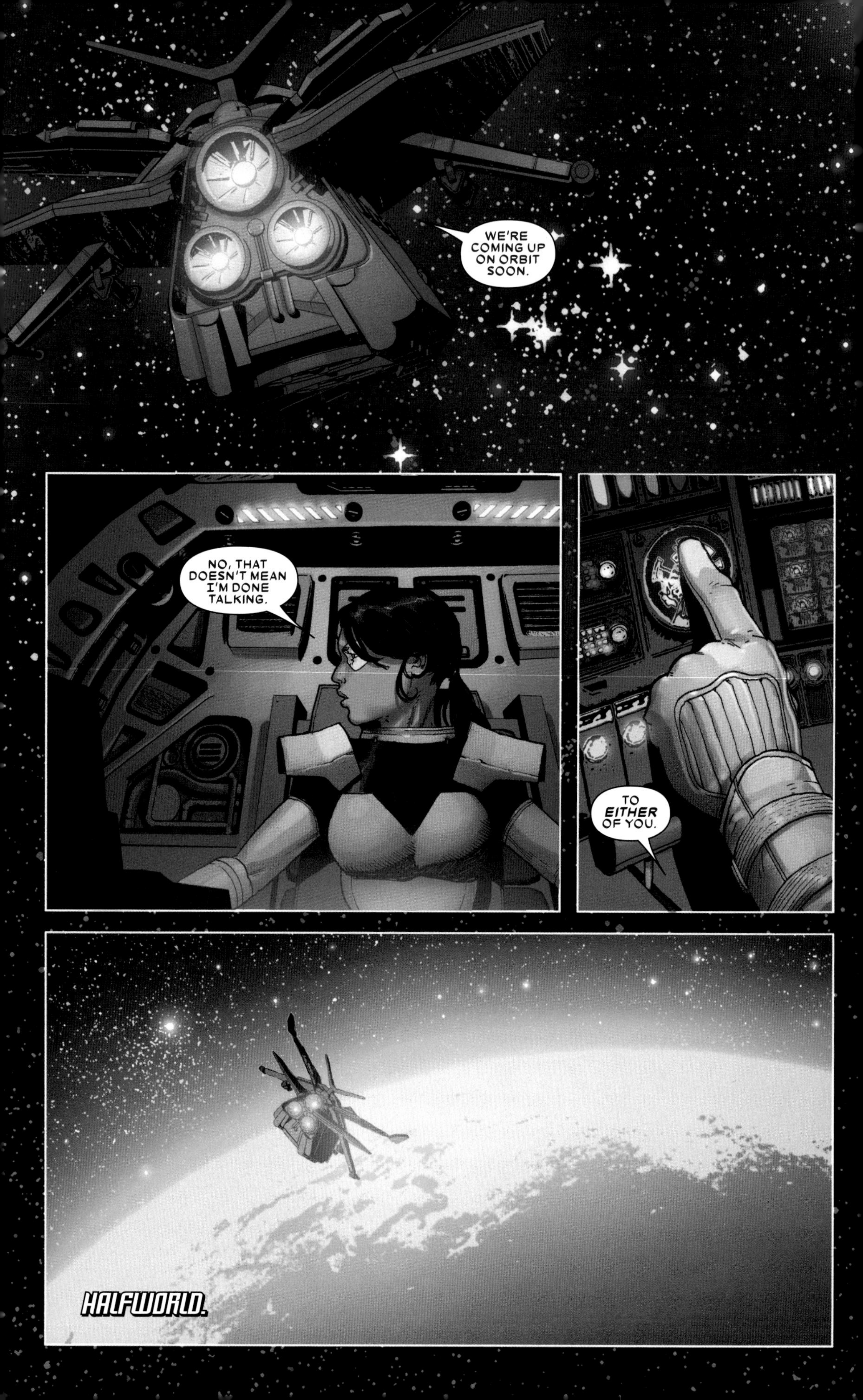
WE'RE COMING UP ON ORBIT SOON.
NO, THAT DOESN'T MEAN I'M DONE TALKING.
TO EITHER OF YOU.
HALFWORLD.

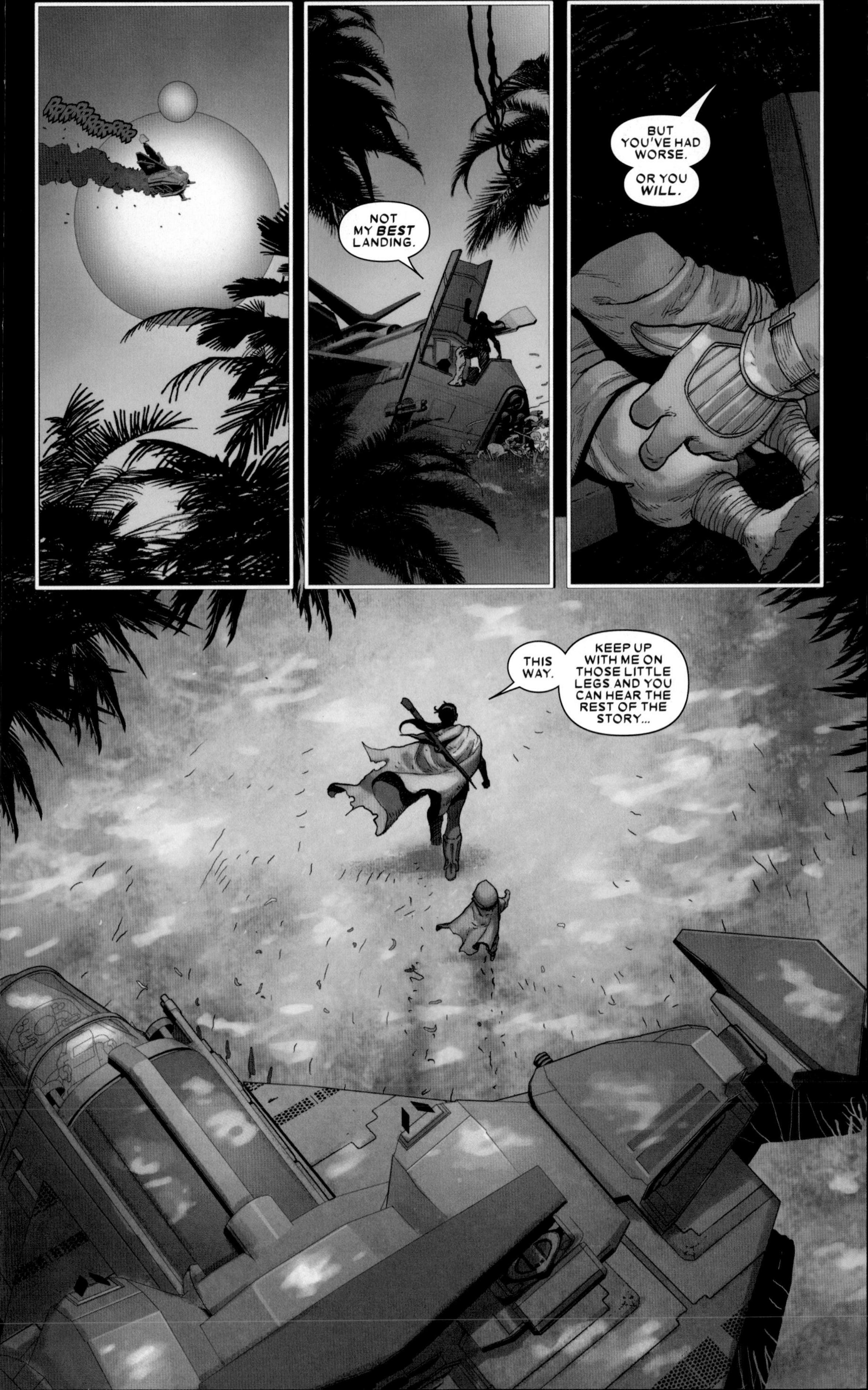
RRRRRRRRRRR
NOT MY BEST LANDING.
BUT YOU'VE HAD WORSE.
OR YOU WILL.
THIS WAY.
KEEP UP WITH ME ON THOSE LITTLE LEGS AND YOU CAN HEAR THE REST OF THE STORY...

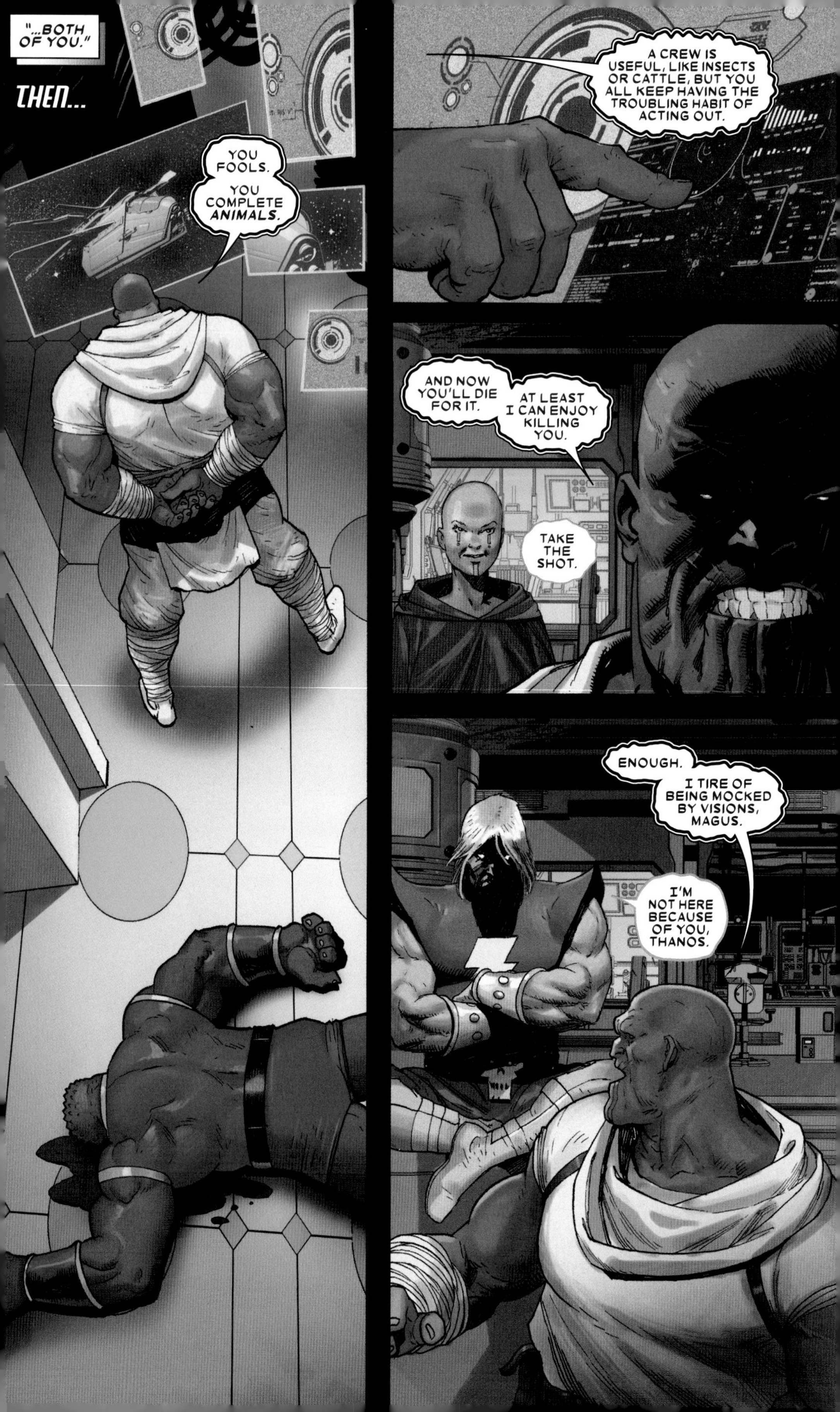
"...BOTH OF YOU."
THEN...
YOU FOOLS.
YOU COMPLETE ANIMALS.
A CREW IS USEFUL, LIKE INSECTS OR CATTLE, BUT YOU ALL KEEP HAVING THE TROUBLING HABIT OF ACTING OUT.
AND NOW YOU'LL DIE FOR IT.
AT LEAST I CAN ENJOY KILLING YOU.
TAKE THE SHOT.
ENOUGH.
I TIRE OF BEING MOCKED BY VISIONS, MAGUS.
I'M NOT HERE BECAUSE OF YOU, THANOS.

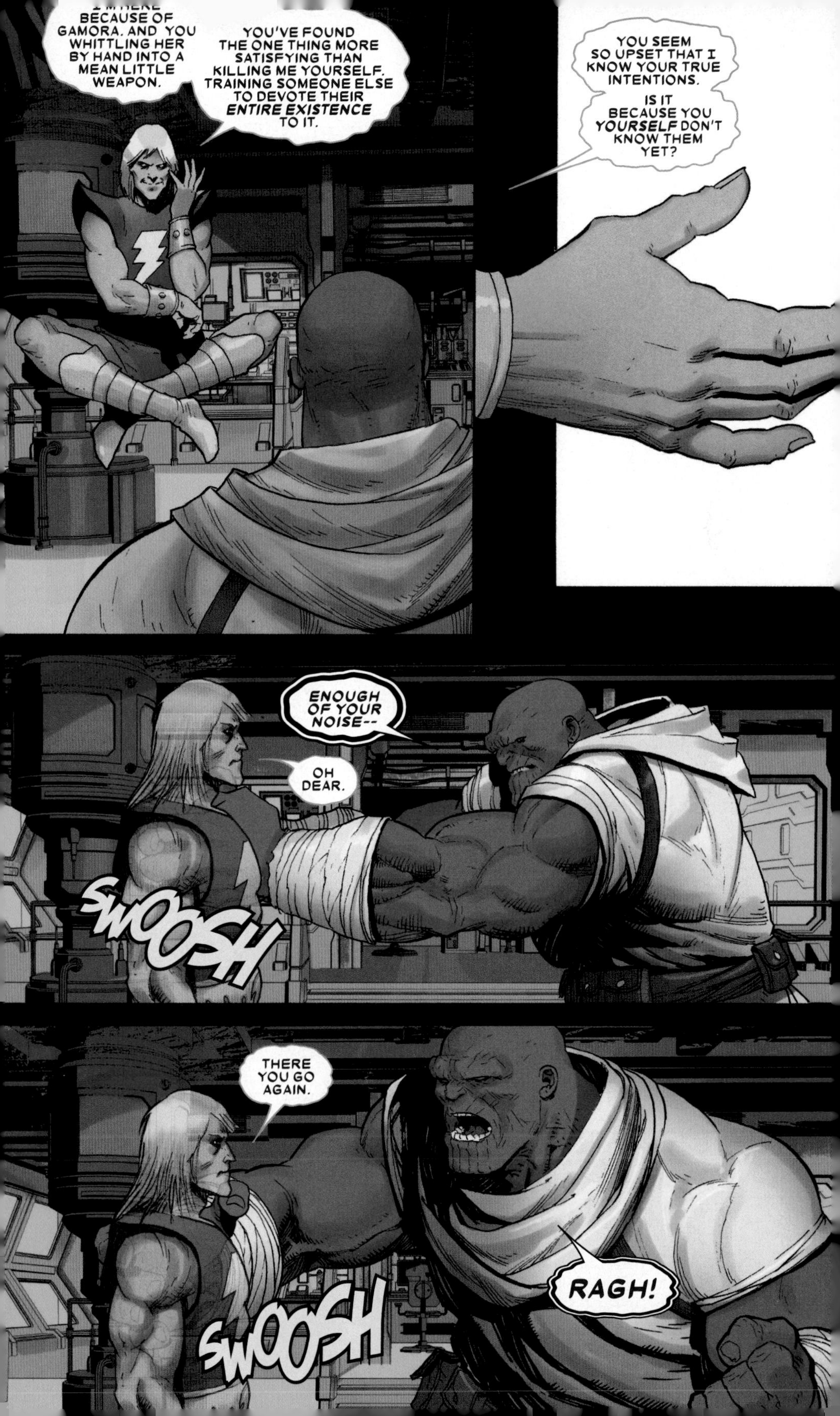
BECAUSE OF GAMORA. AND YOU WHITTLING HER BY HAND INTO A MEAN LITTLE WEAPON.
YOU'VE FOUND THE ONE THING MORE SATISFYING THAN KILLING ME YOURSELF. TRAINING SOMEONE ELSE TO DEVOTE THEIR *ENTIRE EXISTENCE* TO IT.
YOU SEEM SO UPSET THAT I KNOW YOUR TRUE INTENTIONS.
IS IT BECAUSE YOU *YOURSELF* DON'T KNOW THEM YET?
ENOUGH OF YOUR NOISE--
OH DEAR.
SWOOSH
THERE YOU GO AGAIN.
RAGH!
SWOOSH

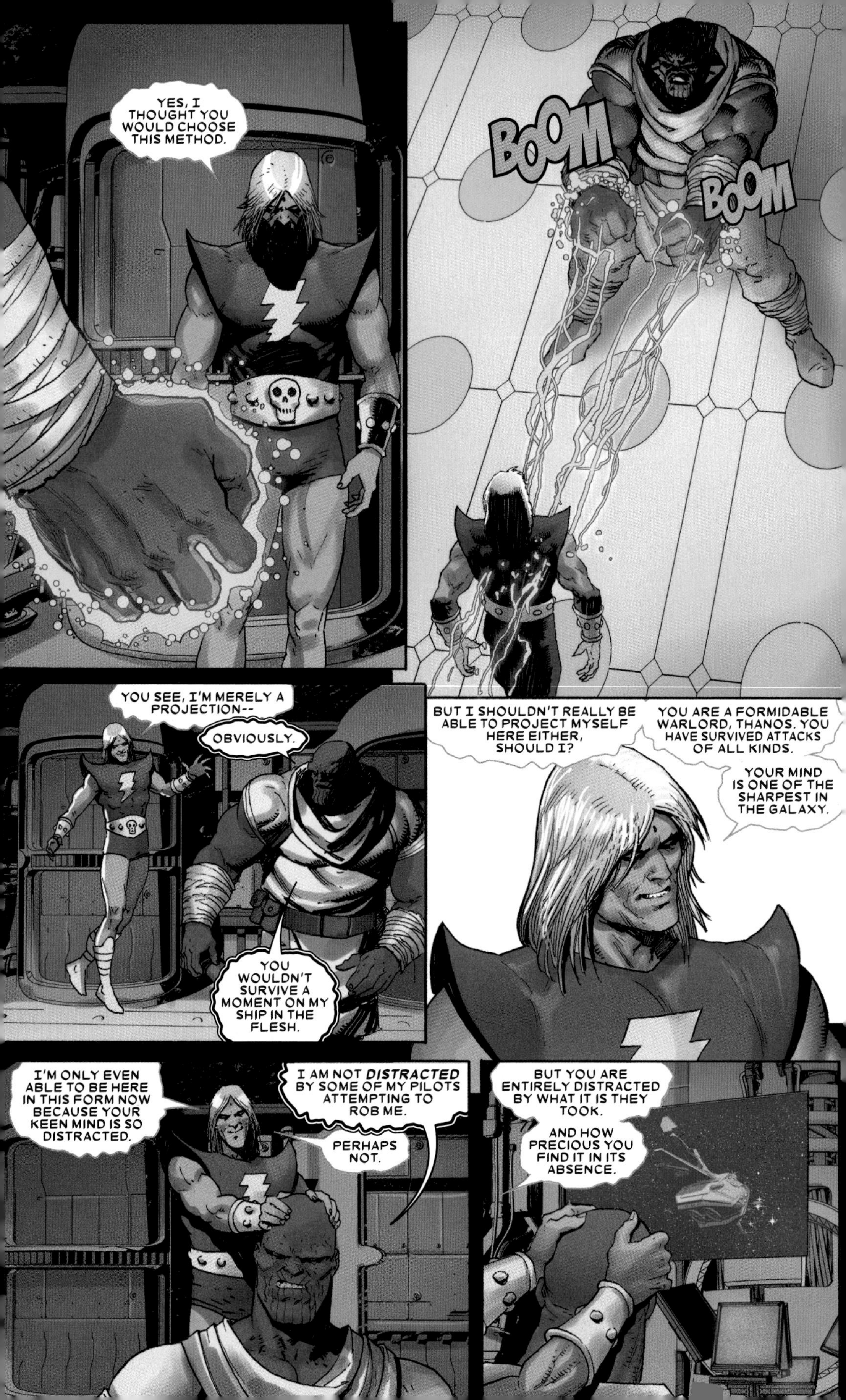
YES, I THOUGHT YOU WOULD CHOOSE THIS METHOD.
BOOM
BOOM
YOU SEE, I'M MERELY A PROJECTION--
OBVIOUSLY.
YOU WOULDN'T SURVIVE A MOMENT ON MY SHIP IN THE FLESH.
BUT I SHOULDN'T REALLY BE ABLE TO PROJECT MYSELF HERE EITHER, SHOULD I?
YOU ARE A FORMIDABLE WARLORD, THANOS. YOU HAVE SURVIVED ATTACKS OF ALL KINDS.
YOUR MIND IS ONE OF THE SHARPEST IN THE GALAXY.
I'M ONLY EVEN ABLE TO BE HERE IN THIS FORM NOW BECAUSE YOUR KEEN MIND IS SO DISTRACTED.
I AM NOT *DISTRACTED* BY SOME OF MY PILOTS ATTEMPTING TO ROB ME.
PERHAPS NOT.
BUT YOU ARE ENTIRELY DISTRACTED BY WHAT IT IS THEY TOOK.
AND HOW PRECIOUS YOU FIND IT IN ITS ABSENCE.

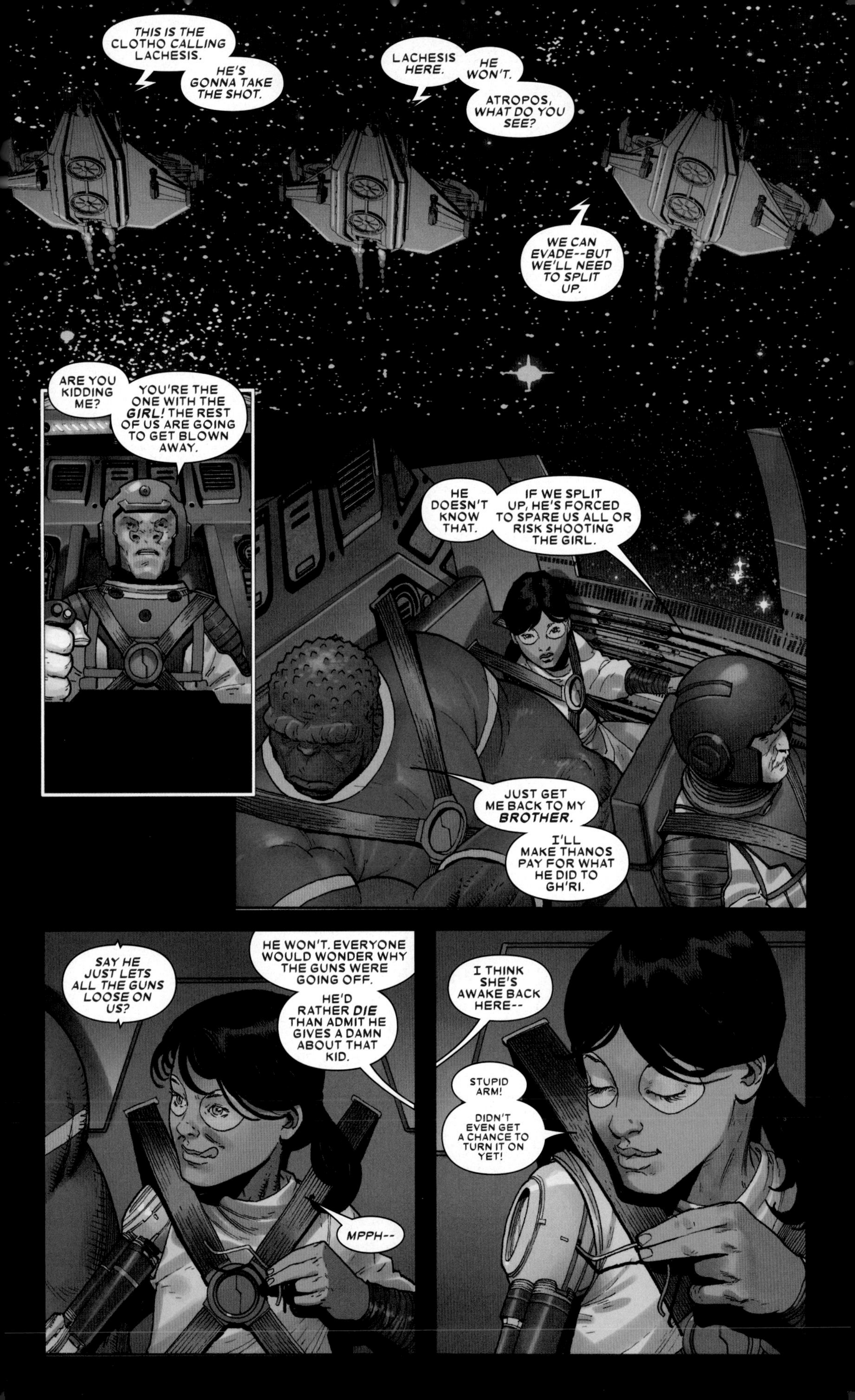
THIS IS THE CLOTHO CALLING LACHESIS.
HE'S GONNA TAKE THE SHOT.
LACHESIS HERE.
HE WON'T.
ATROPOS, WHAT DO YOU SEE?
WE CAN EVADE--BUT WE'LL NEED TO SPLIT UP.
ARE YOU KIDDING ME?
YOU'RE THE ONE WITH THE GIRL! THE REST OF US ARE GOING TO GET BLOWN AWAY.
HE DOESN'T KNOW THAT.
IF WE SPLIT UP, HE'S FORCED TO SPARE US ALL OR RISK SHOOTING THE GIRL.
JUST GET ME BACK TO MY BROTHER.
I'LL MAKE THANOS PAY FOR WHAT HE DID TO GH'RI.
SAY HE JUST LETS ALL THE GUNS LOOSE ON US?
HE WON'T. EVERYONE WOULD WONDER WHY THE GUNS WERE GOING OFF.
HE'D RATHER DIE THAN ADMIT HE GIVES A DAMN ABOUT THAT KID.
MPPH--
I THINK SHE'S AWAKE BACK HERE--
STUPID ARM!
DIDN'T EVEN GET A CHANCE TO TURN IT ON YET!

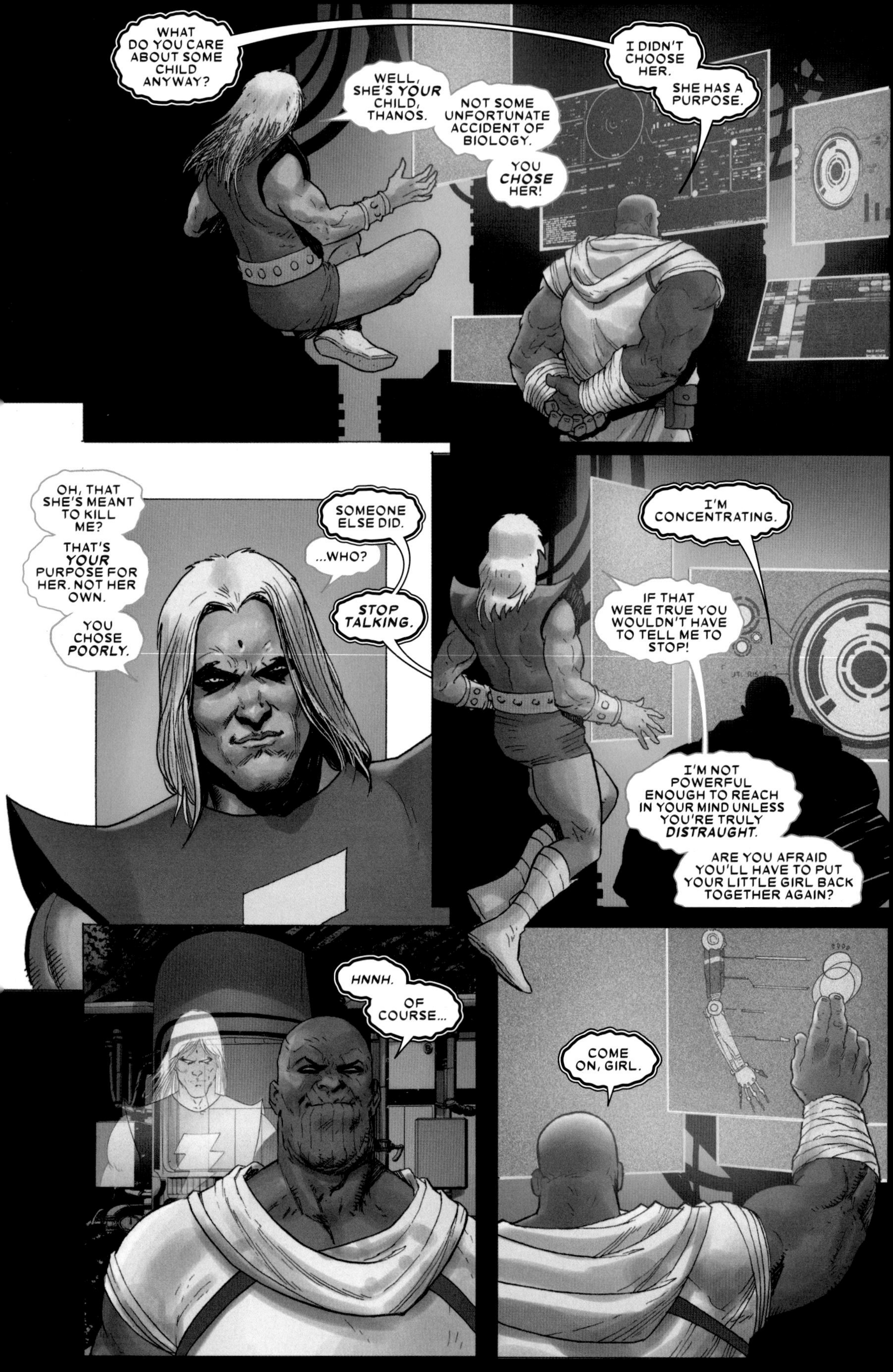
WHAT DO YOU CARE ABOUT SOME CHILD ANYWAY?
I DIDN'T CHOOSE HER.
SHE HAS A PURPOSE.
WELL, SHE'S YOUR CHILD, THANOS.
NOT SOME UNFORTUNATE ACCIDENT OF BIOLOGY.
YOU CHOSE HER!
OH, THAT SHE'S MEANT TO KILL ME?
THAT'S YOUR PURPOSE FOR HER. NOT HER OWN.
YOU CHOSE POORLY.
SOMEONE ELSE DID.
...WHO?
STOP TALKING.
I'M CONCENTRATING.
IF THAT WERE TRUE YOU WOULDN'T HAVE TO TELL ME TO STOP!
I'M NOT POWERFUL ENOUGH TO REACH IN YOUR MIND UNLESS YOU'RE TRULY DISTRAUGHT.
ARE YOU AFRAID YOU'LL HAVE TO PUT YOUR LITTLE GIRL BACK TOGETHER AGAIN?
HNNH.
OF COURSE...
COME ON, GIRL.

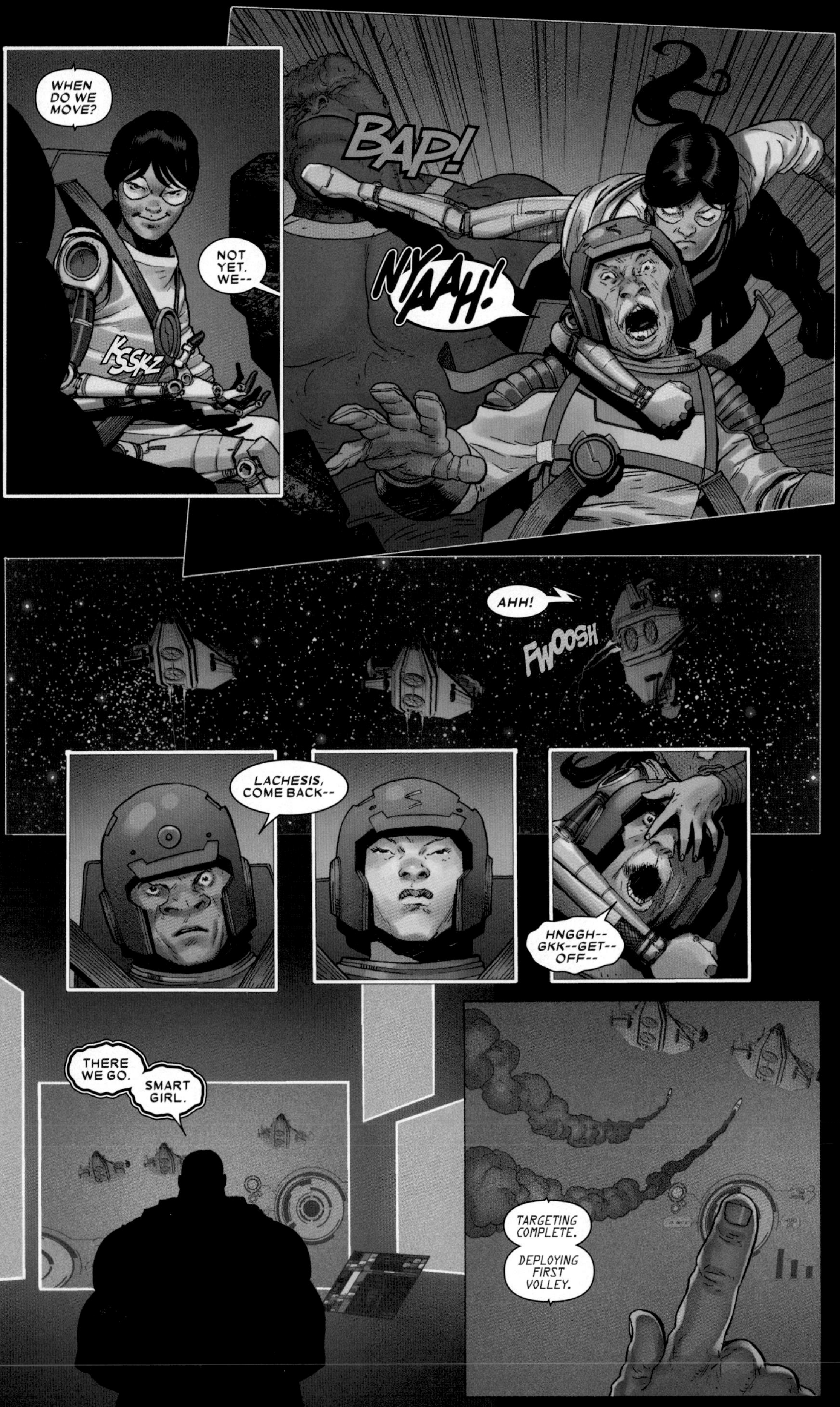
WHEN DO WE MOVE?
NOT YET. WE--
KSSKZ
BAP!
NYAAH!
AHH!
FWOOSH
LACHESIS, COME BACK--
HNGGH-- GKK--GET-- OFF--
THERE WE GO.
SMART GIRL.
TARGETING COMPLETE.
DEPLOYING FIRST VOLLEY.

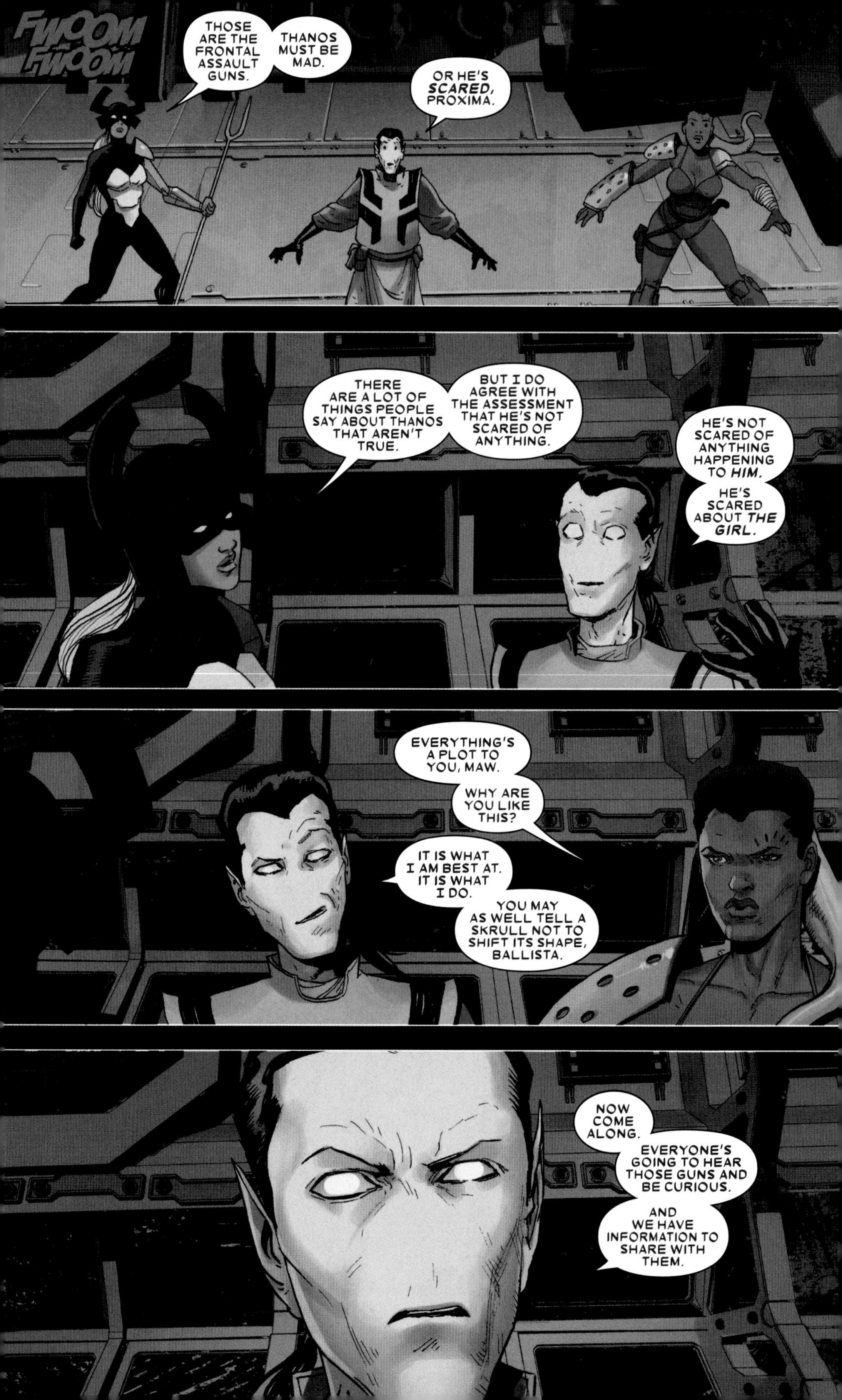
FWOOM FWOOM
THOSE ARE THE FRONTAL ASSAULT GUNS.
THANOS MUST BE MAD.
OR HE'S *SCARED,* PROXIMA.
THERE ARE A LOT OF THINGS PEOPLE SAY ABOUT THANOS THAT AREN'T TRUE.
BUT I DO AGREE WITH THE ASSESSMENT THAT HE'S NOT SCARED OF ANYTHING.
HE'S NOT SCARED OF ANYTHING HAPPENING TO *HIM.*
HE'S SCARED ABOUT *THE GIRL.*
EVERYTHING'S A PLOT TO YOU, MAW.
WHY ARE YOU LIKE THIS?
IT IS WHAT I AM BEST AT. IT IS WHAT I DO.
YOU MAY AS WELL TELL A SKRULL NOT TO SHIFT ITS SHAPE, BALLISTA.
NOW COME ALONG.
EVERYONE'S GOING TO HEAR THOSE GUNS AND BE CURIOUS.
AND WE HAVE INFORMATION TO SHARE WITH THEM.

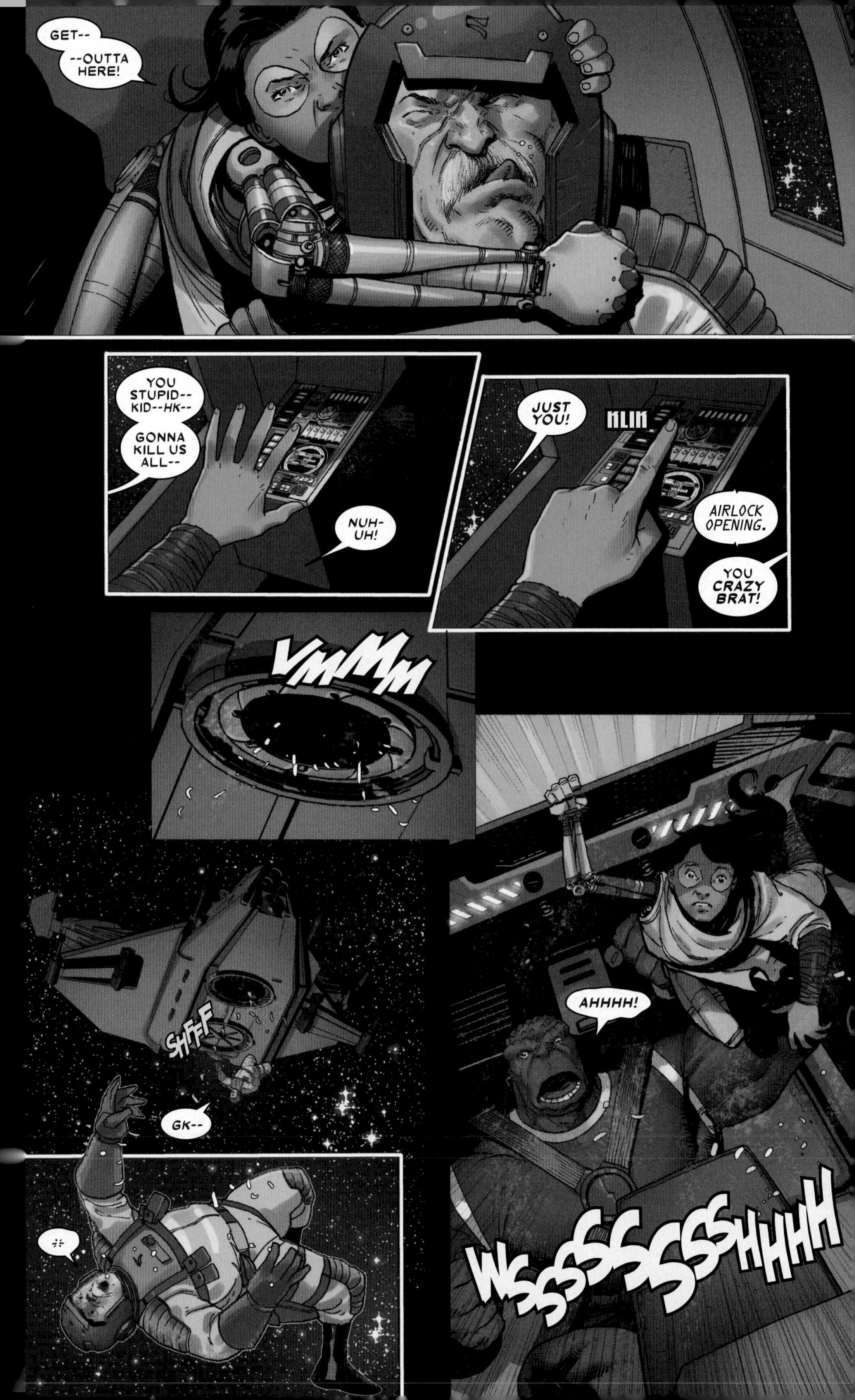
GET--
--OUTTA HERE!
YOU STUPID-- KID--HK--
GONNA KILL US ALL--
NUH-UH!
JUST YOU!
KLIK
AIRLOCK OPENING.
YOU CRAZY BRAT!
VMMM
SHFFF
GK--
AHHHH!
WSSSSSSSSHHHH

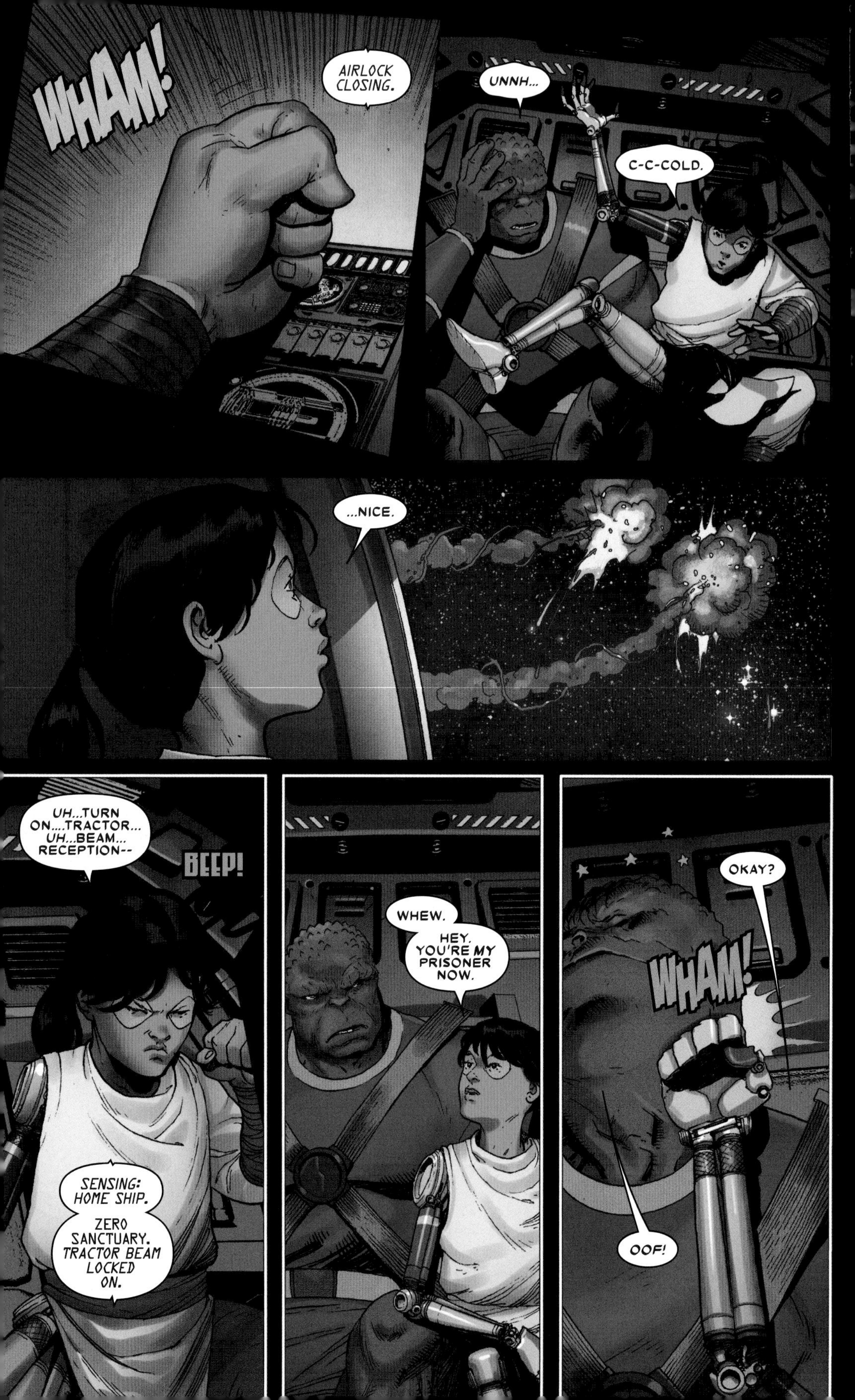
WHAM!
AIRLOCK CLOSING.
UNNH...
C-C-COLD.
...NICE.
UH...TURN ON....TRACTOR... UH...BEAM... RECEPTION--
BEEP!
SENSING: HOME SHIP.
ZERO SANCTUARY. TRACTOR BEAM LOCKED ON.
WHEW.
HEY. YOU'RE MY PRISONER NOW.
OKAY?
WHAM!
OOF!

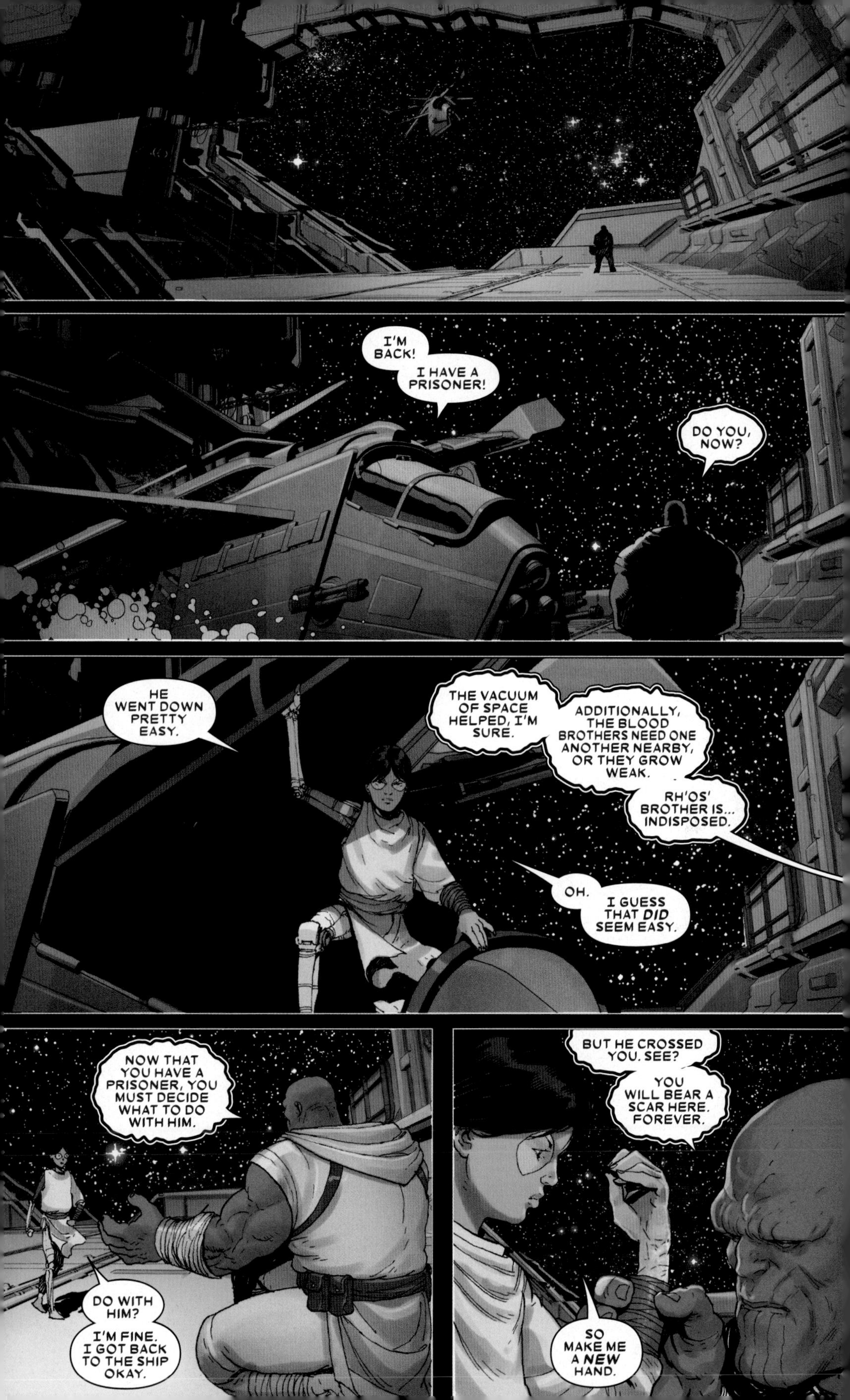
I'M BACK!
I HAVE A PRISONER!
DO YOU, NOW?
HE WENT DOWN PRETTY EASY.
THE VACUUM OF SPACE HELPED, I'M SURE.
ADDITIONALLY, THE BLOOD BROTHERS NEED ONE ANOTHER NEARBY, OR THEY GROW WEAK.
RH'OS' BROTHER IS... INDISPOSED.
OH.
I GUESS THAT *DID* SEEM EASY.
NOW THAT YOU HAVE A PRISONER, YOU MUST DECIDE WHAT TO DO WITH HIM.
DO WITH HIM?
I'M FINE. I GOT BACK TO THE SHIP OKAY.
BUT HE CROSSED YOU. SEE?
YOU WILL BEAR A SCAR HERE. FOREVER.
SO MAKE ME A *NEW* HAND.

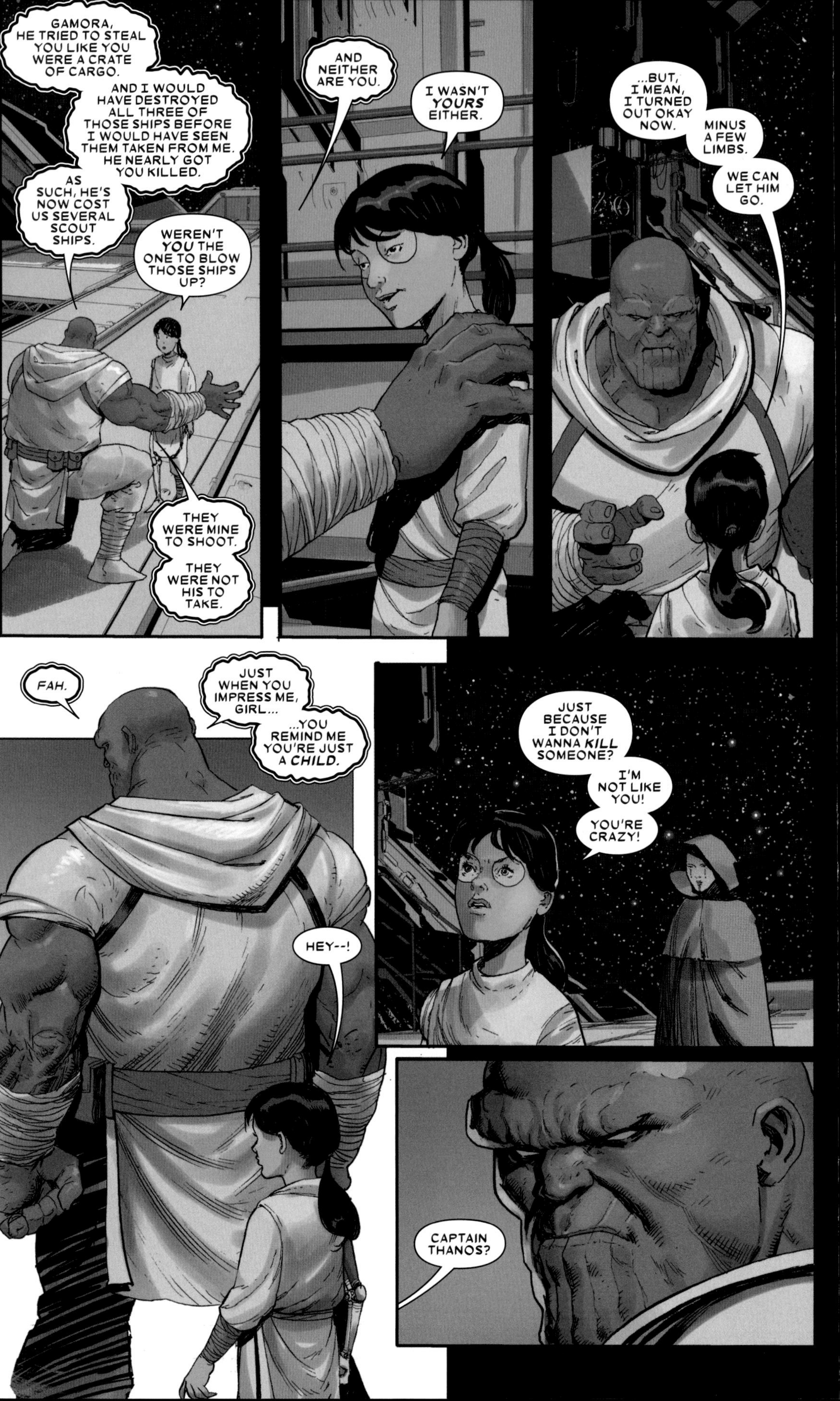
GAMORA, HE TRIED TO STEAL YOU LIKE YOU WERE A CRATE OF CARGO.
AND I WOULD HAVE DESTROYED ALL THREE OF THOSE SHIPS BEFORE I WOULD HAVE SEEN THEM TAKEN FROM ME. HE NEARLY GOT YOU KILLED.
AS SUCH, HE'S NOW COST US SEVERAL SCOUT SHIPS.
WEREN'T *YOU* THE ONE TO BLOW THOSE SHIPS UP?
THEY WERE MINE TO SHOOT.
THEY WERE NOT HIS TO TAKE.
AND NEITHER ARE YOU.
I WASN'T *YOURS* EITHER.
...BUT, I MEAN, I TURNED OUT OKAY NOW.
MINUS A FEW LIMBS.
WE CAN LET HIM GO.
FAH.
JUST WHEN YOU IMPRESS ME, GIRL...
...YOU REMIND ME YOU'RE JUST A *CHILD.*
HEY--!
JUST BECAUSE I DON'T WANNA *KILL* SOMEONE?
I'M NOT LIKE YOU!
YOU'RE CRAZY!
CAPTAIN THANOS?

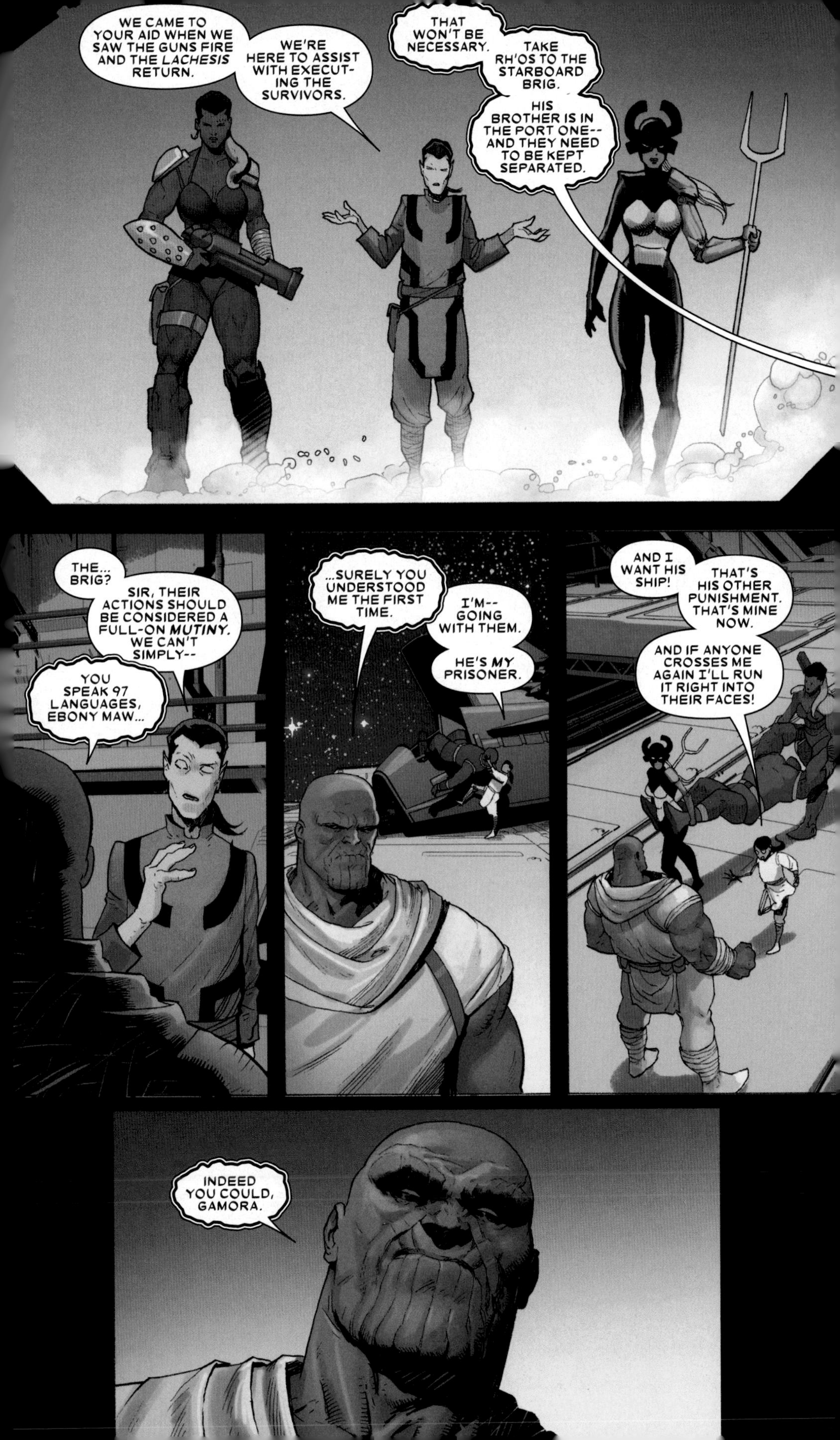
WE CAME TO YOUR AID WHEN WE SAW THE GUNS FIRE AND THE *LACHESIS* RETURN.
WE'RE HERE TO ASSIST WITH EXECUTING THE SURVIVORS.
THAT WON'T BE NECESSARY.
TAKE RH'OS TO THE STARBOARD BRIG.
HIS BROTHER IS IN THE PORT ONE-- AND THEY NEED TO BE KEPT SEPARATED.
THE... BRIG?
SIR, THEIR ACTIONS SHOULD BE CONSIDERED A FULL-ON *MUTINY.* WE CAN'T SIMPLY--
YOU SPEAK 97 LANGUAGES, EBONY MAW...
...SURELY YOU UNDERSTOOD ME THE FIRST TIME.
I'M-- GOING WITH THEM.
HE'S *MY* PRISONER.
AND I WANT HIS SHIP!
THAT'S HIS OTHER PUNISHMENT. THAT'S MINE NOW.
AND IF ANYONE CROSSES ME AGAIN I'LL RUN IT RIGHT INTO THEIR FACES!
INDEED YOU COULD, GAMORA.

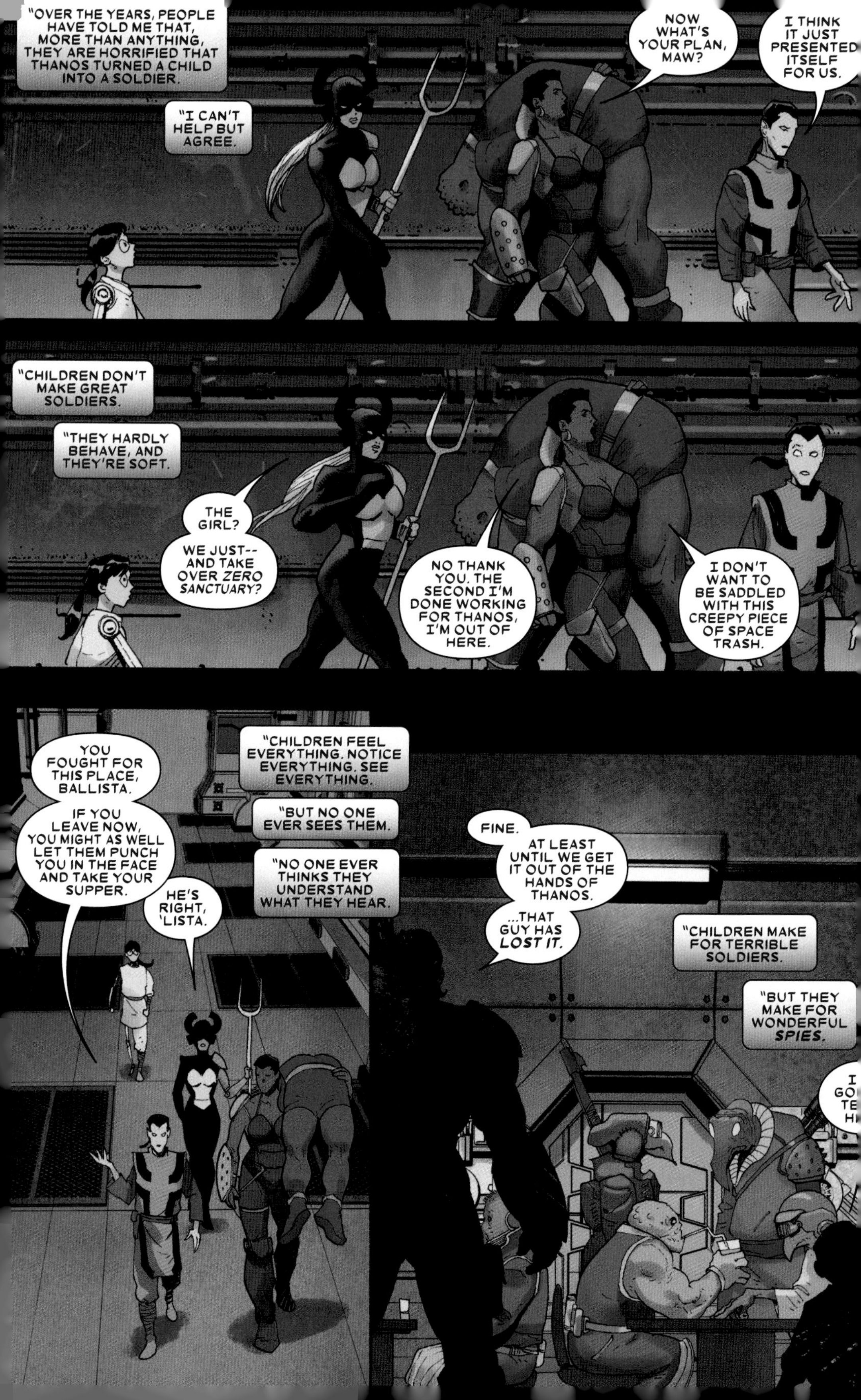
"OVER THE YEARS, PEOPLE HAVE TOLD ME THAT, MORE THAN ANYTHING, THEY ARE HORRIFIED THAT THANOS TURNED A CHILD INTO A SOLDIER.
"I CAN'T HELP BUT AGREE.
NOW WHAT'S YOUR PLAN, MAW?
I THINK IT JUST PRESENTED ITSELF FOR US.
"CHILDREN DON'T MAKE GREAT SOLDIERS.
"THEY HARDLY BEHAVE, AND THEY'RE SOFT.
THE GIRL?
WE JUST-- AND TAKE OVER *ZERO SANCTUARY*?
NO THANK YOU. THE SECOND I'M DONE WORKING FOR THANOS, I'M OUT OF HERE.
I DON'T WANT TO BE SADDLED WITH THIS CREEPY PIECE OF SPACE TRASH.
YOU FOUGHT FOR THIS PLACE, BALLISTA.
IF YOU LEAVE NOW, YOU MIGHT AS WELL LET THEM PUNCH YOU IN THE FACE AND TAKE YOUR SUPPER.
HE'S RIGHT, 'LISTA.
"CHILDREN FEEL EVERYTHING. NOTICE EVERYTHING. SEE EVERYTHING.
"BUT NO ONE EVER SEES THEM.
"NO ONE EVER THINKS THEY UNDERSTAND WHAT THEY HEAR.
FINE.
AT LEAST UNTIL WE GET IT OUT OF THE HANDS OF THANOS.
...THAT GUY HAS *LOST IT.*
"CHILDREN MAKE FOR TERRIBLE SOLDIERS.
"BUT THEY MAKE FOR WONDERFUL *SPIES.*

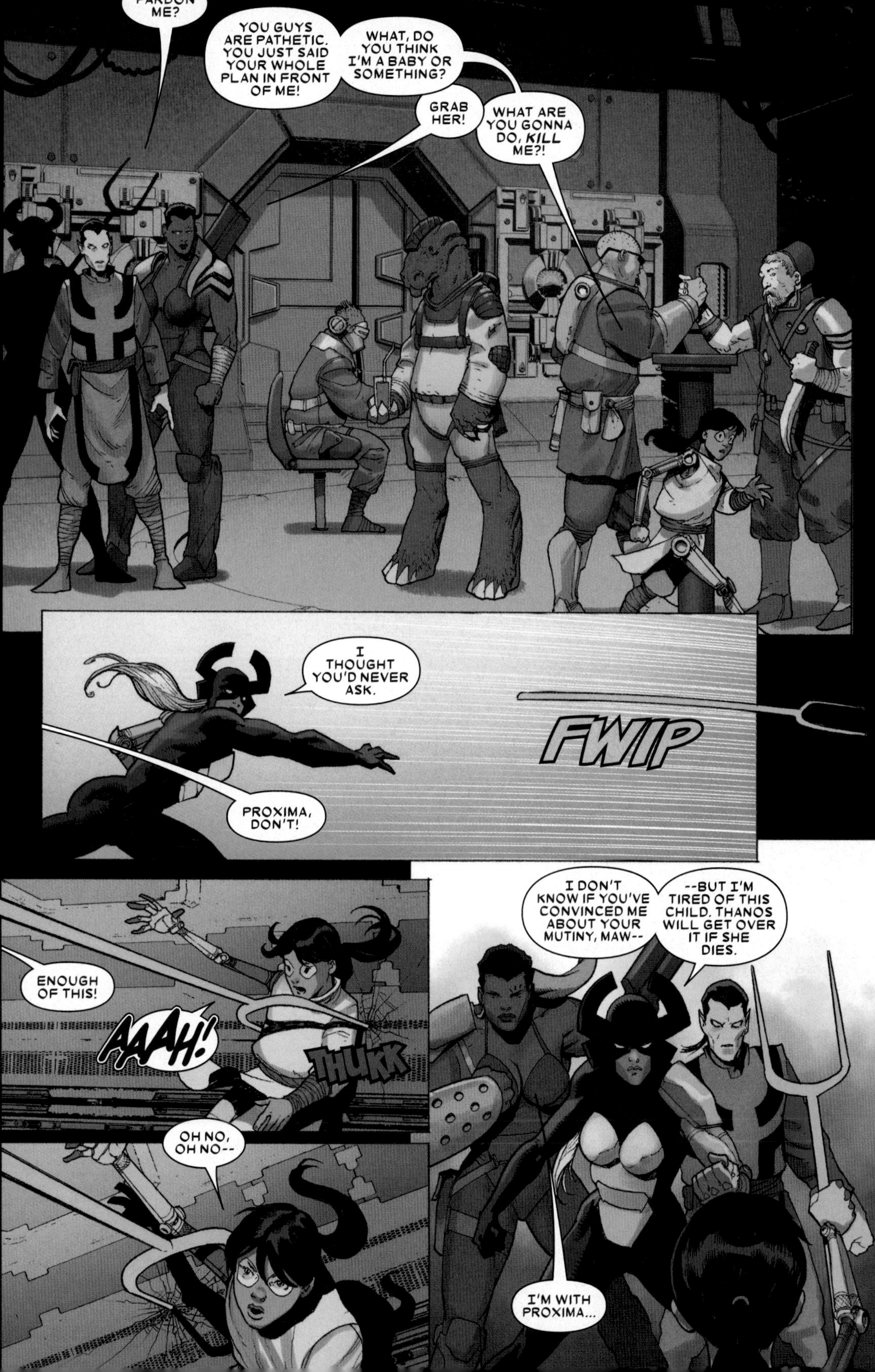
PARDON ME?
YOU GUYS ARE PATHETIC. YOU JUST SAID YOUR WHOLE PLAN IN FRONT OF ME!
WHAT, DO YOU THINK I'M A BABY OR SOMETHING?
GRAB HER!
WHAT ARE YOU GONNA DO, KILL ME?!
I THOUGHT YOU'D NEVER ASK.
FWIP
PROXIMA, DON'T!
ENOUGH OF THIS!
AAAH!
THUKK
OH NO, OH NO--
I DON'T KNOW IF YOU'VE CONVINCED ME ABOUT YOUR MUTINY, MAW--
--BUT I'M TIRED OF THIS CHILD. THANOS WILL GET OVER IT IF SHE DIES.
I'M WITH PROXIMA...

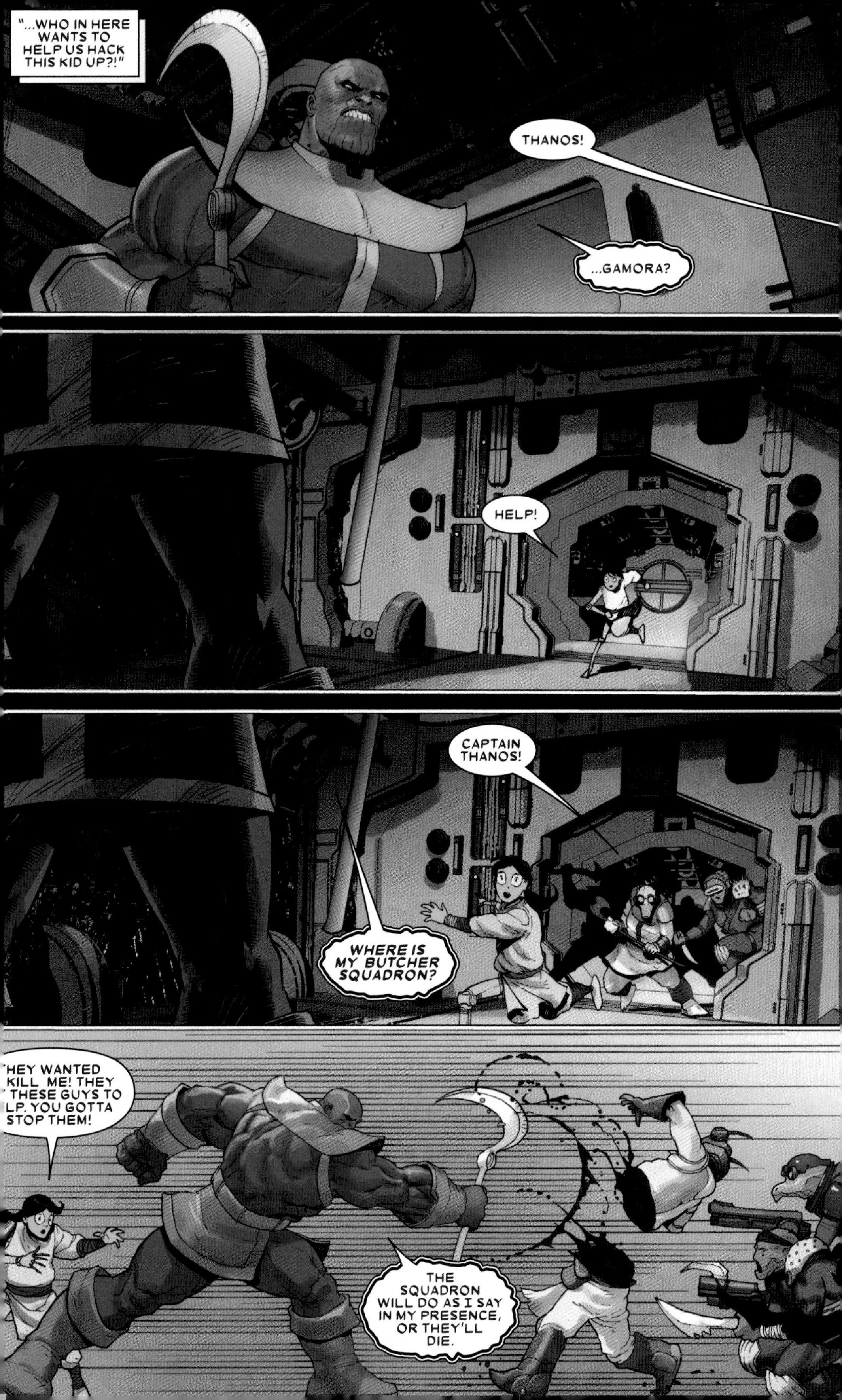
"...WHO IN HERE WANTS TO HELP US HACK THIS KID UP?!"
THANOS!
...GAMORA?
HELP!
CAPTAIN THANOS!
WHERE IS MY BUTCHER SQUADRON?
HEY WANTED KILL ME! THEY THESE GUYS TO LP. YOU GOTTA STOP THEM!
THE SQUADRON WILL DO AS I SAY IN MY PRESENCE, OR THEY'LL DIE.

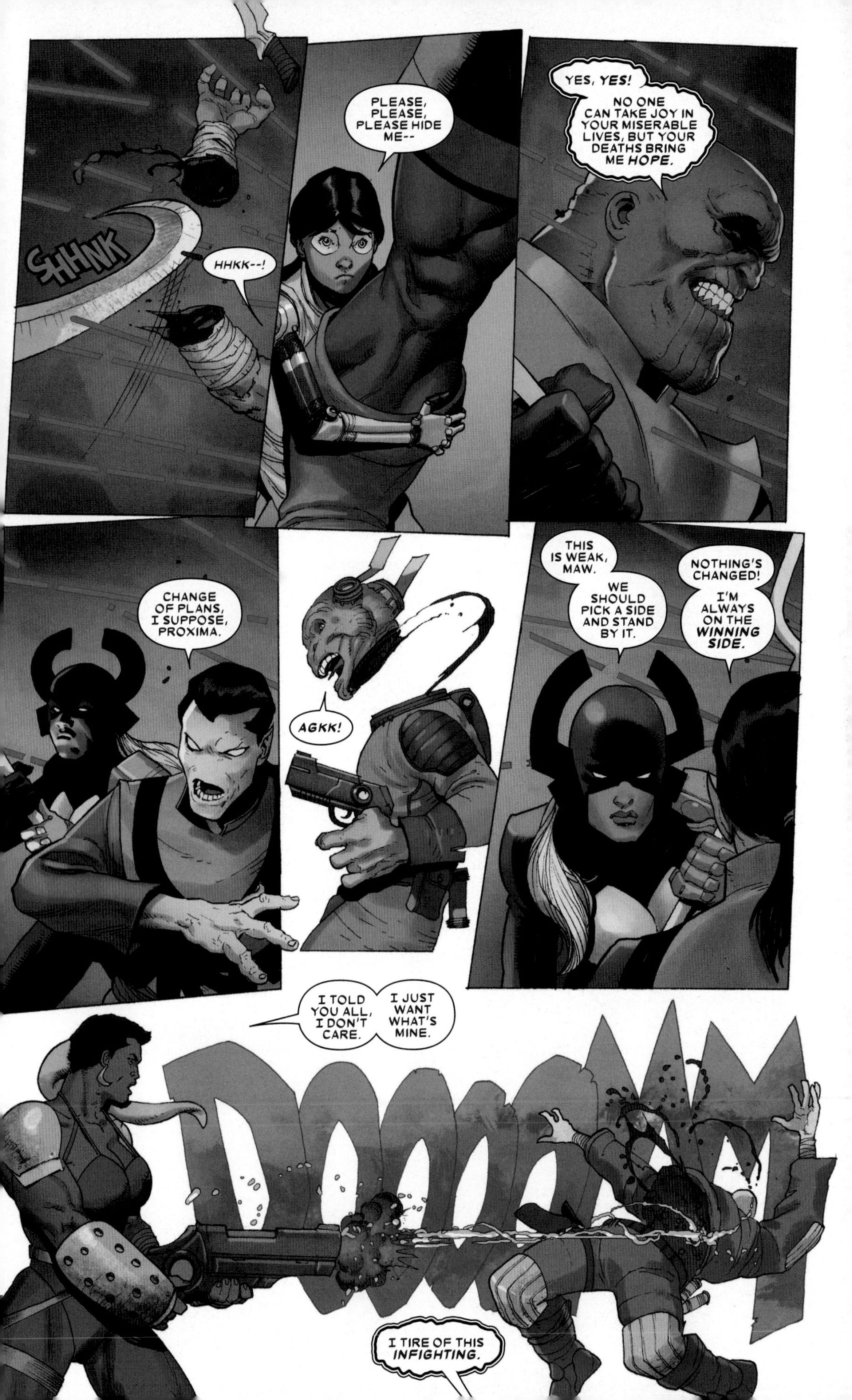
SHHNK
HHKK--!
PLEASE, PLEASE, PLEASE HIDE ME--
YES, *YES!*
NO ONE CAN TAKE JOY IN YOUR MISERABLE LIVES, BUT YOUR DEATHS BRING ME *HOPE.*
CHANGE OF PLANS, I SUPPOSE, PROXIMA.
AGKK!
THIS IS WEAK, MAW.
WE SHOULD PICK A SIDE AND STAND BY IT.
NOTHING'S CHANGED!
I'M ALWAYS ON THE *WINNING SIDE.*
I TOLD YOU ALL, I DON'T CARE.
I JUST WANT WHAT'S MINE.
I TIRE OF THIS *INFIGHTING.*

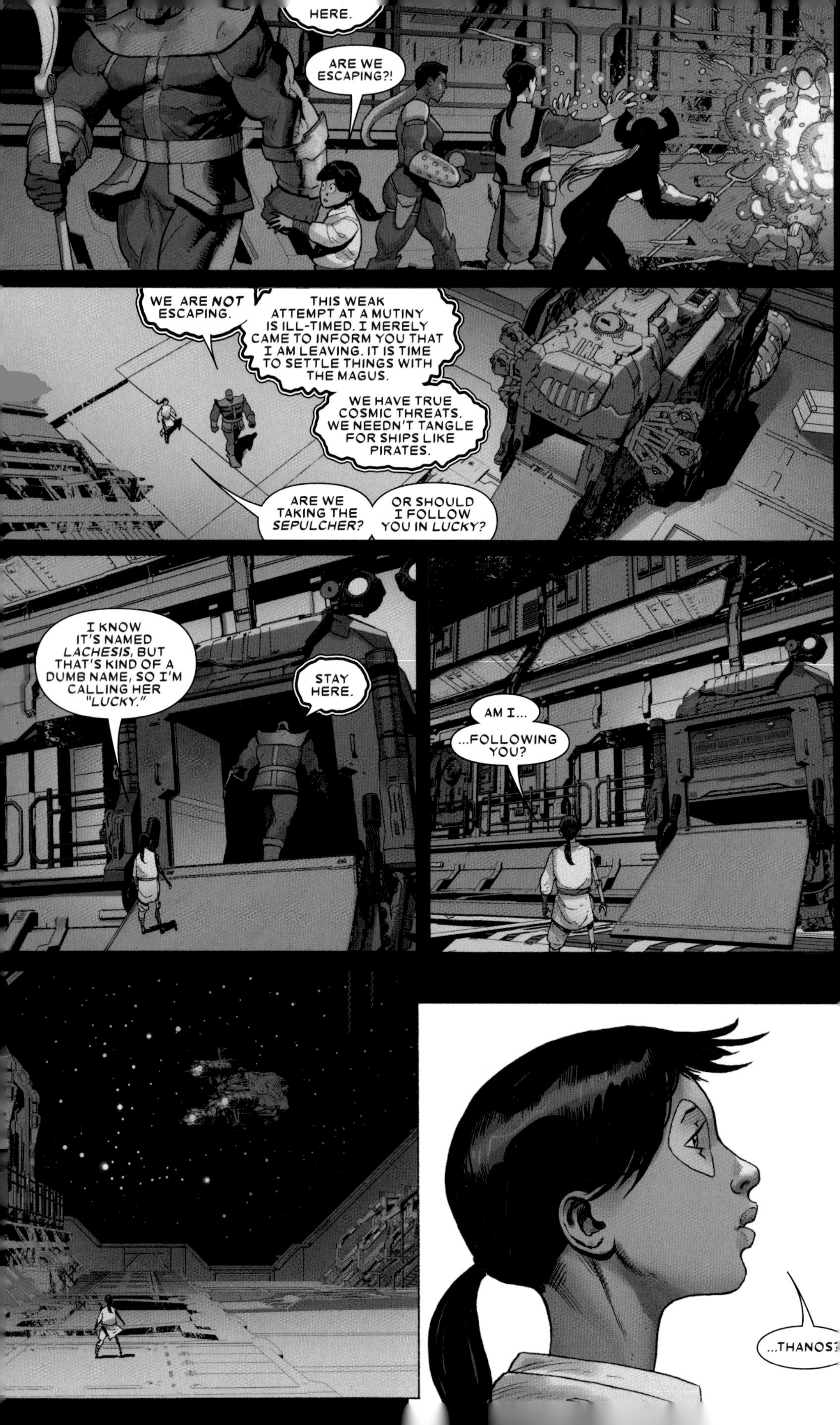
HERE.
ARE WE ESCAPING?!
WE ARE NOT ESCAPING.
THIS WEAK ATTEMPT AT A MUTINY IS ILL-TIMED. I MERELY CAME TO INFORM YOU THAT I AM LEAVING. IT IS TIME TO SETTLE THINGS WITH THE MAGUS.
WE HAVE TRUE COSMIC THREATS. WE NEEDN'T TANGLE FOR SHIPS LIKE PIRATES.
ARE WE TAKING THE SEPULCHER?
OR SHOULD I FOLLOW YOU IN LUCKY?
I KNOW IT'S NAMED LACHESIS, BUT THAT'S KIND OF A DUMB NAME, SO I'M CALLING HER "LUCKY."
STAY HERE.
AM I...
...FOLLOWING YOU?
...THANOS?

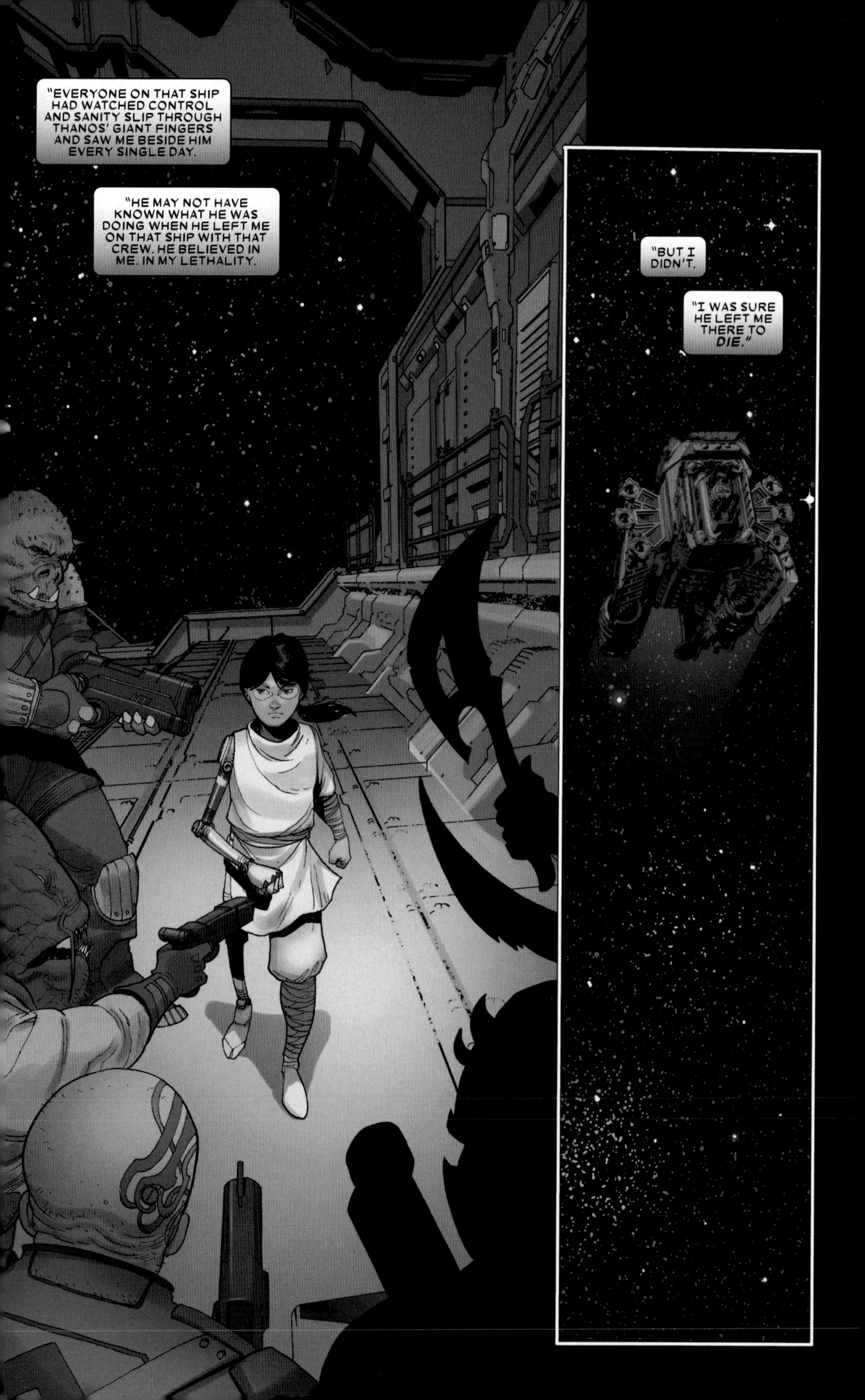
"EVERYONE ON THAT SHIP HAD WATCHED CONTROL AND SANITY SLIP THROUGH THANOS' GIANT FINGERS AND SAW ME BESIDE HIM EVERY SINGLE DAY.
"HE MAY NOT HAVE KNOWN WHAT HE WAS DOING WHEN HE LEFT ME ON THAT SHIP WITH THAT CREW. HE BELIEVED IN ME. IN MY LETHALITY.
"BUT I DIDN'T.
"I WAS SURE HE LEFT ME THERE TO DIE."

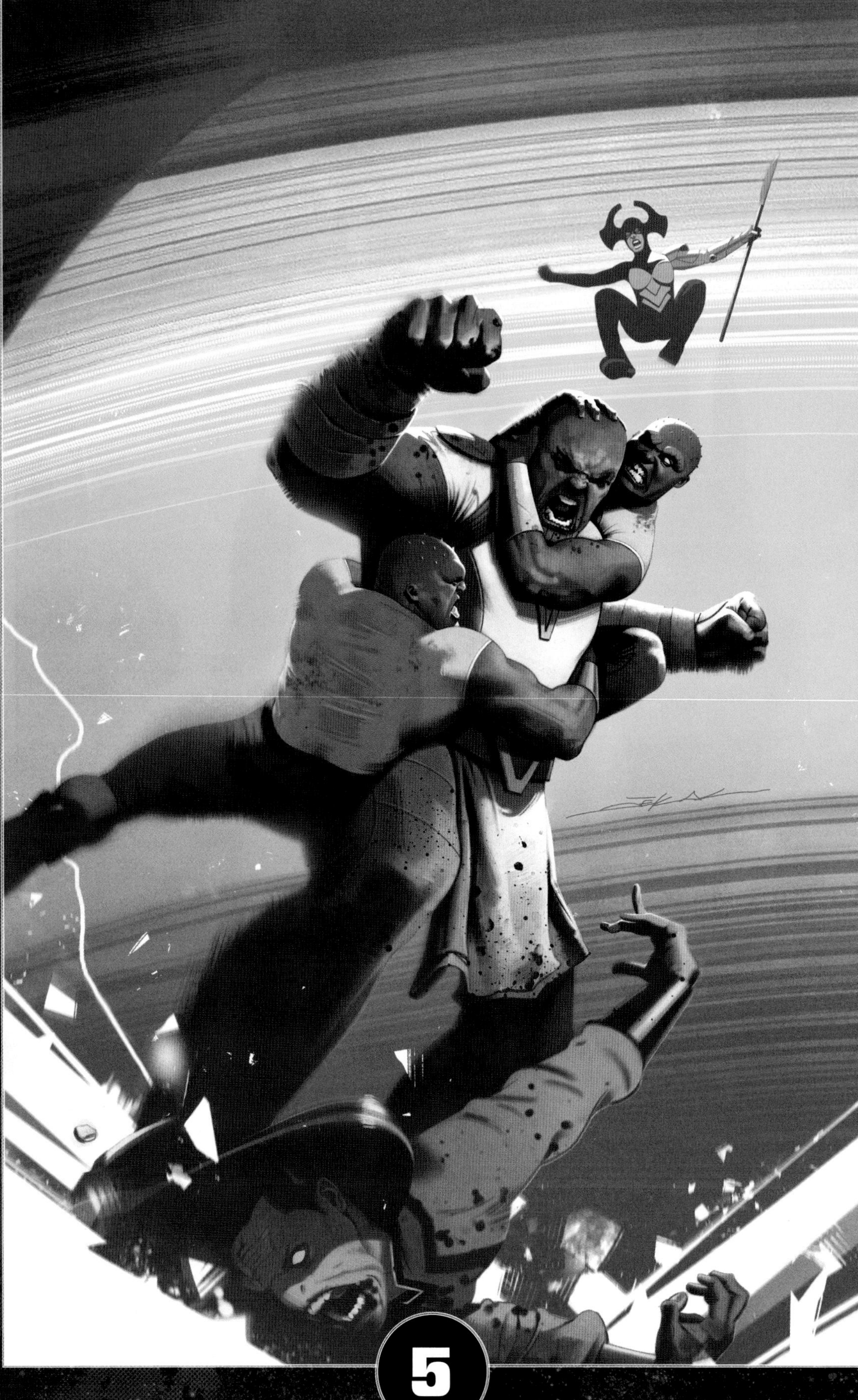

5

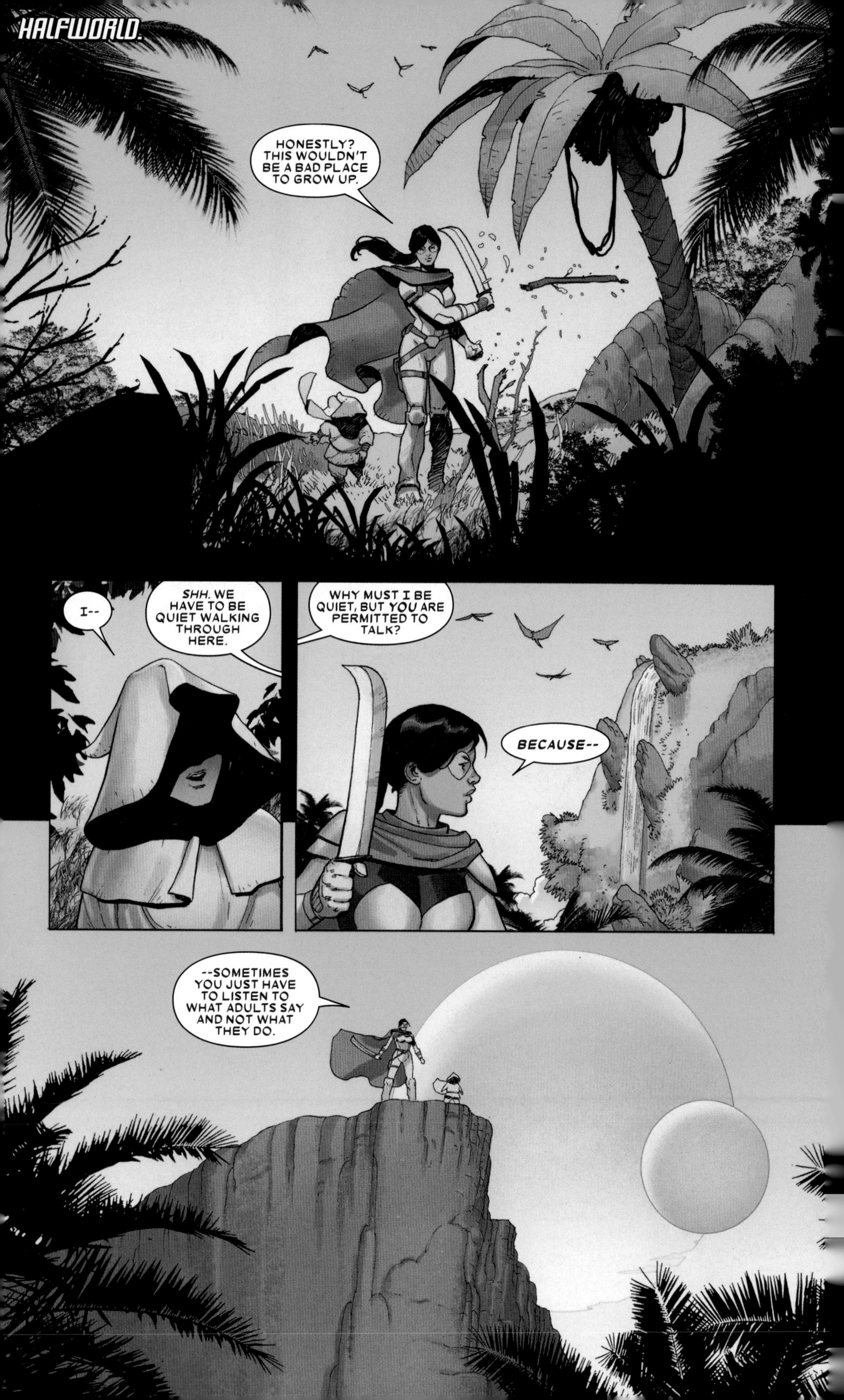
HALFWORLD.
HONESTLY? THIS WOULDN'T BE A BAD PLACE TO GROW UP.
I--
SHH. WE HAVE TO BE QUIET WALKING THROUGH HERE.
WHY MUST I BE QUIET, BUT YOU ARE PERMITTED TO TALK?
BECAUSE--
--SOMETIMES YOU JUST HAVE TO LISTEN TO WHAT ADULTS SAY AND NOT WHAT THEY DO.

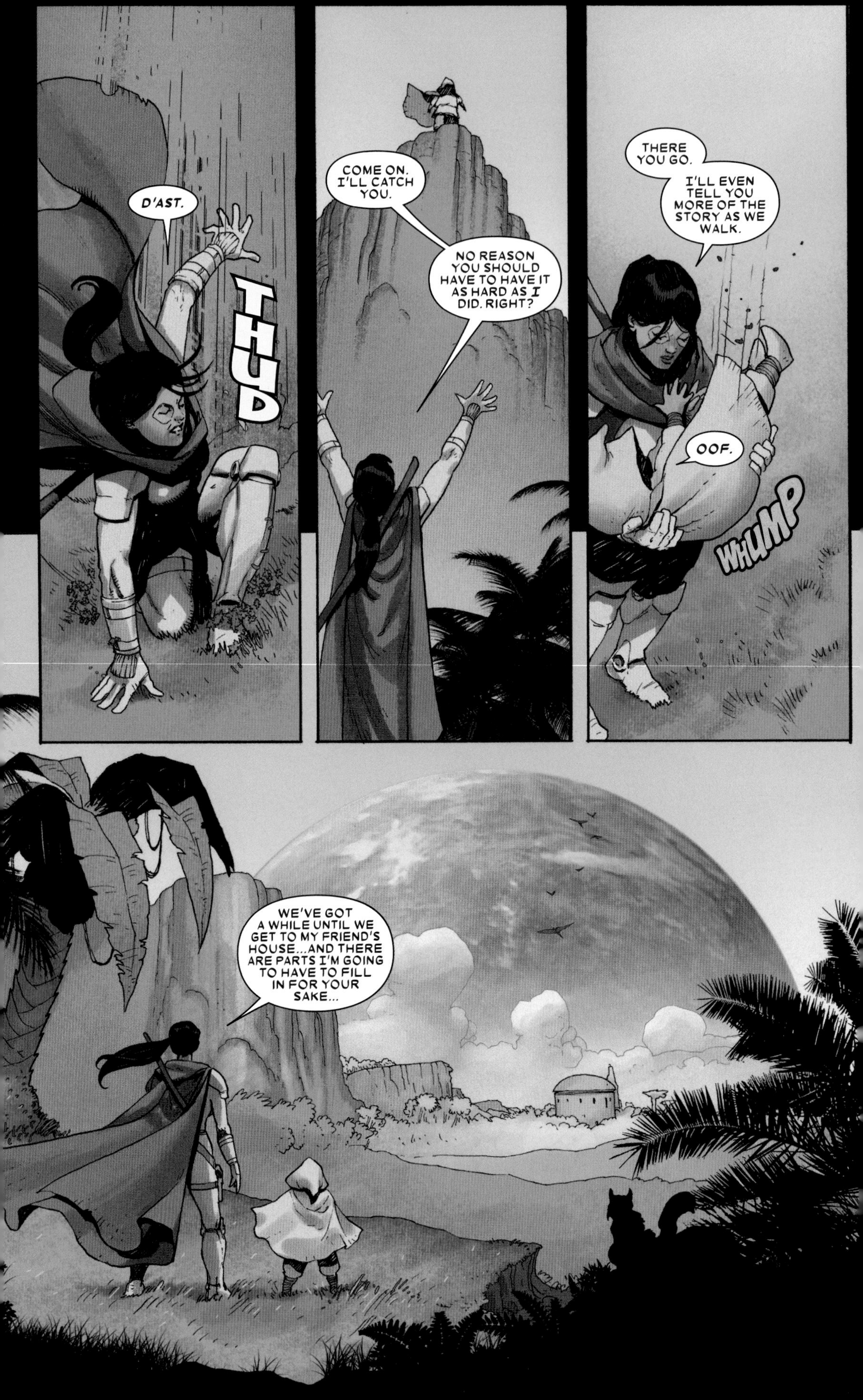
D'AST.
THUD
COME ON. I'LL CATCH YOU.
NO REASON YOU SHOULD HAVE TO HAVE IT AS HARD AS *I* DID. RIGHT?
THERE YOU GO.
I'LL EVEN TELL YOU MORE OF THE STORY AS WE WALK.
OOF.
WHUMP
WE'VE GOT A WHILE UNTIL WE GET TO MY FRIEND'S HOUSE...AND THERE ARE PARTS I'M GOING TO HAVE TO FILL IN FOR YOUR SAKE...

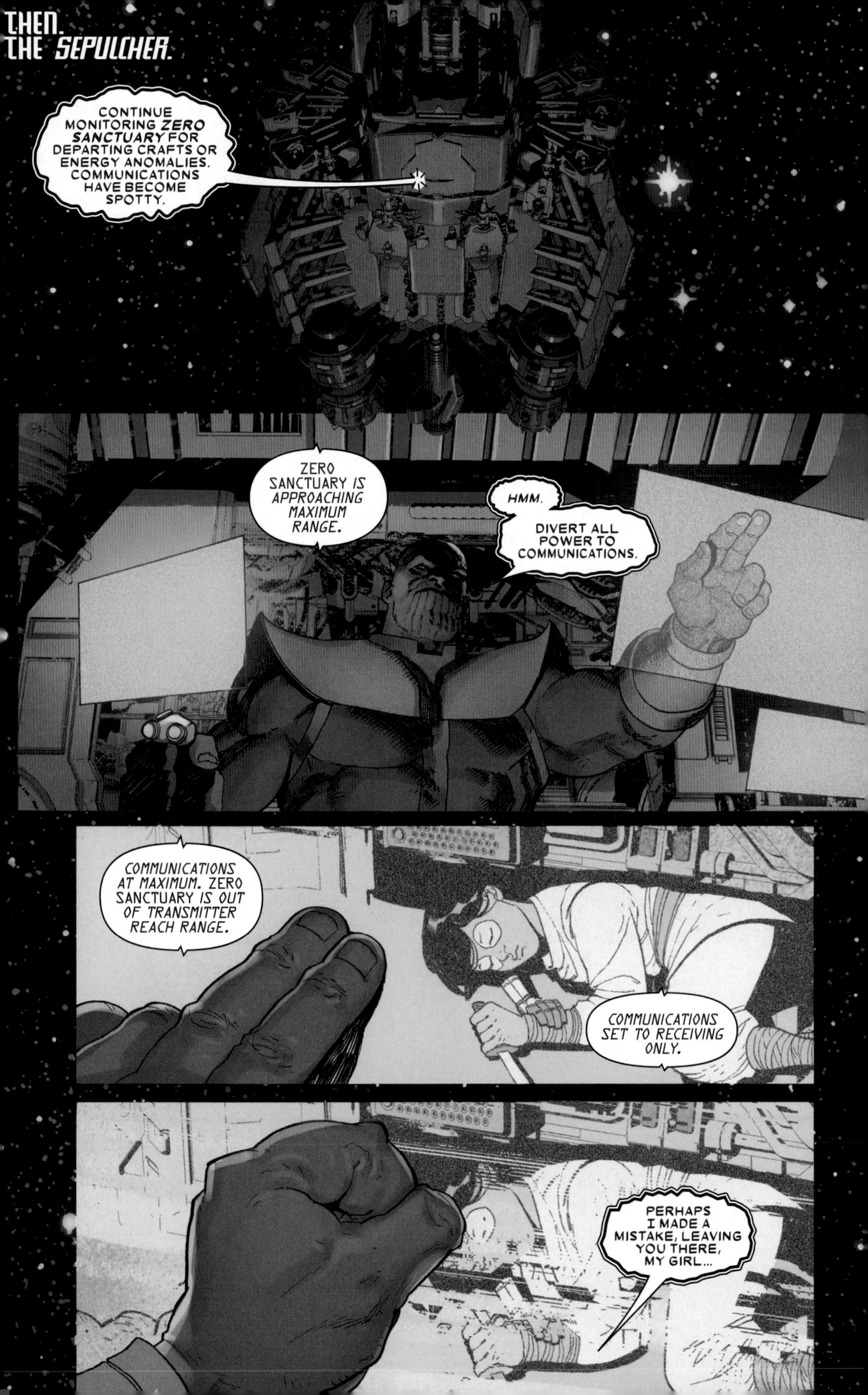
THEN.
THE SEPULCHER.
CONTINUE MONITORING ZERO SANCTUARY FOR DEPARTING CRAFTS OR ENERGY ANOMALIES. COMMUNICATIONS HAVE BECOME SPOTTY.
ZERO SANCTUARY IS APPROACHING MAXIMUM RANGE.
HMM.
DIVERT ALL POWER TO COMMUNICATIONS.
COMMUNICATIONS AT MAXIMUM. ZERO SANCTUARY IS OUT OF TRANSMITTER REACH RANGE.
COMMUNICATIONS SET TO RECEIVING ONLY.
PERHAPS I MADE A MISTAKE, LEAVING YOU THERE, MY GIRL...

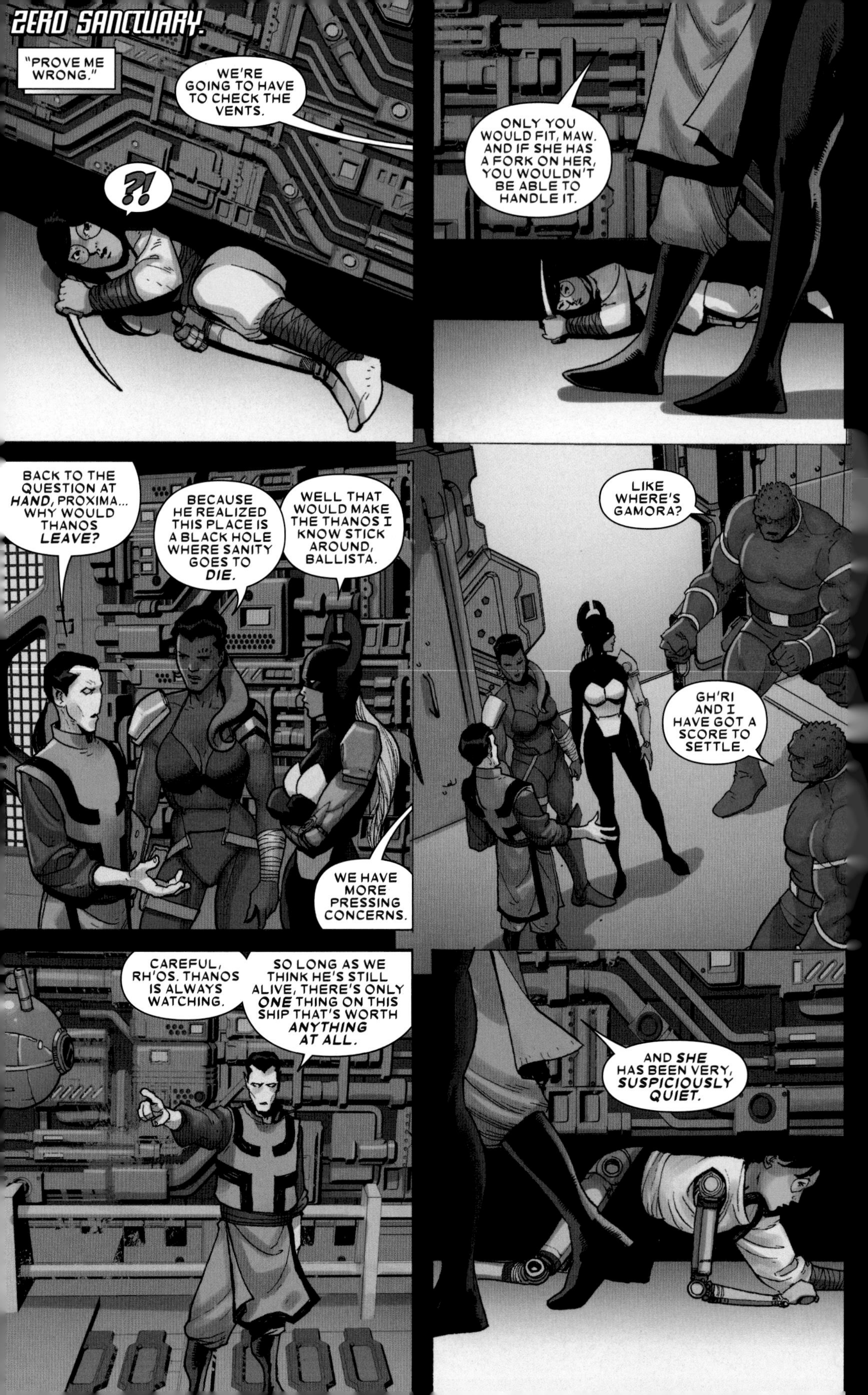
ZERO SANCTUARY.
"PROVE ME WRONG."
WE'RE GOING TO HAVE TO CHECK THE VENTS.
?!
ONLY YOU WOULD FIT, MAW. AND IF SHE HAS A FORK ON HER, YOU WOULDN'T BE ABLE TO HANDLE IT.
BACK TO THE QUESTION AT HAND, PROXIMA... WHY WOULD THANOS LEAVE?
BECAUSE HE REALIZED THIS PLACE IS A BLACK HOLE WHERE SANITY GOES TO DIE.
WELL THAT WOULD MAKE THE THANOS I KNOW STICK AROUND, BALLISTA.
WE HAVE MORE PRESSING CONCERNS.
LIKE WHERE'S GAMORA?
GH'RI AND I HAVE GOT A SCORE TO SETTLE.
CAREFUL, RH'OS. THANOS IS ALWAYS WATCHING.
SO LONG AS WE THINK HE'S STILL ALIVE, THERE'S ONLY ONE THING ON THIS SHIP THAT'S WORTH ANYTHING AT ALL.
AND SHE HAS BEEN VERY, SUSPICIOUSLY QUIET.

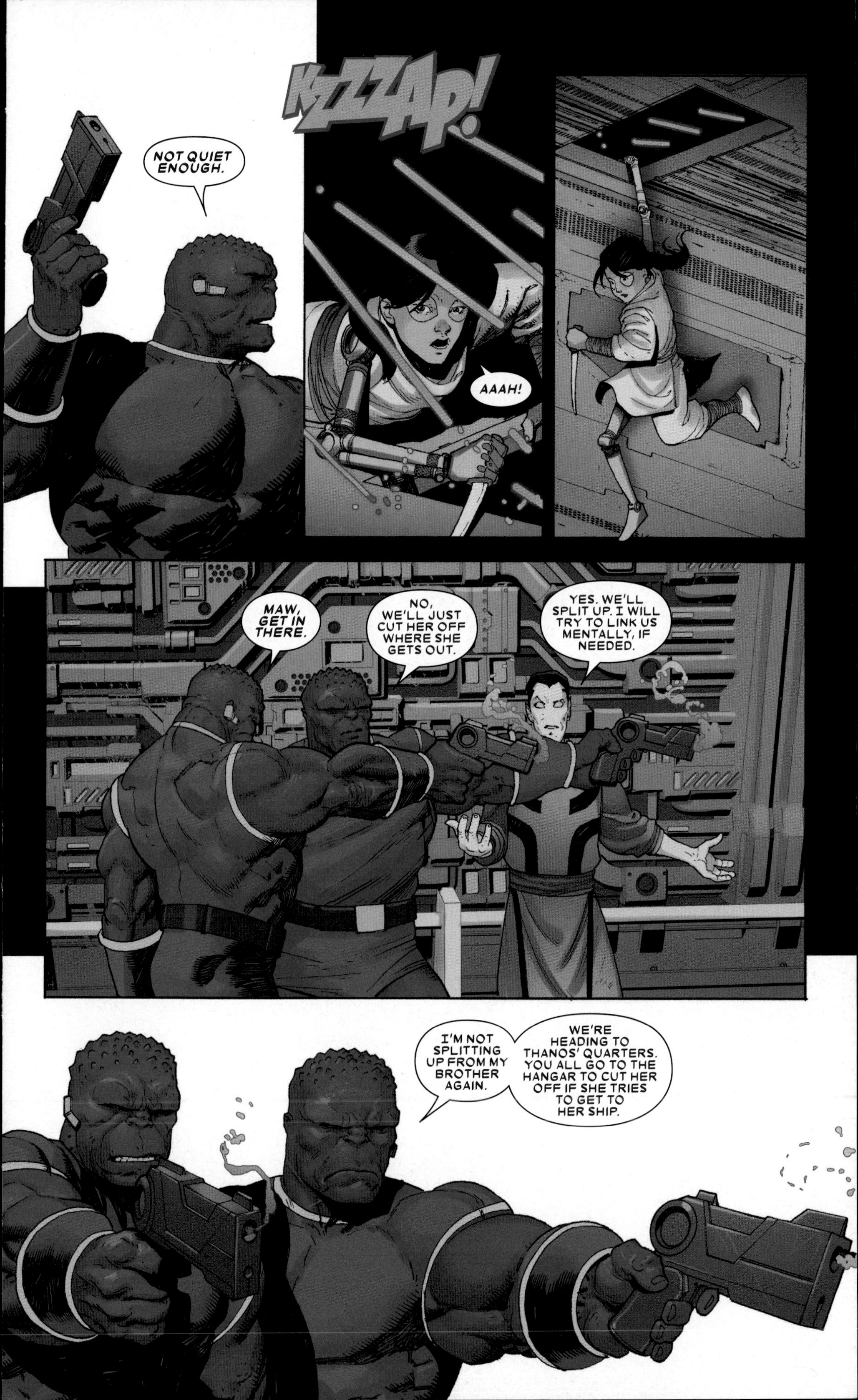
KZZZZAP!
NOT QUIET ENOUGH.
AAAH!
MAW, GET IN THERE.
NO, WE'LL JUST CUT HER OFF WHERE SHE GETS OUT.
YES. WE'LL SPLIT UP. I WILL TRY TO LINK US MENTALLY, IF NEEDED.
I'M NOT SPLITTING UP FROM MY BROTHER AGAIN.
WE'RE HEADING TO THANOS' QUARTERS. YOU ALL GO TO THE HANGAR TO CUT HER OFF IF SHE TRIES TO GET TO HER SHIP.

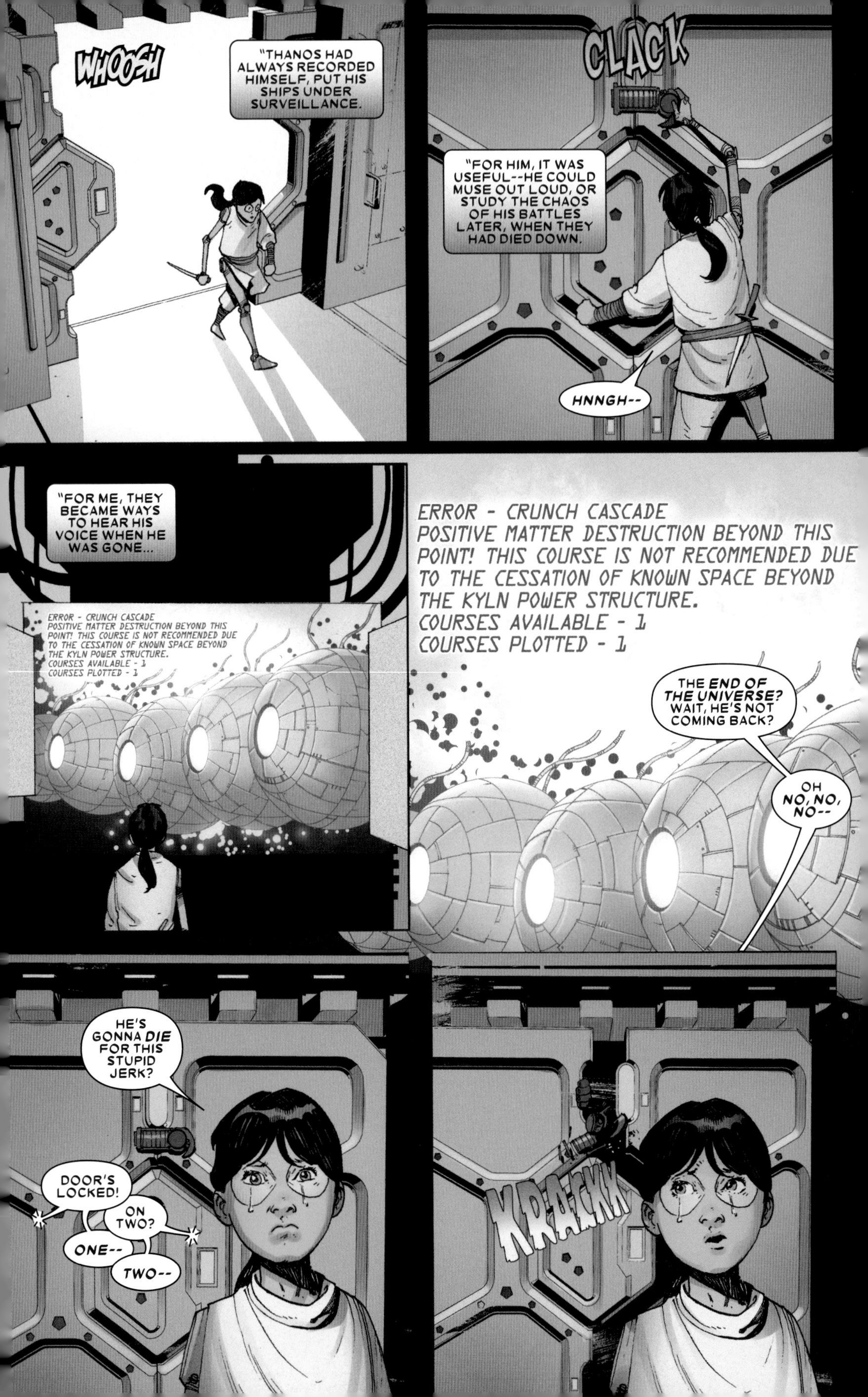
WHOOSH
"THANOS HAD ALWAYS RECORDED HIMSELF, PUT HIS SHIPS UNDER SURVEILLANCE.
CLACK
"FOR HIM, IT WAS USEFUL--HE COULD MUSE OUT LOUD, OR STUDY THE CHAOS OF HIS BATTLES LATER, WHEN THEY HAD DIED DOWN.
HNNGH--
"FOR ME, THEY BECAME WAYS TO HEAR HIS VOICE WHEN HE WAS GONE...
ERROR - CRUNCH CASCADE
POSITIVE MATTER DESTRUCTION BEYOND THIS POINT! THIS COURSE IS NOT RECOMMENDED DUE TO THE CESSATION OF KNOWN SPACE BEYOND THE KYLN POWER STRUCTURE.
COURSES AVAILABLE - 1
COURSES PLOTTED - 1
THE END OF THE UNIVERSE? WAIT, HE'S NOT COMING BACK?
OH NO, NO, NO--
HE'S GONNA DIE FOR THIS STUPID JERK?
DOOR'S LOCKED!
ON TWO?
ONE--
TWO--
KRAKKK

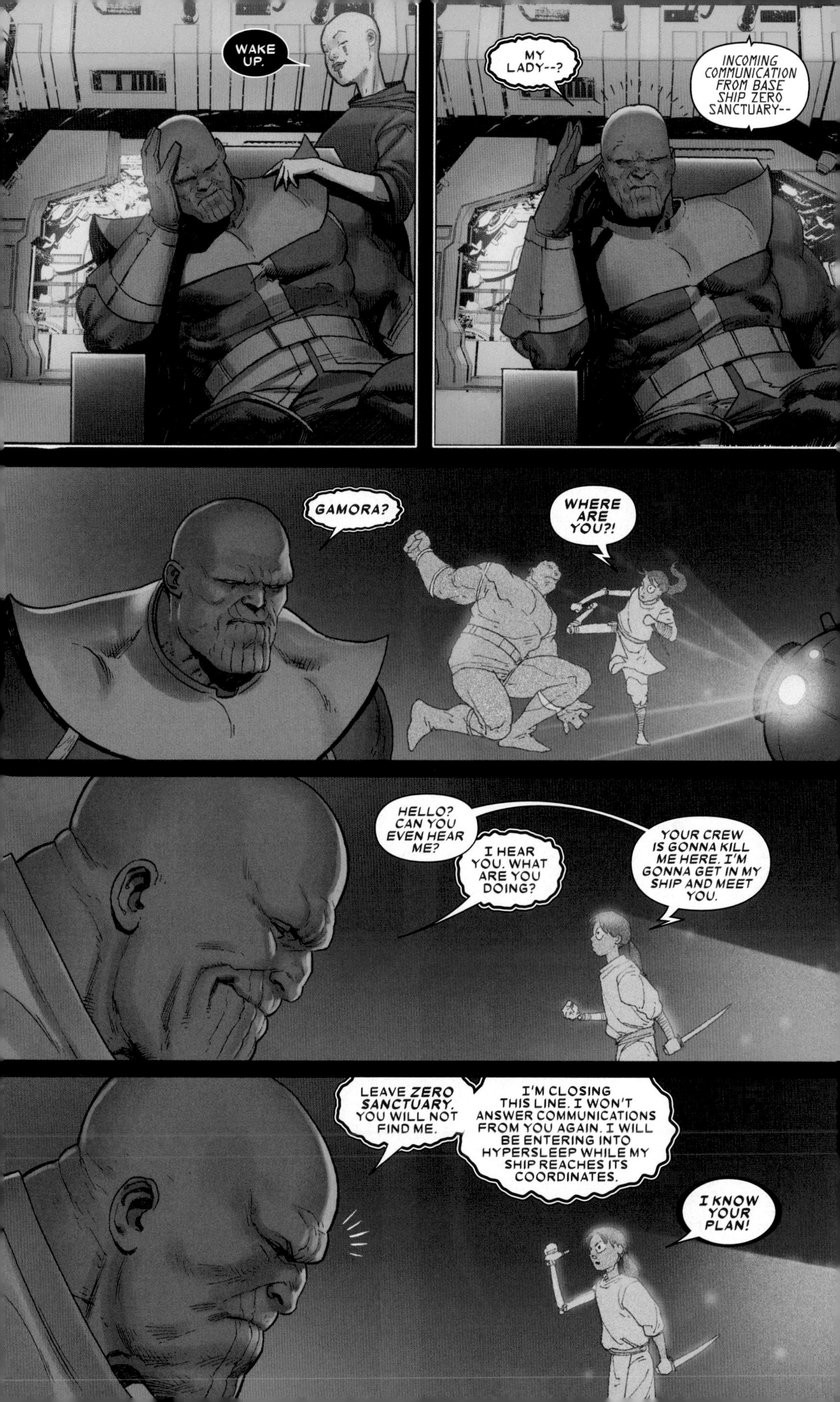
WAKE UP.
MY LADY--?
INCOMING COMMUNICATION FROM BASE SHIP ZERO SANCTUARY--
GAMORA?
WHERE ARE YOU?!
HELLO? CAN YOU EVEN HEAR ME?
I HEAR YOU. WHAT ARE YOU DOING?
YOUR CREW IS GONNA KILL ME HERE. I'M GONNA GET IN MY SHIP AND MEET YOU.
LEAVE ZERO SANCTUARY. YOU WILL NOT FIND ME.
I'M CLOSING THIS LINE. I WON'T ANSWER COMMUNICATIONS FROM YOU AGAIN. I WILL BE ENTERING INTO HYPERSLEEP WHILE MY SHIP REACHES ITS COORDINATES.
I KNOW YOUR PLAN!

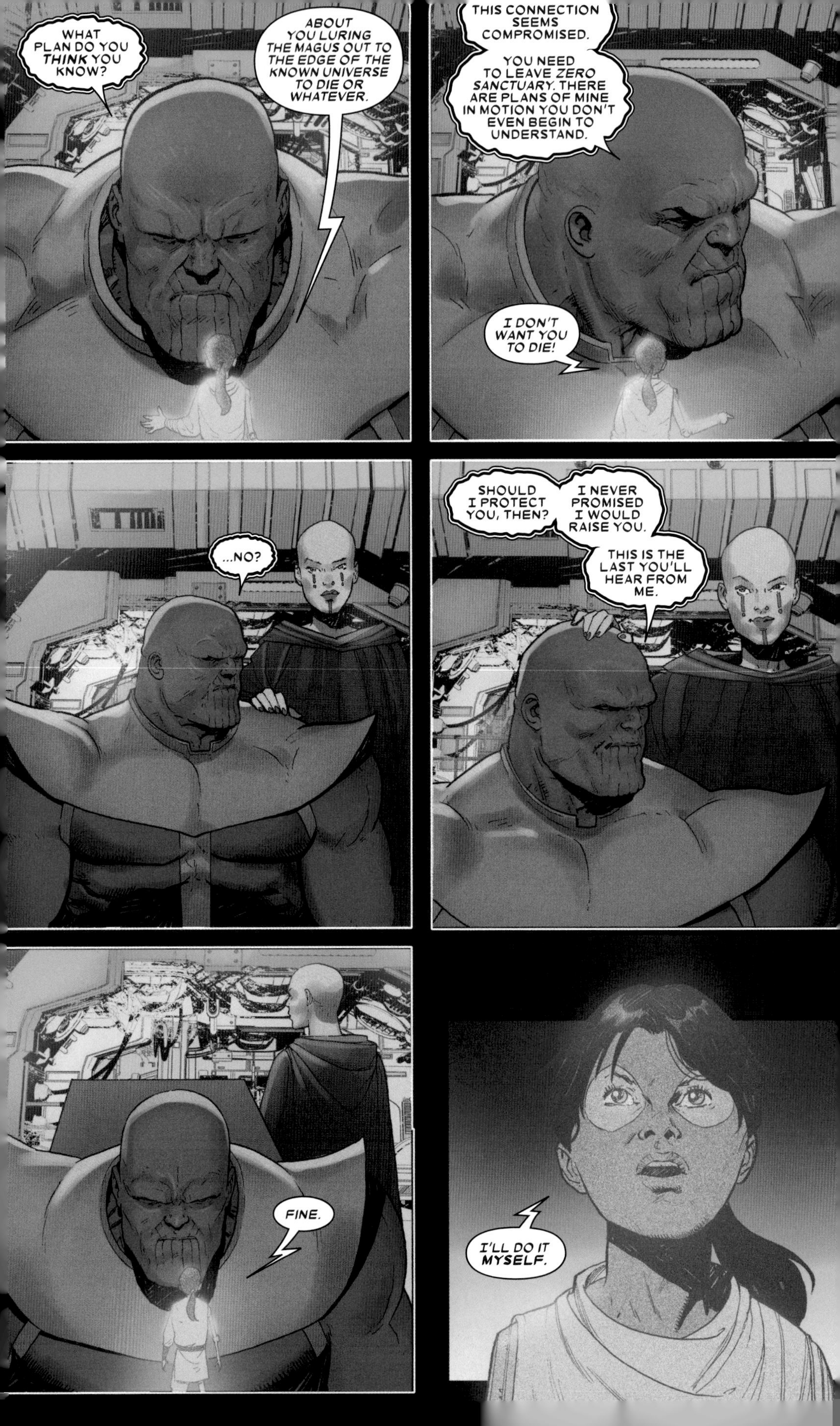
WHAT PLAN DO YOU *THINK* YOU KNOW?
ABOUT YOU LURING THE MAGUS OUT TO THE EDGE OF THE KNOWN UNIVERSE TO DIE OR WHATEVER.
THIS CONNECTION SEEMS COMPROMISED.
YOU NEED TO LEAVE *ZERO SANCTUARY*. THERE ARE PLANS OF MINE IN MOTION YOU DON'T EVEN BEGIN TO UNDERSTAND.
I DON'T WANT YOU TO DIE!
...NO?
SHOULD I PROTECT YOU, THEN?
I NEVER PROMISED I WOULD RAISE YOU.
THIS IS THE LAST YOU'LL HEAR FROM ME.
FINE.
I'LL DO IT *MYSELF*.

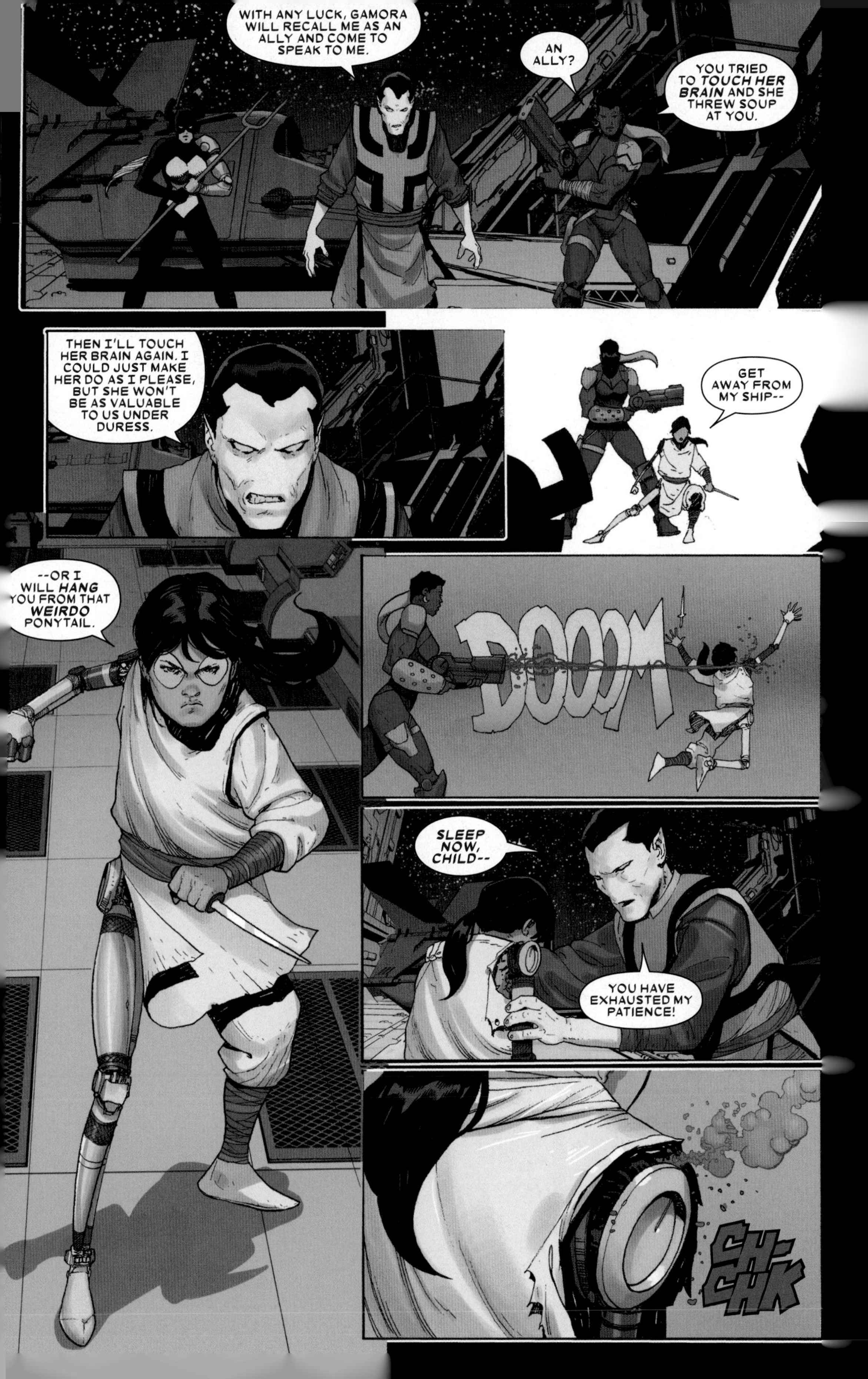
WITH ANY LUCK, GAMORA WILL RECALL ME AS AN ALLY AND COME TO SPEAK TO ME.
AN ALLY?
YOU TRIED TO TOUCH HER BRAIN AND SHE THREW SOUP AT YOU.
THEN I'LL TOUCH HER BRAIN AGAIN. I COULD JUST MAKE HER DO AS I PLEASE, BUT SHE WON'T BE AS VALUABLE TO US UNDER DURESS.
GET AWAY FROM MY SHIP--
--OR I WILL HANG YOU FROM THAT WEIRDO PONYTAIL.
DOOOM
SLEEP NOW, CHILD--
YOU HAVE EXHAUSTED MY PATIENCE!
CH-CHK

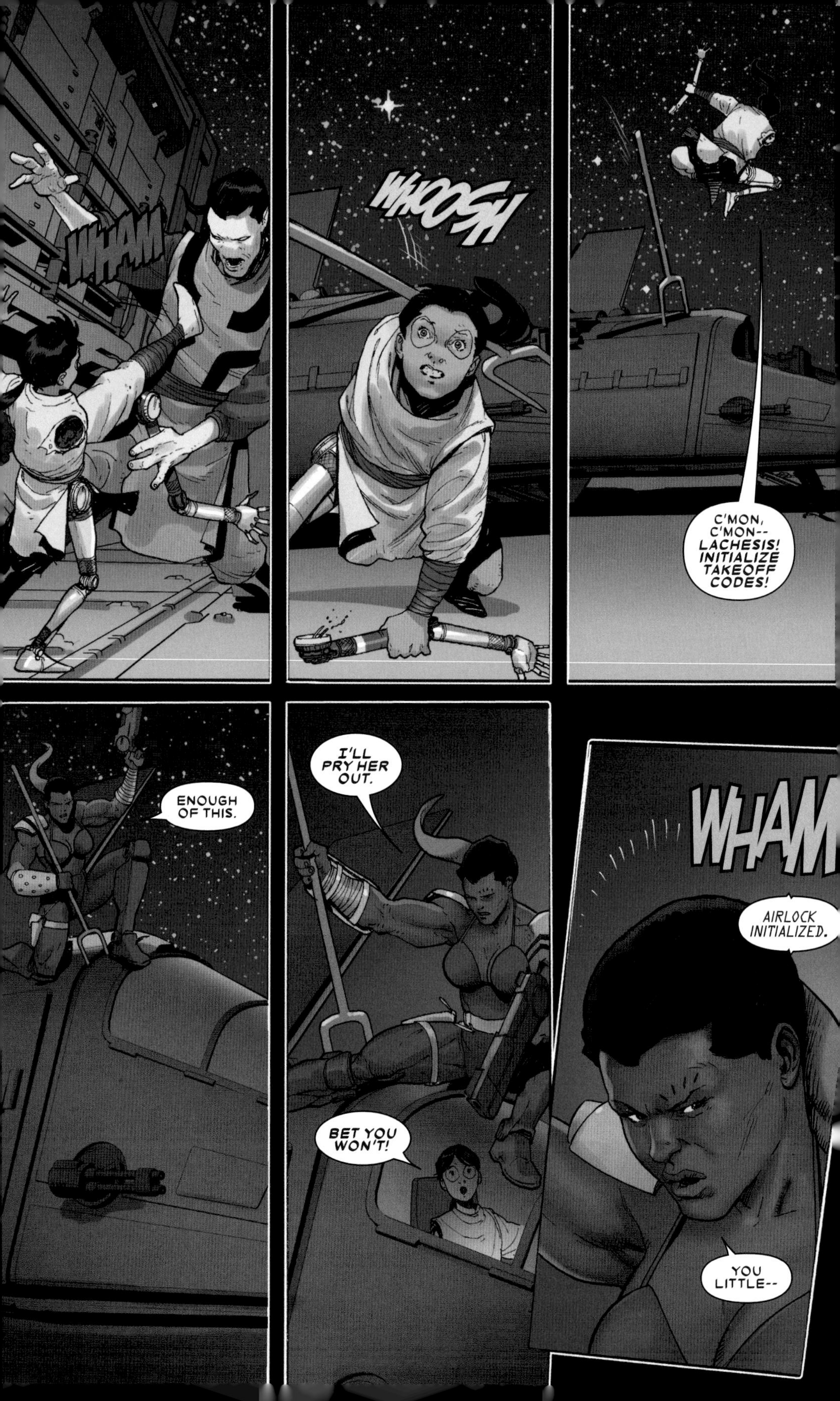
WHAM
WHOOSH
C'MON, C'MON-- LACHESIS! INITIALIZE TAKEOFF CODES!
ENOUGH OF THIS.
I'LL PRY HER OUT.
BET YOU WON'T!
WHAM
AIRLOCK INITIALIZED.
YOU LITTLE--

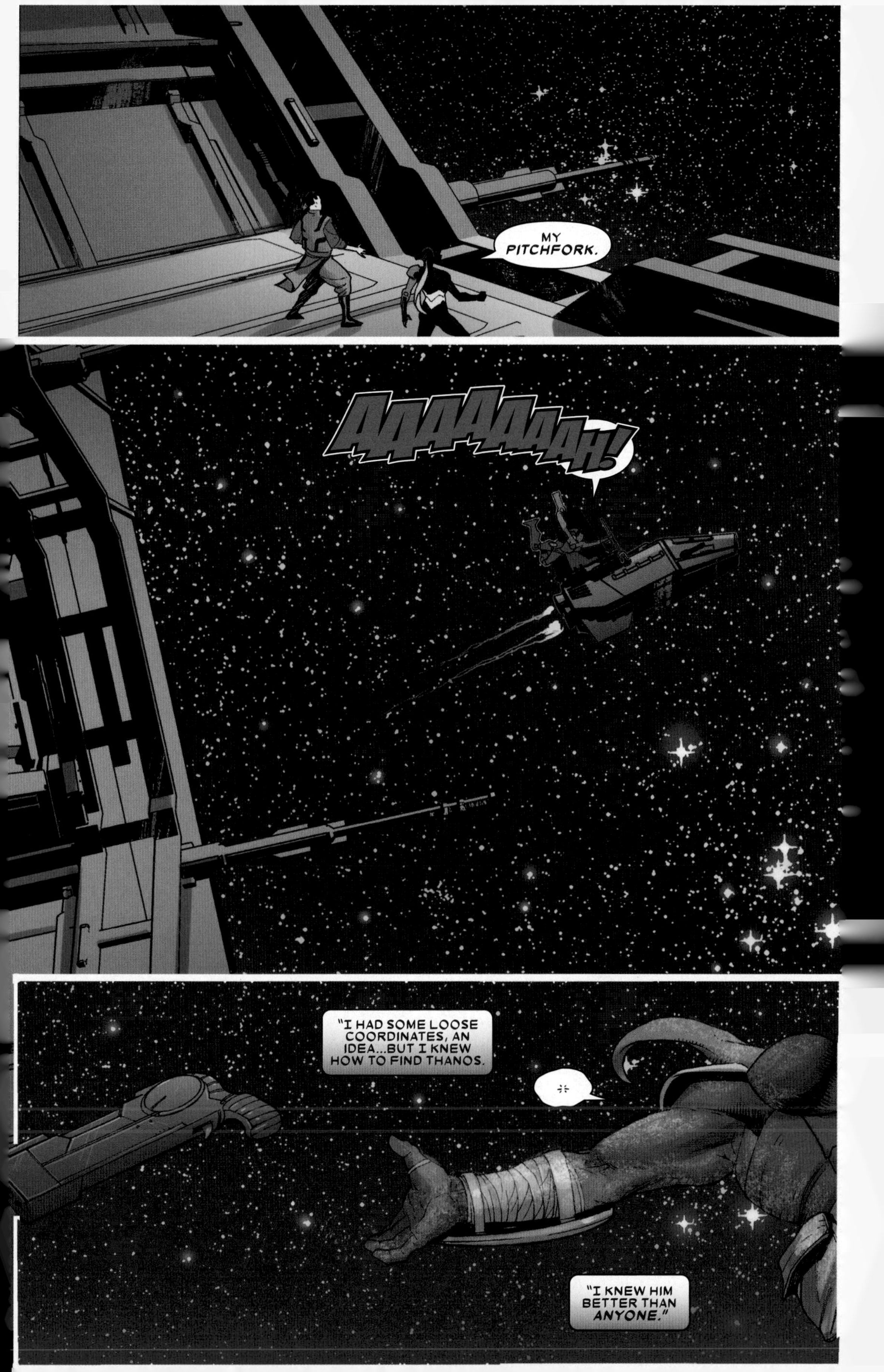
MY PITCHFORK.
AAAAAAAAH!
"I HAD SOME LOOSE COORDINATES, AN IDEA...BUT I KNEW HOW TO FIND THANOS.
"I KNEW HIM BETTER THAN ANYONE."

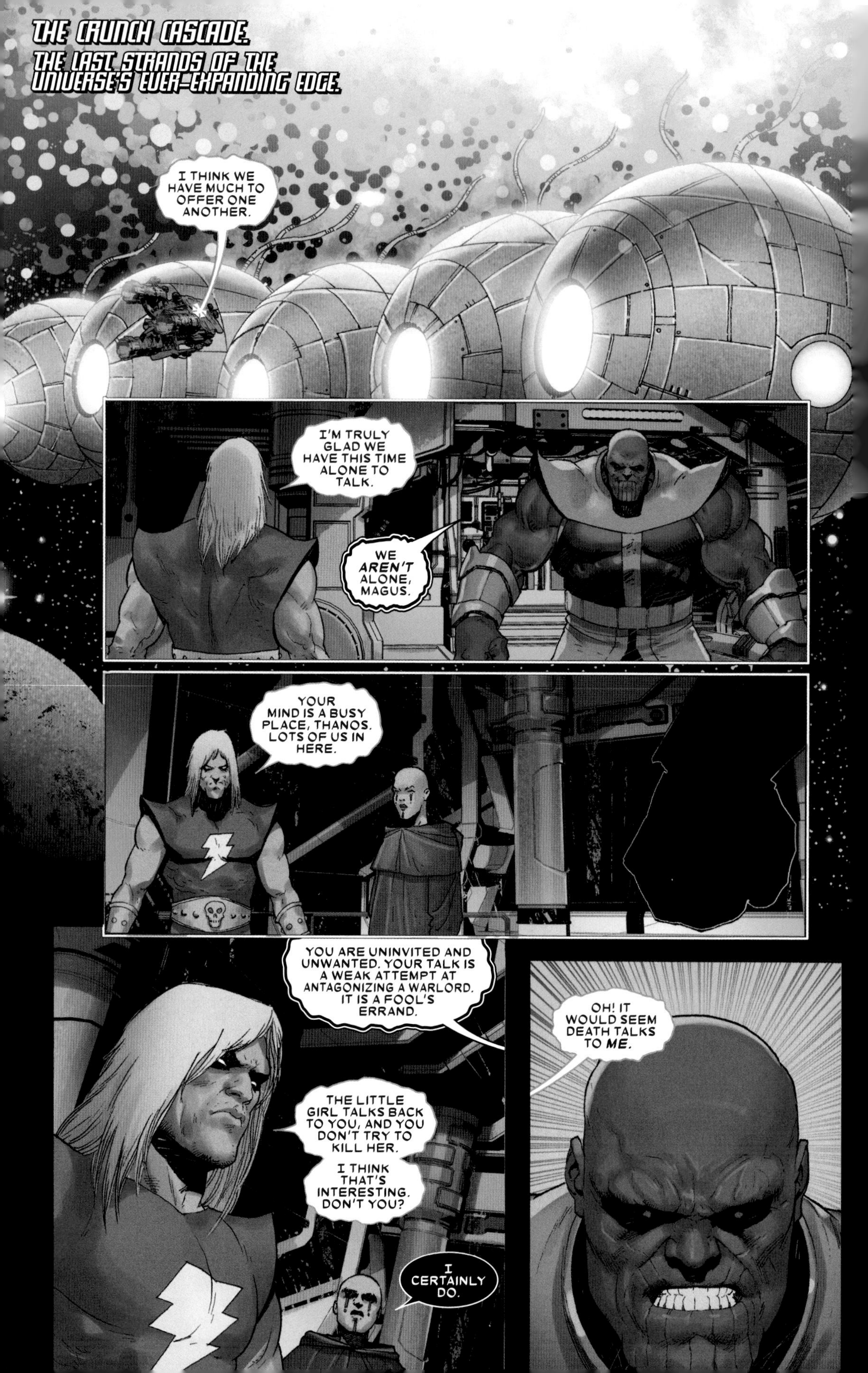
THE CRUNCH CASCADE.
THE LAST STRANDS OF THE UNIVERSE'S EVER-EXPANDING EDGE.
I THINK WE HAVE MUCH TO OFFER ONE ANOTHER.
I'M TRULY GLAD WE HAVE THIS TIME ALONE TO TALK.
WE AREN'T ALONE, MAGUS.
YOUR MIND IS A BUSY PLACE, THANOS. LOTS OF US IN HERE.
YOU ARE UNINVITED AND UNWANTED. YOUR TALK IS A WEAK ATTEMPT AT ANTAGONIZING A WARLORD. IT IS A FOOL'S ERRAND.
OH! IT WOULD SEEM DEATH TALKS TO ME.
THE LITTLE GIRL TALKS BACK TO YOU, AND YOU DON'T TRY TO KILL HER.
I THINK THAT'S INTERESTING. DON'T YOU?
I CERTAINLY DO.

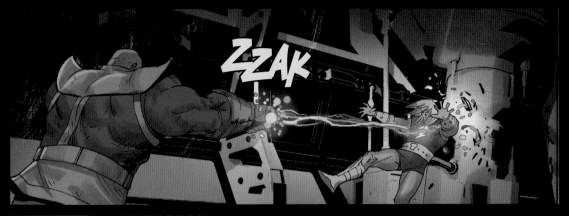

ZZAK

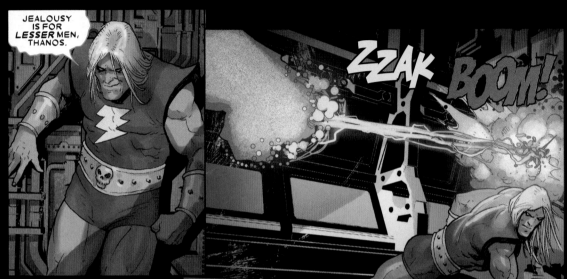

JEALOUSY IS FOR *LESSER* MEN, THANOS.

ZZAK

BOOM!

YOU STUPID ANIMAL.

YOU THOUGHT TO LURE ME OUT HERE TO *KILL* ME?

I AM MORE A GOD THAN YOU WILL *EVER* BE.

SO MANY FLY INTO THE HEAVENS AND CALL THEMSELVES "GODS" AND I LAUGH. WHERE ARE *THEIR* FOLLOWERS?

WHERE-- ARE-- *YOURS?*

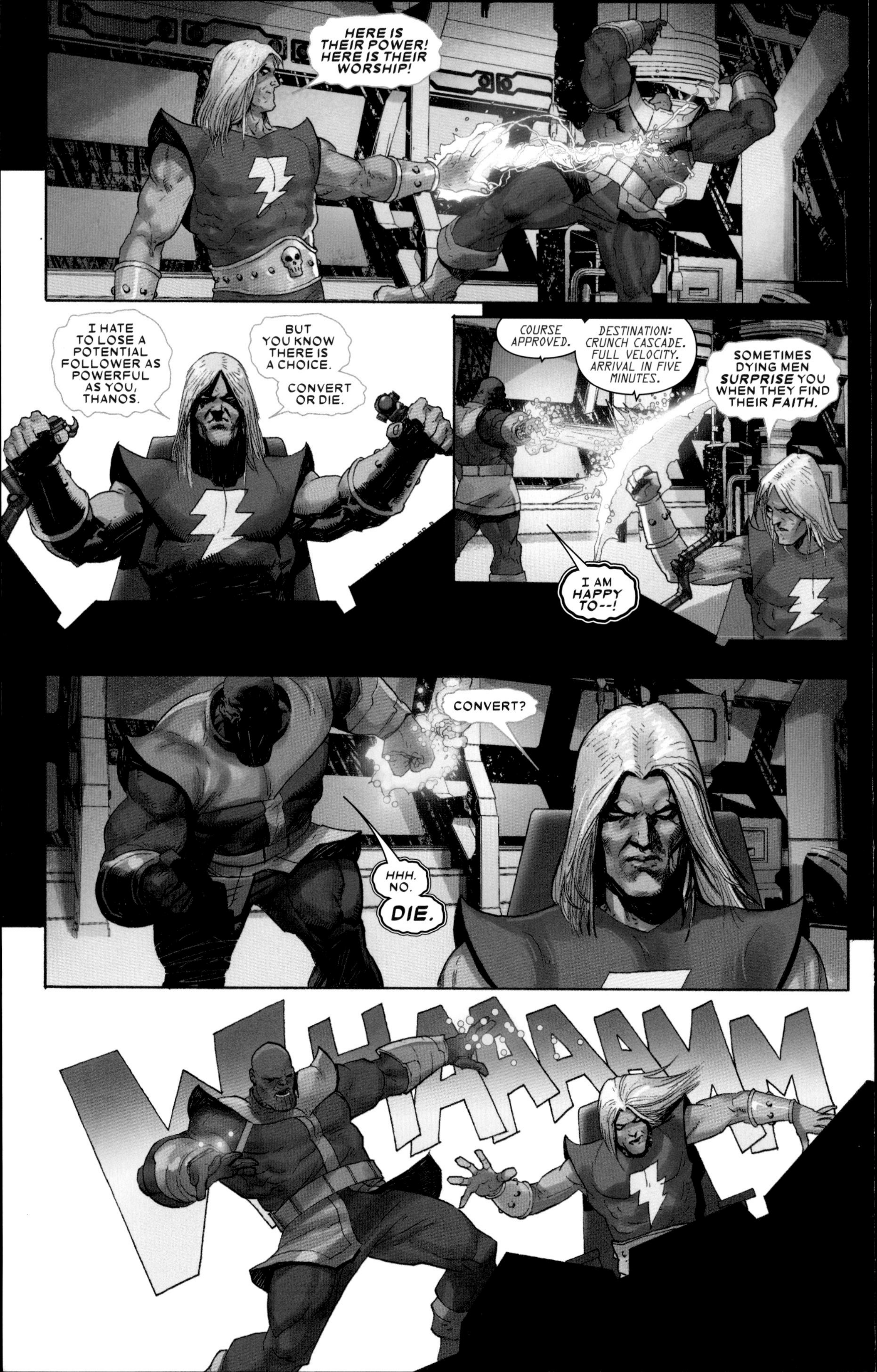
HERE IS THEIR POWER! HERE IS THEIR WORSHIP!
I HATE TO LOSE A POTENTIAL FOLLOWER AS POWERFUL AS YOU, THANOS.
BUT YOU KNOW THERE IS A CHOICE.
CONVERT OR DIE.
COURSE APPROVED.
DESTINATION: CRUNCH CASCADE. FULL VELOCITY. ARRIVAL IN FIVE MINUTES.
SOMETIMES DYING MEN SURPRISE YOU WHEN THEY FIND THEIR FAITH.
I AM HAPPY TO--!
CONVERT?
HHH. NO.
DIE.
WHAAAMM

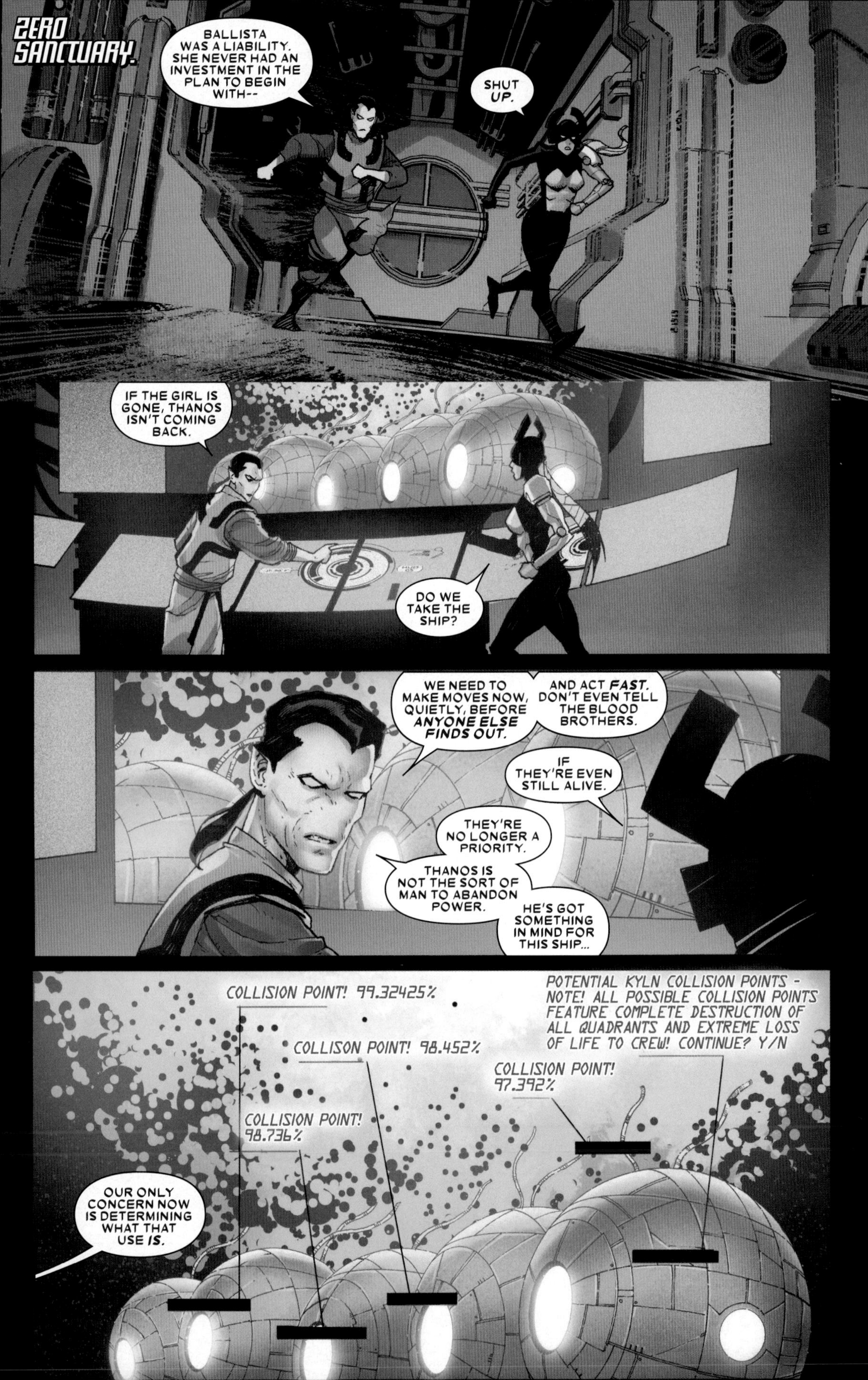
ZERO SANCTUARY.
BALLISTA WAS A LIABILITY. SHE NEVER HAD AN INVESTMENT IN THE PLAN TO BEGIN WITH--
SHUT UP.
IF THE GIRL IS GONE, THANOS ISN'T COMING BACK.
DO WE TAKE THE SHIP?
WE NEED TO MAKE MOVES NOW, QUIETLY, BEFORE ANYONE ELSE FINDS OUT.
AND ACT FAST. DON'T EVEN TELL THE BLOOD BROTHERS.
IF THEY'RE EVEN STILL ALIVE.
THEY'RE NO LONGER A PRIORITY.
THANOS IS NOT THE SORT OF MAN TO ABANDON POWER.
HE'S GOT SOMETHING IN MIND FOR THIS SHIP...
COLLISION POINT! 99.32425%
POTENTIAL KYLN COLLISION POINTS - NOTE! ALL POSSIBLE COLLISION POINTS FEATURE COMPLETE DESTRUCTION OF ALL QUADRANTS AND EXTREME LOSS OF LIFE TO CREW! CONTINUE? Y/N
COLLISON POINT! 98.452%
COLLISION POINT! 97.392%
COLLISION POINT! 98.736%
OUR ONLY CONCERN NOW IS DETERMINING WHAT THAT USE IS.

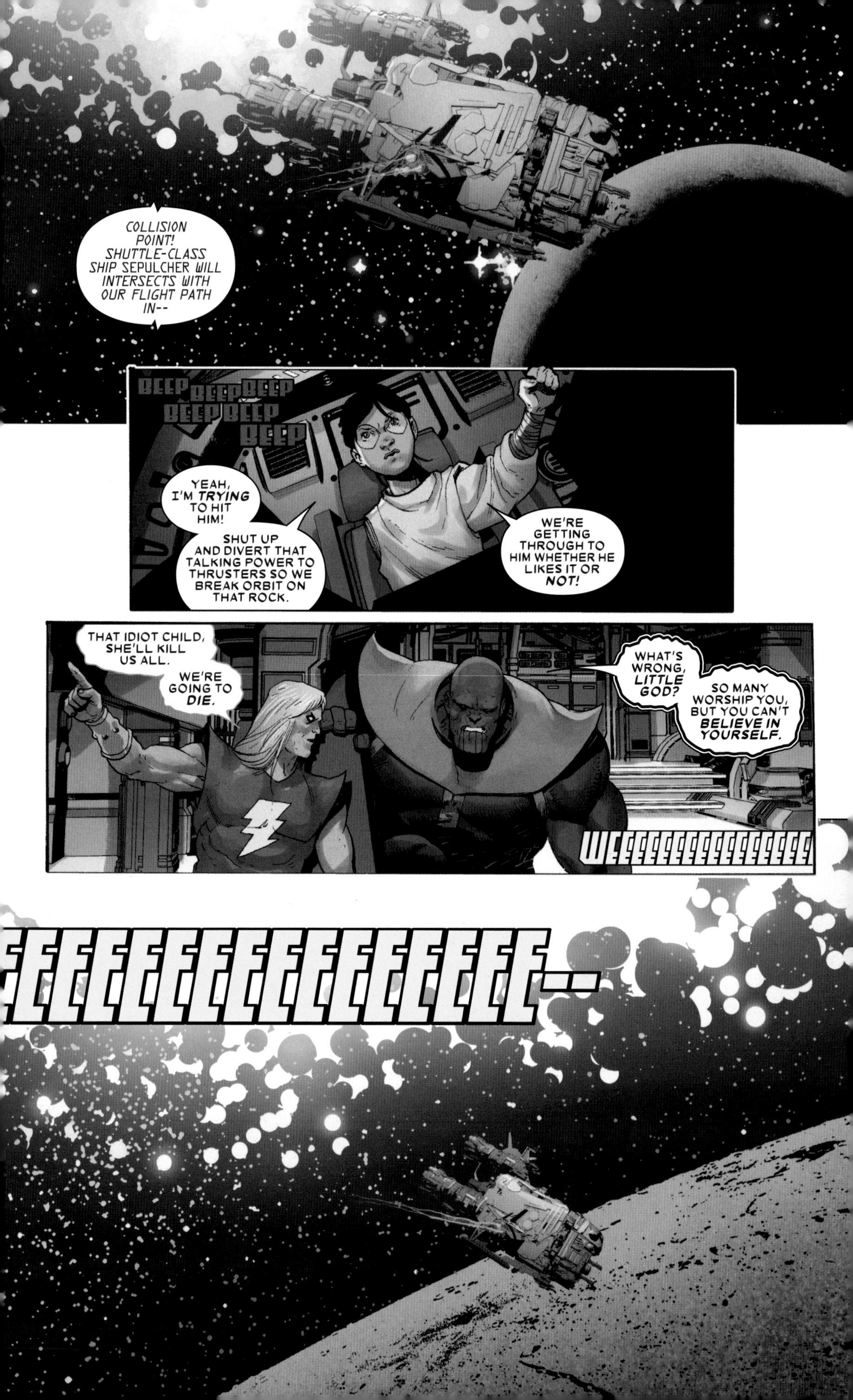
COLLISION POINT! SHUTTLE-CLASS SHIP SEPULCHER WILL INTERSECTS WITH OUR FLIGHT PATH IN--
BEEP BEEP BEEP BEEP BEEP BEEP
YEAH, I'M TRYING TO HIT HIM!
SHUT UP AND DIVERT THAT TALKING POWER TO THRUSTERS SO WE BREAK ORBIT ON THAT ROCK.
WE'RE GETTING THROUGH TO HIM WHETHER HE LIKES IT OR NOT!
THAT IDIOT CHILD, SHE'LL KILL US ALL.
WE'RE GOING TO DIE.
WHAT'S WRONG, LITTLE GOD?
SO MANY WORSHIP YOU, BUT YOU CAN'T BELIEVE IN YOURSELF.
WEEEEEEEEEEEEEEE
EEEEEEEEEEEEEEEE--

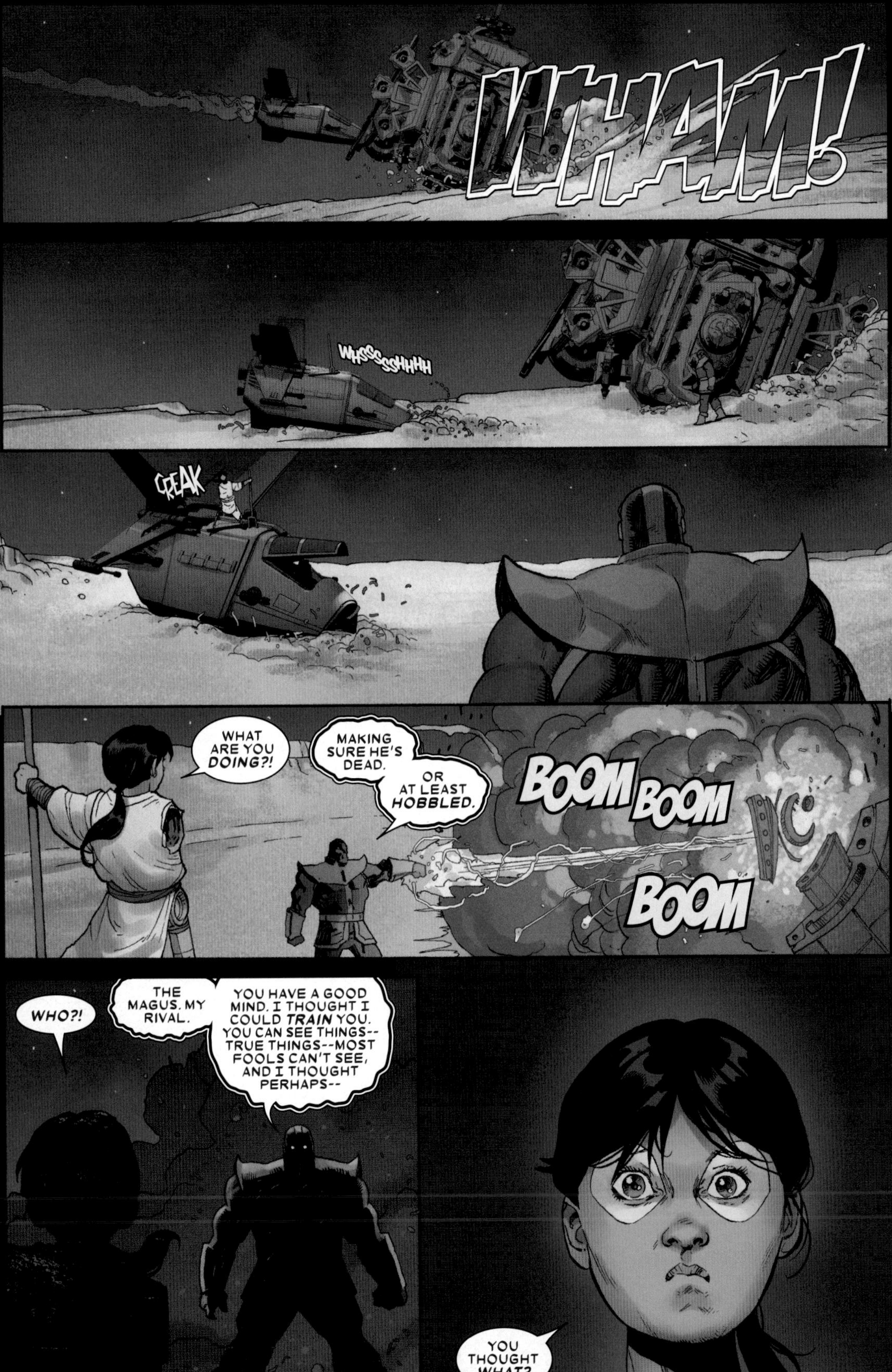
WHAM!
WHSSSSHHHH
CREAK
WHAT ARE YOU DOING?!
MAKING SURE HE'S DEAD.
OR AT LEAST HOBBLED.
BOOM BOOM
BOOM
WHO?!
THE MAGUS. MY RIVAL.
YOU HAVE A GOOD MIND. I THOUGHT I COULD TRAIN YOU. YOU CAN SEE THINGS--TRUE THINGS--MOST FOOLS CAN'T SEE, AND I THOUGHT PERHAPS--
YOU THOUGHT WHAT?

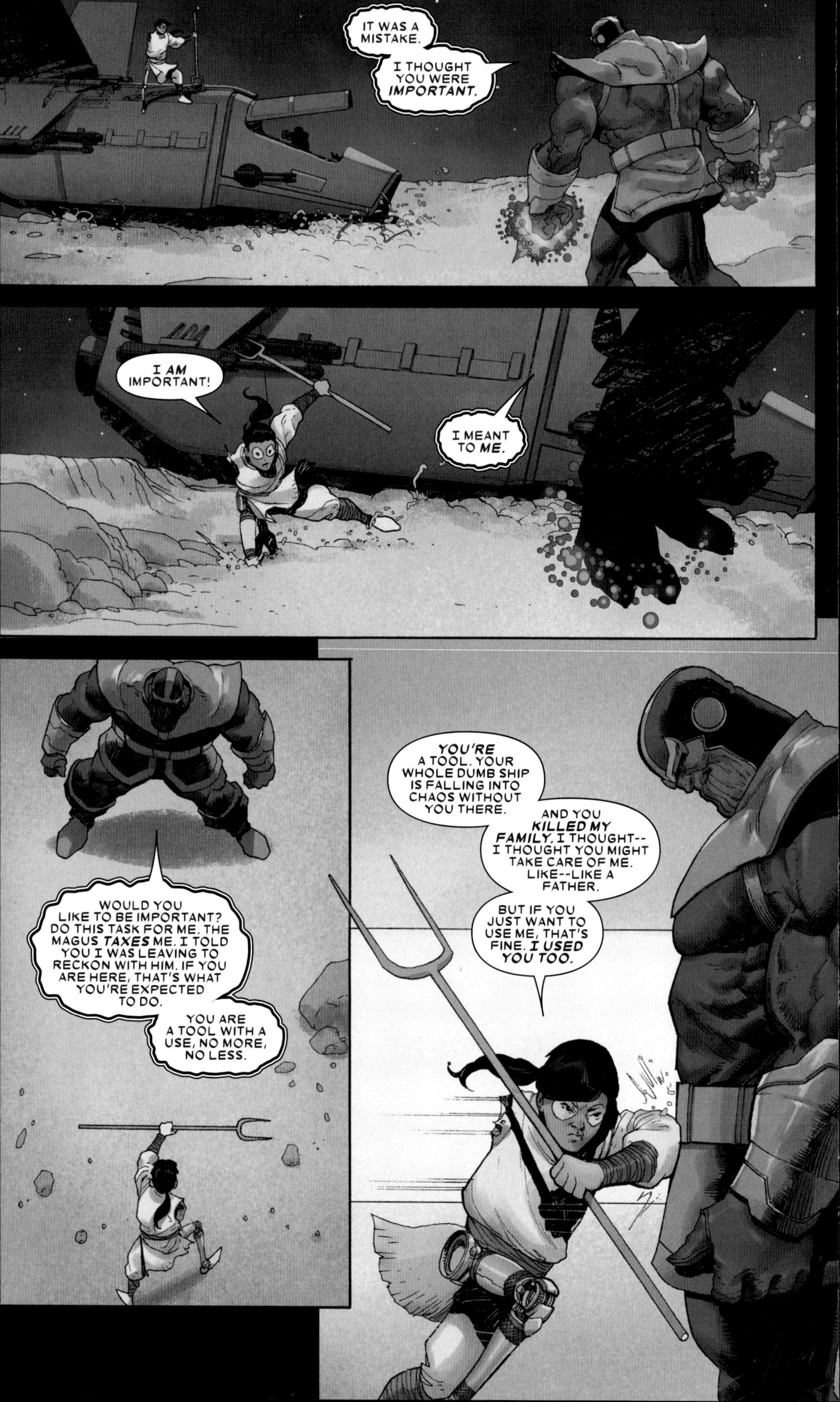

IT WAS A MISTAKE.
I THOUGHT YOU WERE IMPORTANT.
I AM IMPORTANT!
I MEANT TO ME.
WOULD YOU LIKE TO BE IMPORTANT? DO THIS TASK FOR ME. THE MAGUS TAXES ME. I TOLD YOU I WAS LEAVING TO RECKON WITH HIM. IF YOU ARE HERE, THAT'S WHAT YOU'RE EXPECTED TO DO.
YOU ARE A TOOL WITH A USE, NO MORE, NO LESS.
YOU'RE A TOOL. YOUR WHOLE DUMB SHIP IS FALLING INTO CHAOS WITHOUT YOU THERE.
AND YOU KILLED MY FAMILY. I THOUGHT-- I THOUGHT YOU MIGHT TAKE CARE OF ME. LIKE--LIKE A FATHER.
BUT IF YOU JUST WANT TO USE ME, THAT'S FINE. I USED YOU TOO.

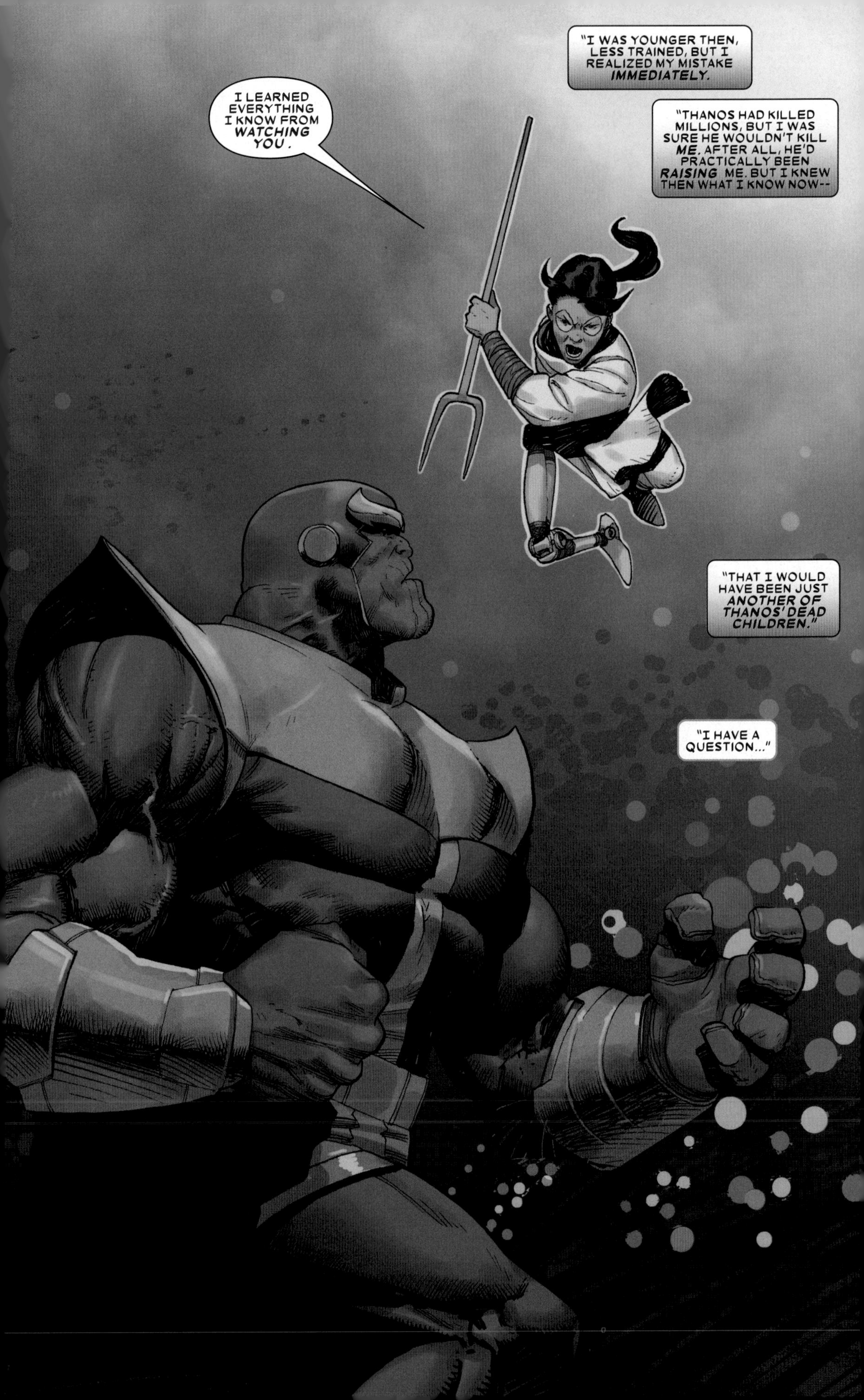
"I WAS YOUNGER THEN, LESS TRAINED, BUT I REALIZED MY MISTAKE IMMEDIATELY.
I LEARNED EVERYTHING I KNOW FROM WATCHING YOU.
"THANOS HAD KILLED MILLIONS, BUT I WAS SURE HE WOULDN'T KILL ME. AFTER ALL, HE'D PRACTICALLY BEEN RAISING ME. BUT I KNEW THEN WHAT I KNOW NOW--
"THAT I WOULD HAVE BEEN JUST ANOTHER OF THANOS' DEAD CHILDREN."
"I HAVE A QUESTION..."

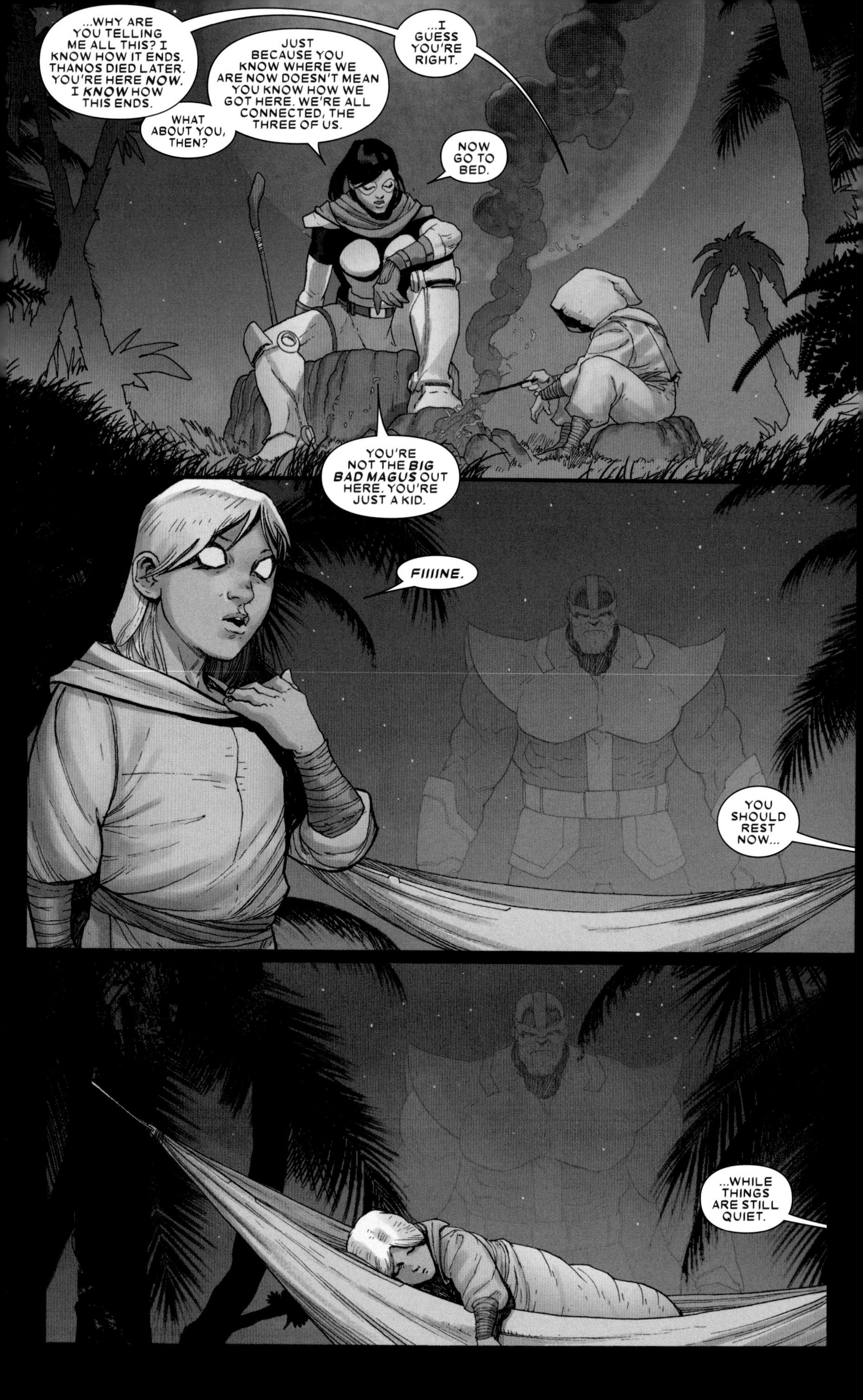
...WHY ARE YOU TELLING ME ALL THIS? I KNOW HOW IT ENDS. THANOS DIED LATER. YOU'RE HERE NOW. I KNOW HOW THIS ENDS.
JUST BECAUSE YOU KNOW WHERE WE ARE NOW DOESN'T MEAN YOU KNOW HOW WE GOT HERE. WE'RE ALL CONNECTED, THE THREE OF US.
WHAT ABOUT YOU, THEN?
...I GUESS YOU'RE RIGHT.
NOW GO TO BED.
YOU'RE NOT THE BIG BAD MAGUS OUT HERE. YOU'RE JUST A KID.
FIIIINE.
YOU SHOULD REST NOW...
...WHILE THINGS ARE STILL QUIET.

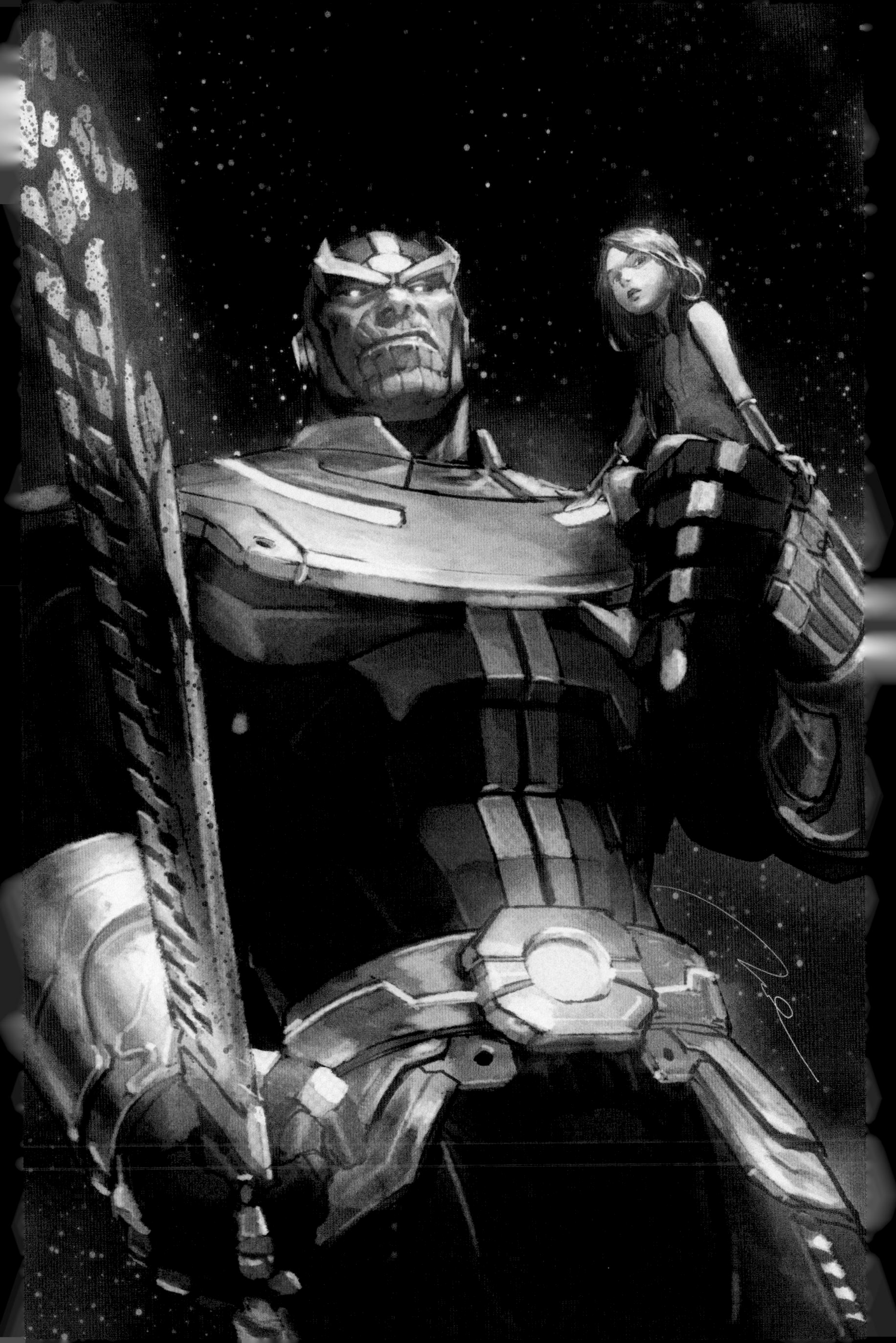

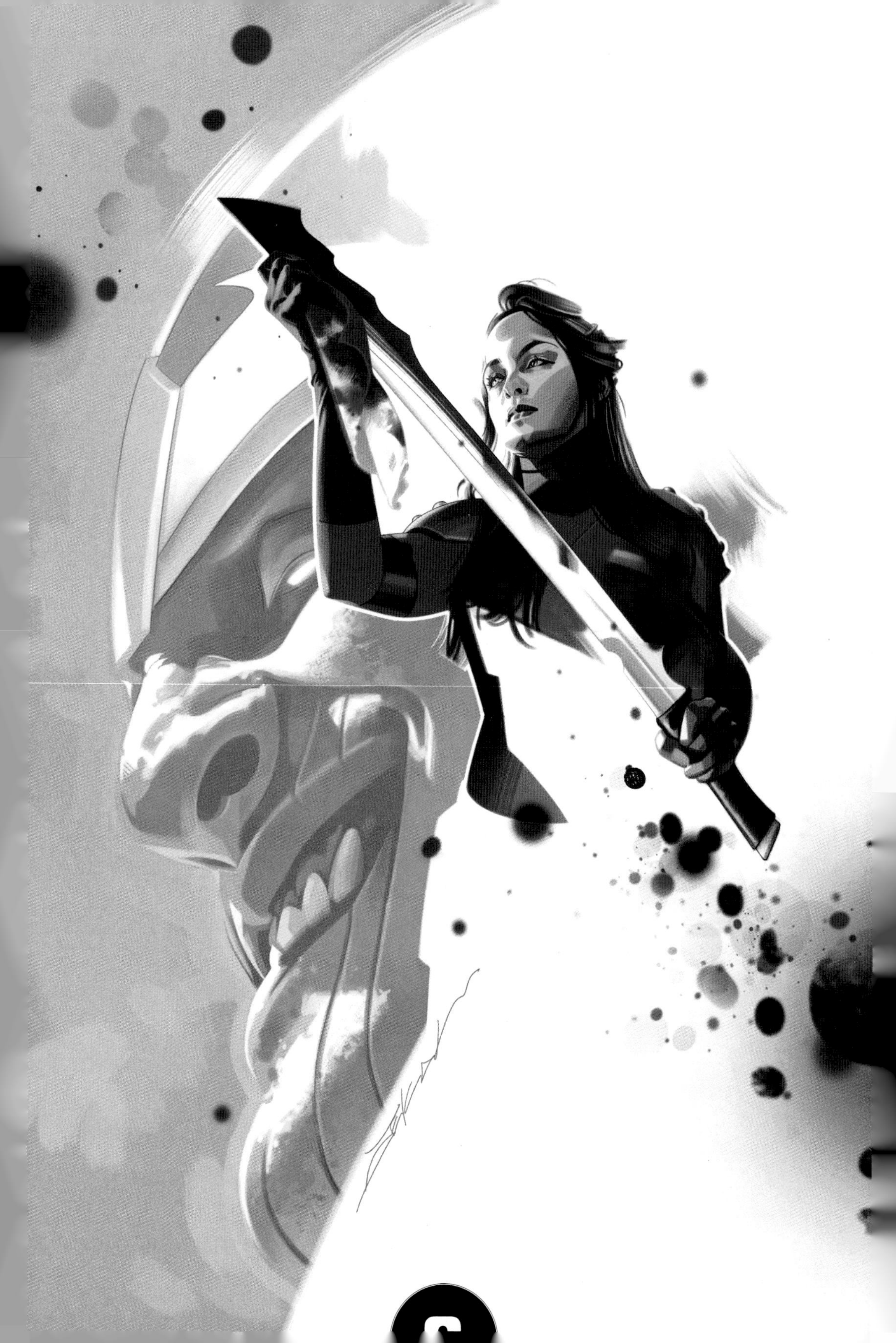

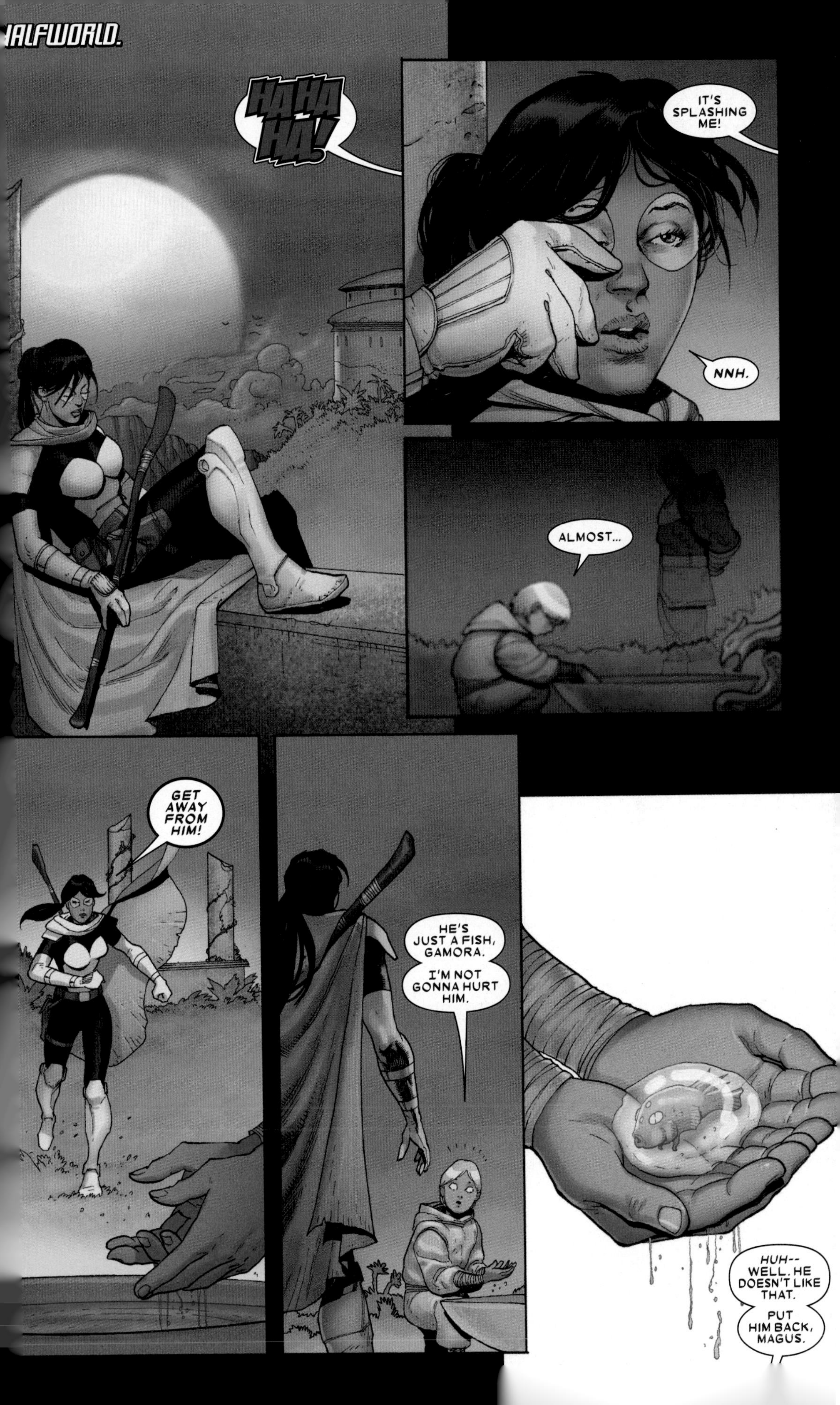
HALFWORLD.
HAHAHA!
IT'S SPLASHING ME!
NNH.
ALMOST...
GET AWAY FROM HIM!
HE'S JUST A FISH, GAMORA.
I'M NOT GONNA HURT HIM.
HUH-- WELL. HE DOESN'T LIKE THAT.
PUT HIM BACK, MAGUS.

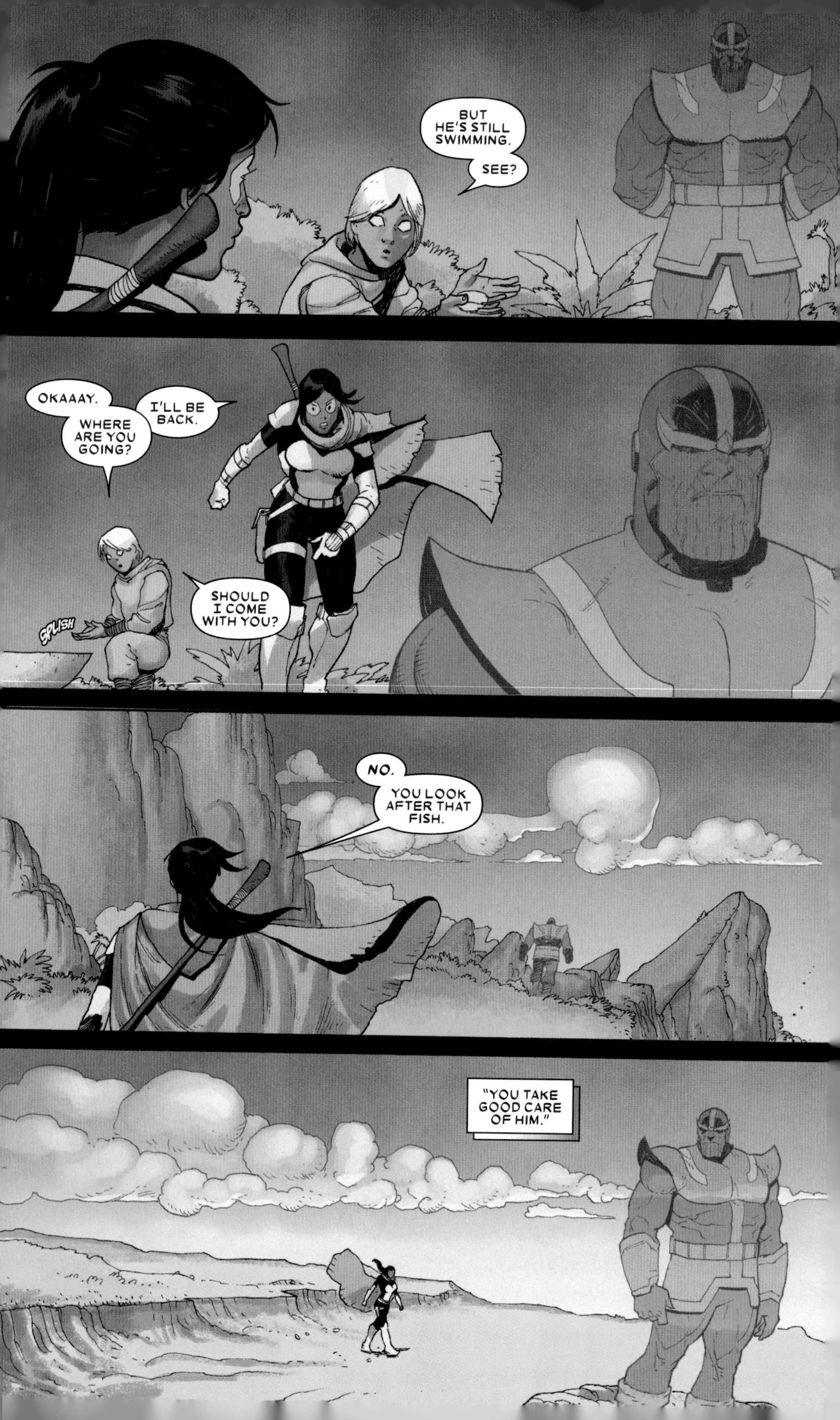

BUT HE'S STILL SWIMMING.
SEE?
OKAAAY.
WHERE ARE YOU GOING?
I'LL BE BACK.
SHOULD I COME WITH YOU?
SPLISH
NO.
YOU LOOK AFTER THAT FISH.
"YOU TAKE GOOD CARE OF HIM."

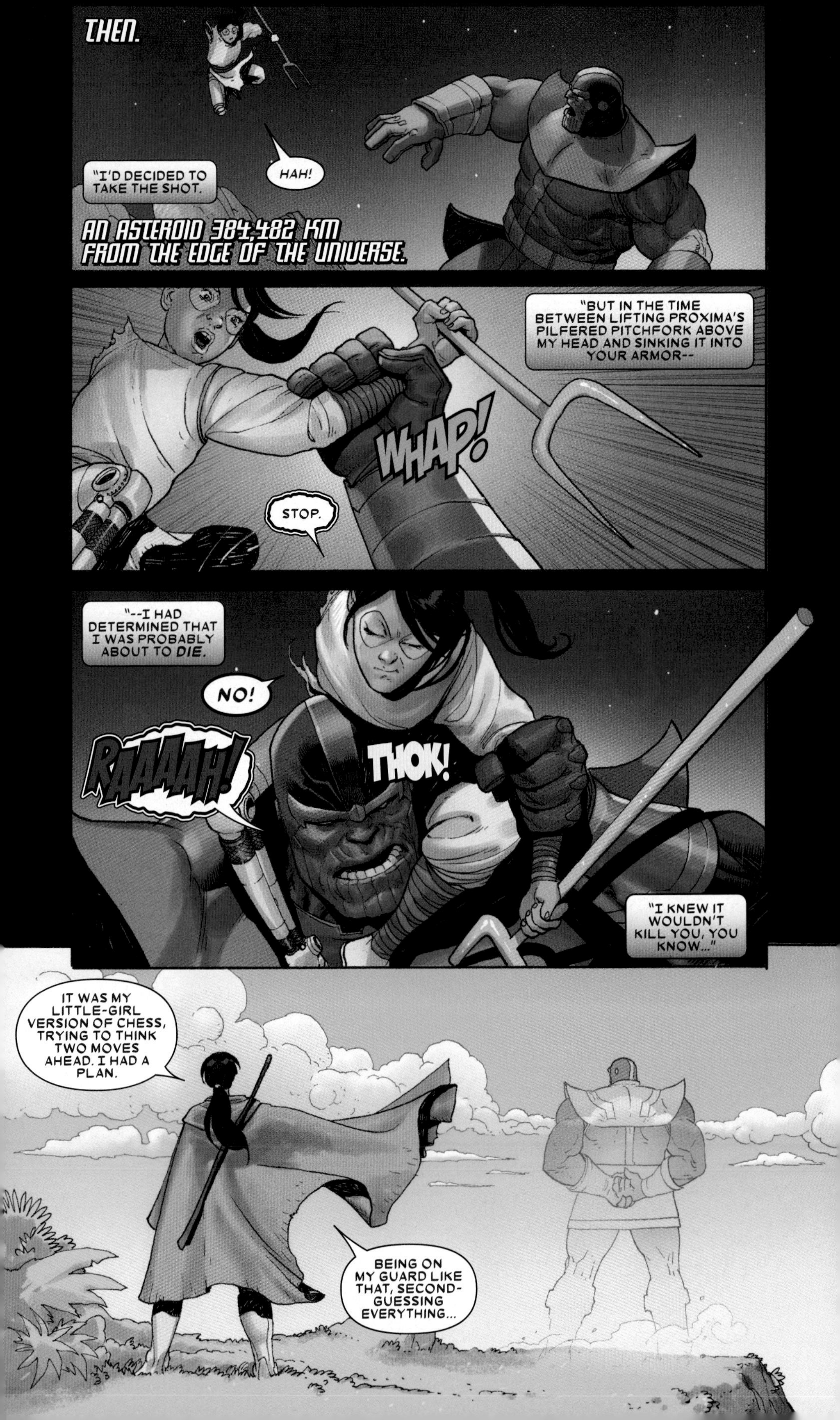
THEN.
"I'D DECIDED TO TAKE THE SHOT.
HAH!
AN ASTEROID 384,482 KM FROM THE EDGE OF THE UNIVERSE.
"BUT IN THE TIME BETWEEN LIFTING PROXIMA'S PILFERED PITCHFORK ABOVE MY HEAD AND SINKING IT INTO YOUR ARMOR--
WHAP!
STOP.
"--I HAD DETERMINED THAT I WAS PROBABLY ABOUT TO *DIE*.
NO!
RAAAAH!
THOK!
"I KNEW IT WOULDN'T KILL YOU, YOU KNOW..."
IT WAS MY LITTLE-GIRL VERSION OF CHESS, TRYING TO THINK TWO MOVES AHEAD. I HAD A PLAN.
BEING ON MY GUARD LIKE THAT, SECOND-GUESSING EVERYTHING...

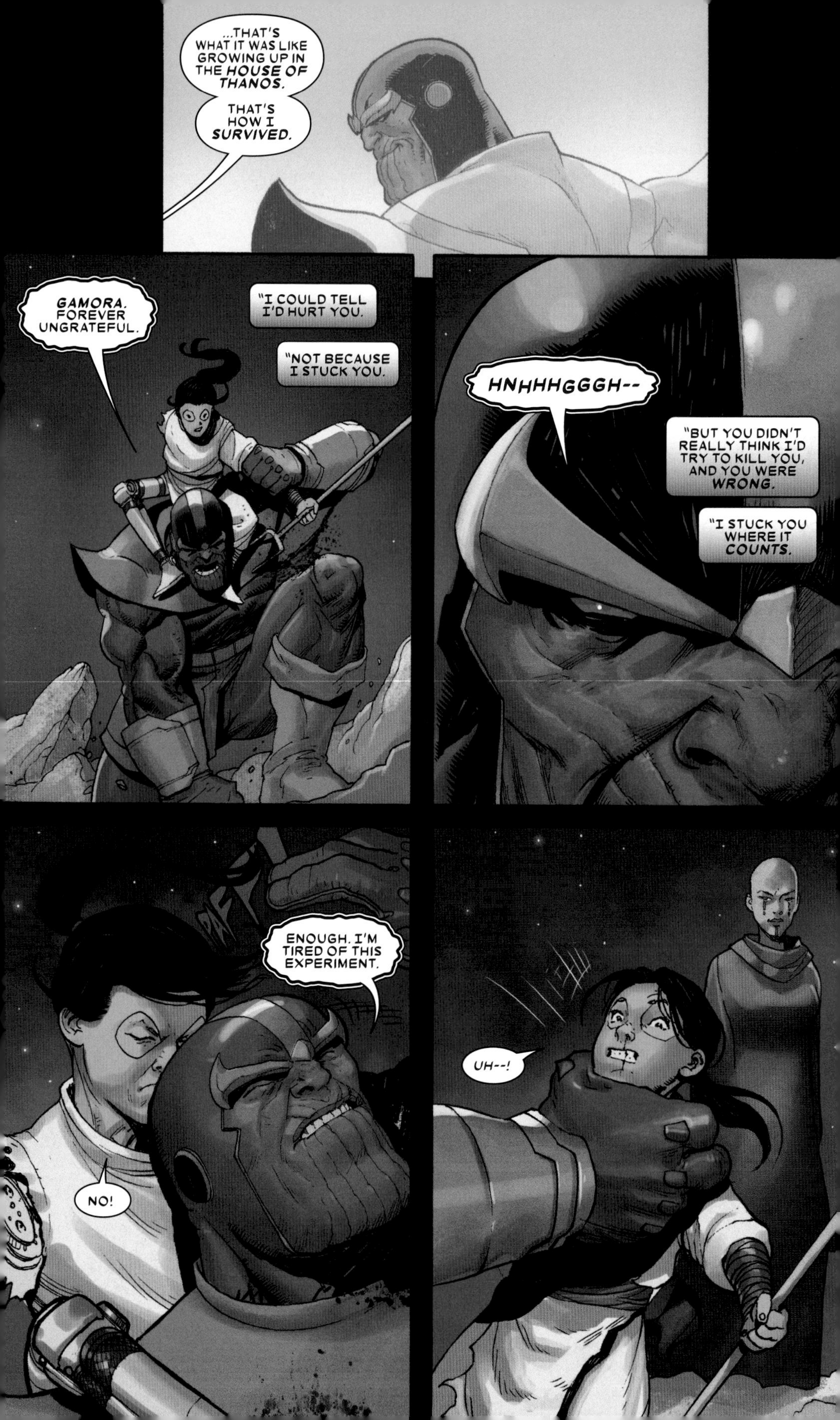

...THAT'S WHAT IT WAS LIKE GROWING UP IN THE *HOUSE OF THANOS.*
THAT'S HOW I *SURVIVED.*
GAMORA. FOREVER UNGRATEFUL.
"I COULD TELL I'D HURT YOU.
"NOT BECAUSE I STUCK YOU.
HNHHHGGGH--
"BUT YOU DIDN'T REALLY THINK I'D TRY TO KILL YOU, AND YOU WERE *WRONG.*
"I STUCK YOU WHERE IT *COUNTS.*
ENOUGH. I'M TIRED OF THIS EXPERIMENT.
NO!
UH--!

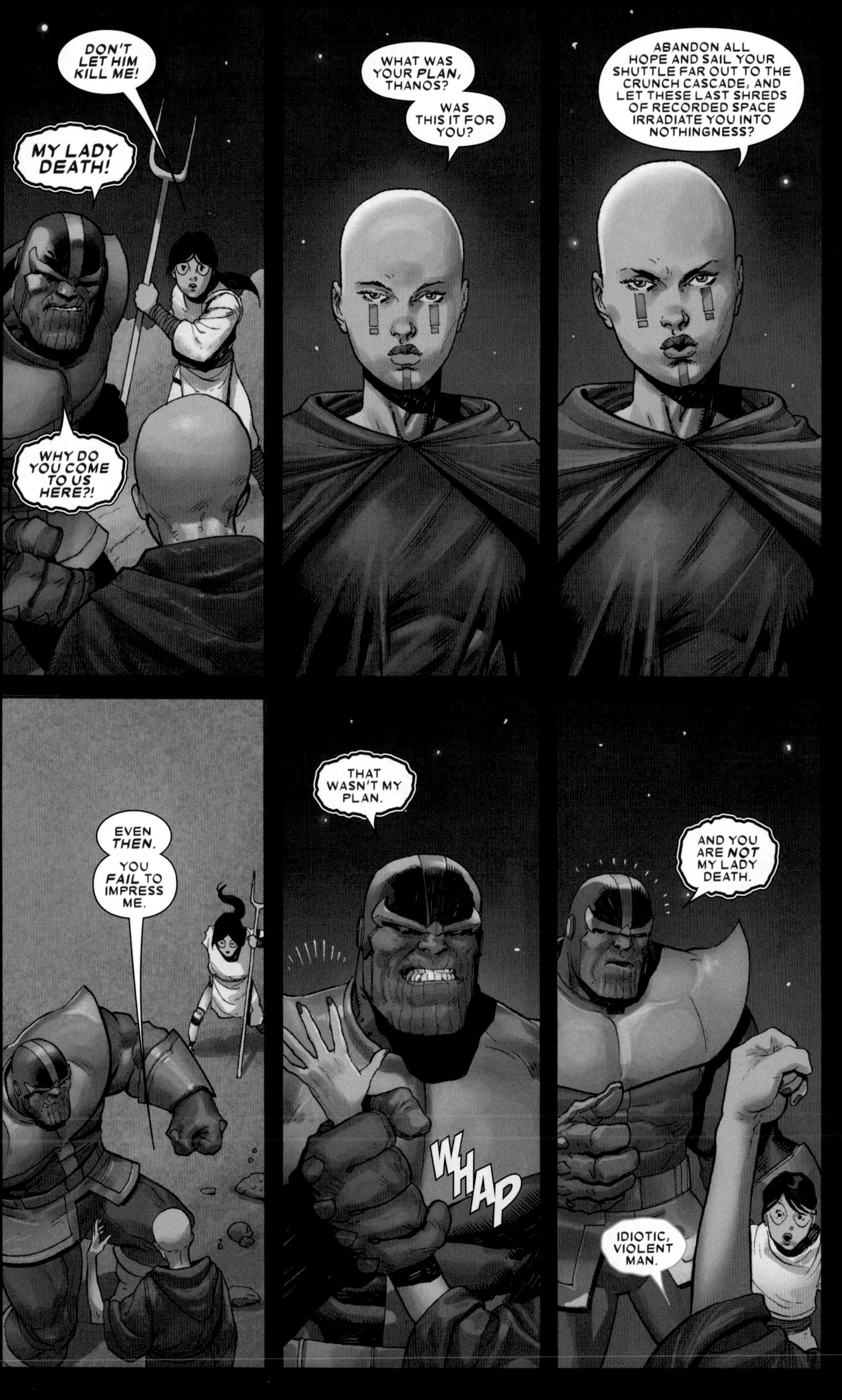

DON'T LET HIM KILL ME!
MY LADY DEATH!
WHY DO YOU COME TO US HERE?!
WHAT WAS YOUR PLAN, THANOS?
WAS THIS IT FOR YOU?
ABANDON ALL HOPE AND SAIL YOUR SHUTTLE FAR OUT TO THE CRUNCH CASCADE, AND LET THESE LAST SHREDS OF RECORDED SPACE IRRADIATE YOU INTO NOTHINGNESS?
EVEN THEN.
YOU FAIL TO IMPRESS ME.
THAT WASN'T MY PLAN.
WHAP
AND YOU ARE NOT MY LADY DEATH.
IDIOTIC, VIOLENT MAN.

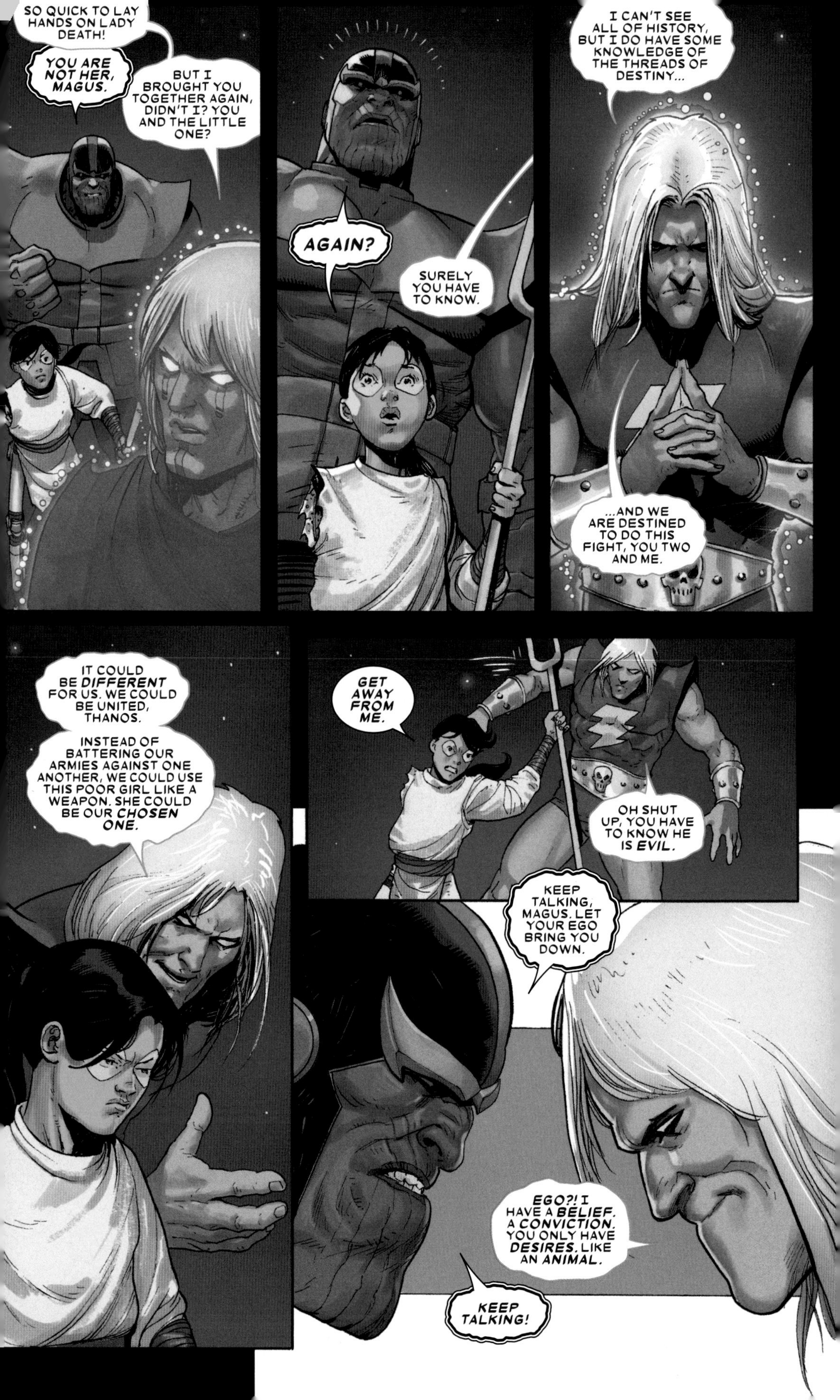

SO QUICK TO LAY HANDS ON LADY DEATH!
YOU ARE NOT HER, MAGUS.
BUT I BROUGHT YOU TOGETHER AGAIN, DIDN'T I? YOU AND THE LITTLE ONE?
AGAIN?
SURELY YOU HAVE TO KNOW.
I CAN'T SEE ALL OF HISTORY, BUT I DO HAVE SOME KNOWLEDGE OF THE THREADS OF DESTINY...
...AND WE ARE DESTINED TO DO THIS FIGHT, YOU TWO AND ME.
IT COULD BE DIFFERENT FOR US. WE COULD BE UNITED, THANOS.
INSTEAD OF BATTERING OUR ARMIES AGAINST ONE ANOTHER, WE COULD USE THIS POOR GIRL LIKE A WEAPON. SHE COULD BE OUR CHOSEN ONE.
GET AWAY FROM ME.
OH SHUT UP, YOU HAVE TO KNOW HE IS EVIL.
KEEP TALKING, MAGUS. LET YOUR EGO BRING YOU DOWN.
EGO?! I HAVE A BELIEF. A CONVICTION. YOU ONLY HAVE DESIRES, LIKE AN ANIMAL.
KEEP TALKING!

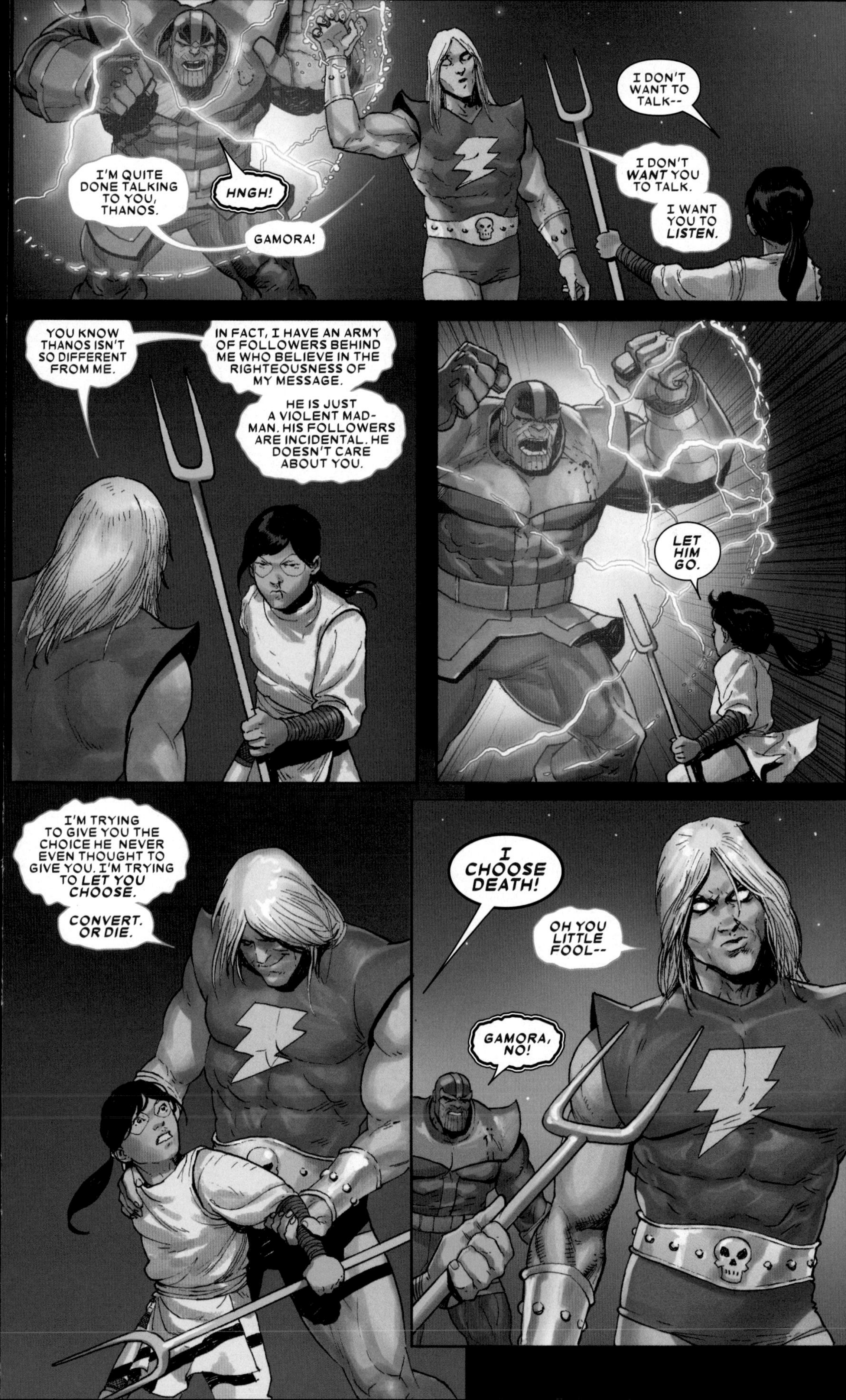
I'M QUITE DONE TALKING TO YOU, THANOS.
HNGH!
GAMORA!
I DON'T WANT TO TALK--
I DON'T WANT YOU TO TALK.
I WANT YOU TO LISTEN.
YOU KNOW THANOS ISN'T SO DIFFERENT FROM ME.
IN FACT, I HAVE AN ARMY OF FOLLOWERS BEHIND ME WHO BELIEVE IN THE RIGHTEOUSNESS OF MY MESSAGE.
HE IS JUST A VIOLENT MAD-MAN. HIS FOLLOWERS ARE INCIDENTAL. HE DOESN'T CARE ABOUT YOU.
LET HIM GO.
I'M TRYING TO GIVE YOU THE CHOICE HE NEVER EVEN THOUGHT TO GIVE YOU. I'M TRYING TO LET YOU CHOOSE.
CONVERT. OR DIE.
I CHOOSE DEATH!
OH YOU LITTLE FOOL--
GAMORA, NO!

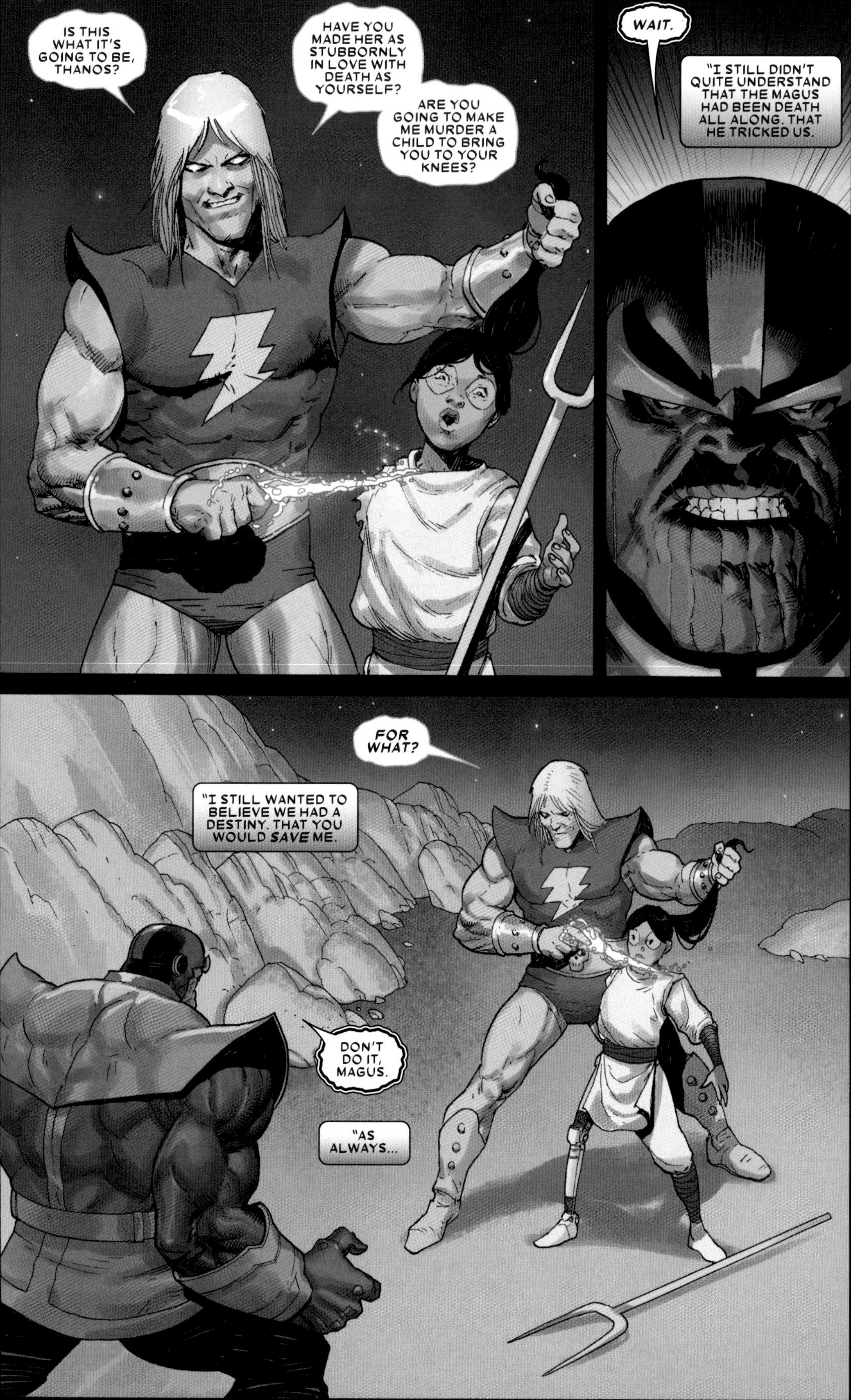
IS THIS WHAT IT'S GOING TO BE, THANOS?
HAVE YOU MADE HER AS STUBBORNLY IN LOVE WITH DEATH AS YOURSELF?
ARE YOU GOING TO MAKE ME MURDER A CHILD TO BRING YOU TO YOUR KNEES?
WAIT.
"I STILL DIDN'T QUITE UNDERSTAND THAT THE MAGUS HAD BEEN DEATH ALL ALONG. THAT HE TRICKED US.
FOR WHAT?
"I STILL WANTED TO BELIEVE WE HAD A DESTINY. THAT YOU WOULD *SAVE* ME.
DON'T DO IT, MAGUS.
"AS ALWAYS...

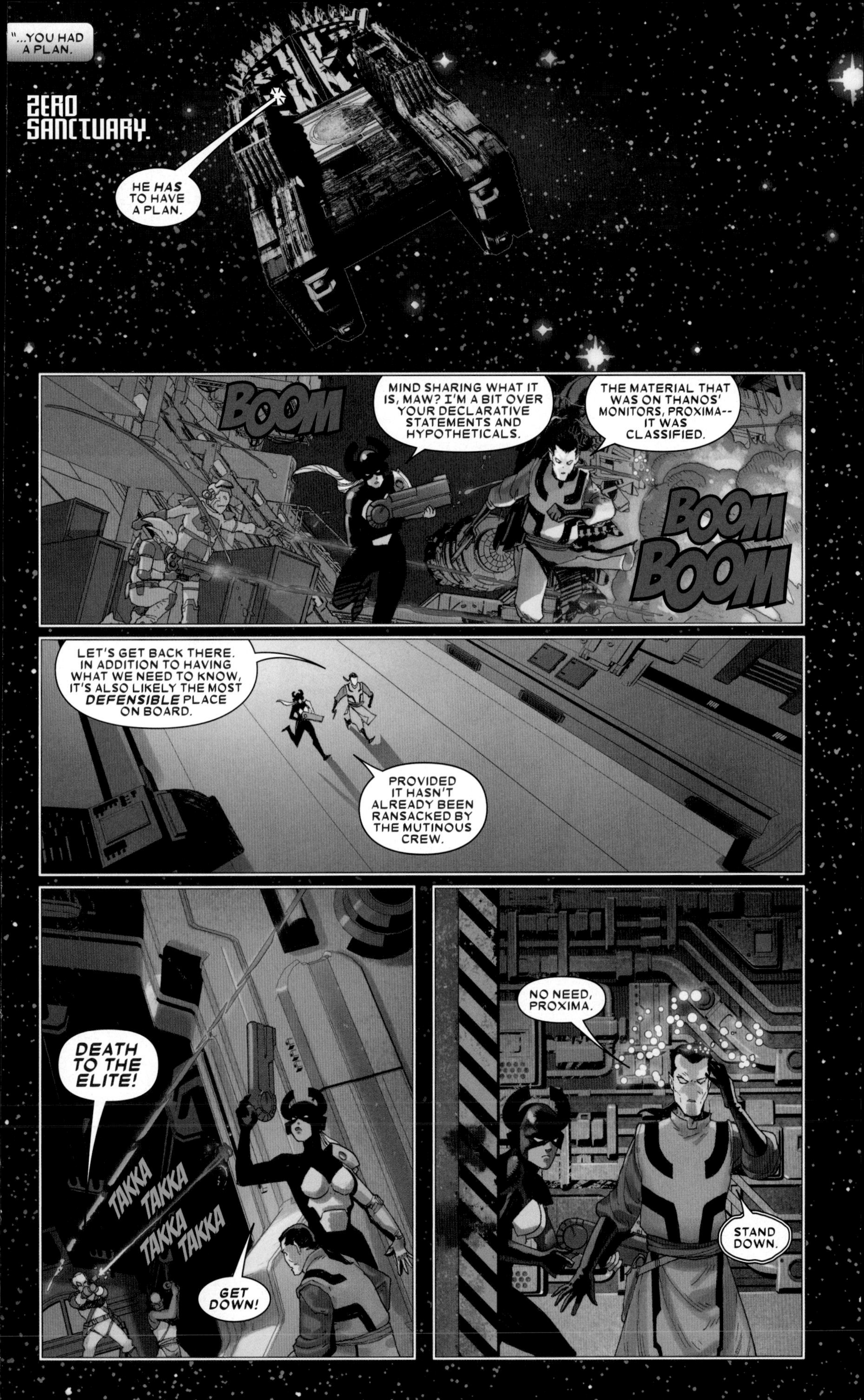
"...YOU HAD A PLAN.
ZERO SANCTUARY.
HE HAS TO HAVE A PLAN.
BOOM
MIND SHARING WHAT IT IS, MAW? I'M A BIT OVER YOUR DECLARATIVE STATEMENTS AND HYPOTHETICALS.
THE MATERIAL THAT WAS ON THANOS' MONITORS, PROXIMA-- IT WAS CLASSIFIED.
BOOM BOOM
LET'S GET BACK THERE. IN ADDITION TO HAVING WHAT WE NEED TO KNOW, IT'S ALSO LIKELY THE MOST DEFENSIBLE PLACE ON BOARD.
PROVIDED IT HASN'T ALREADY BEEN RANSACKED BY THE MUTINOUS CREW.
DEATH TO THE ELITE!
TAKKA TAKKA TAKKA TAKKA
GET DOWN!
NO NEED, PROXIMA.
STAND DOWN.

KIND OF YOU TO SAVE ME.

IT'S NOTHING PERSONAL...

IT'S THAT VOICE OF YOURS. IT'S USEFUL.

AND I'M NOT MUCH OF A *TALKER*.

HM, WELL I DON'T BELIEVE I CAN TALK MY WAY INTO THANOS' *FILES*.

QUICKLY...

I STILL CAN'T SEE A DAMN THING. IT'S ALL CLASSIFIED. HE DIDN'T WANT ANYONE ON BOARD TO SEE WHAT HE'S UP TO.

ION THRUSTERS AT MAXIMUM.

THRUSTERS? *ZERO SANCTUARY* IS KEPT IN ORBITAL STATION-KEEPING MODE UNLESS WE'RE IN HYPERSPACE. AND IT LOOKS LIKE THERE'S A MASSIVE NAVAL PRESENCE ON RADAR UP HERE.

WHY THE HELL WOULD THE *THRUSTERS*--

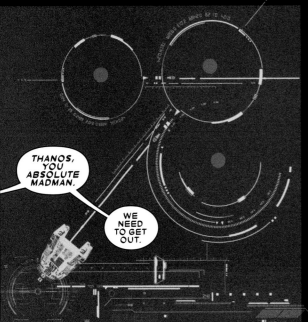

THANOS, YOU ABSOLUTE MADMAN.

WE NEED TO GET OUT.

NOW!

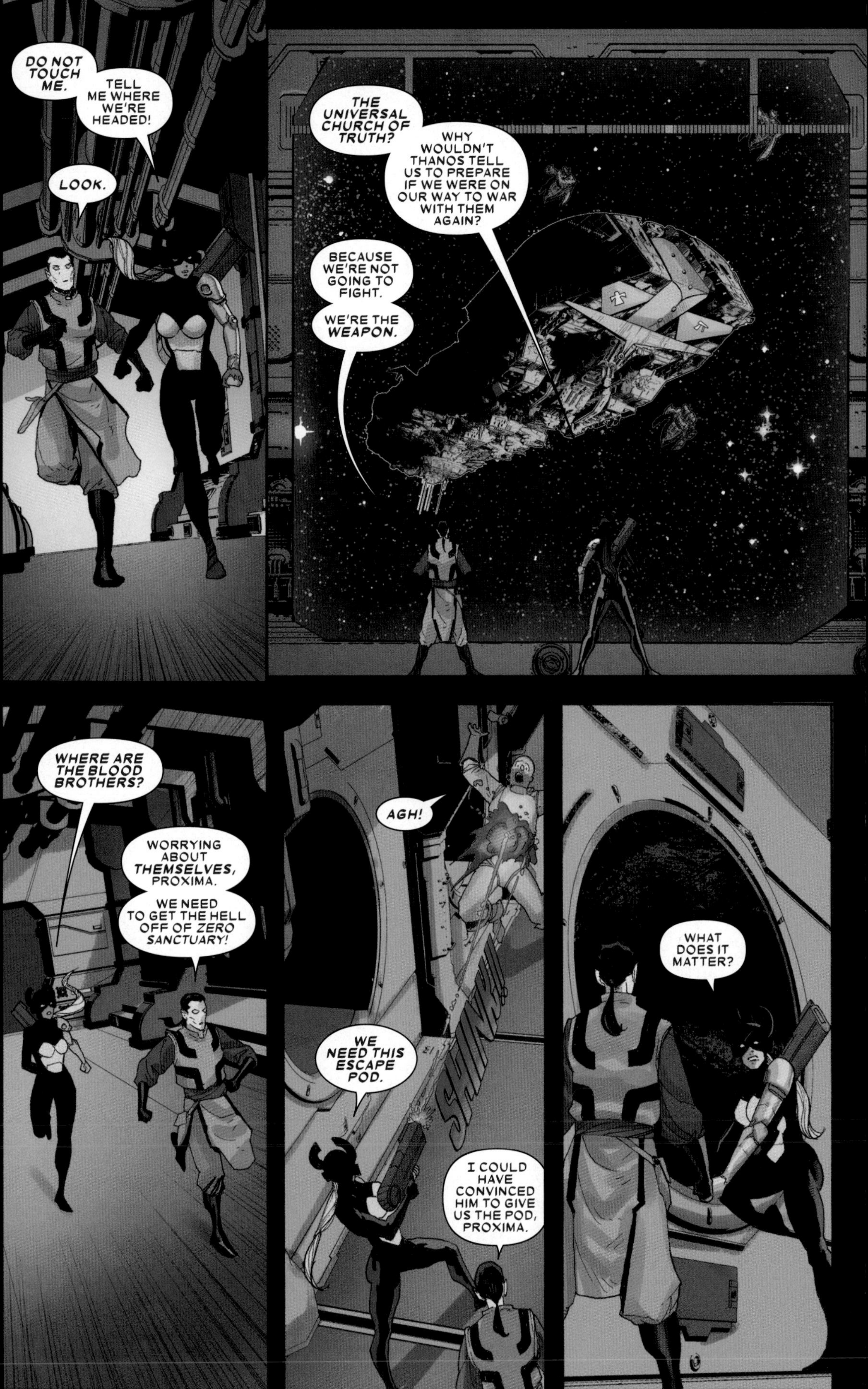
DO NOT TOUCH ME.
TELL ME WHERE WE'RE HEADED!
LOOK.
THE UNIVERSAL CHURCH OF TRUTH?
WHY WOULDN'T THANOS TELL US TO PREPARE IF WE WERE ON OUR WAY TO WAR WITH THEM AGAIN?
BECAUSE WE'RE NOT GOING TO FIGHT.
WE'RE THE WEAPON.
WHERE ARE THE BLOOD BROTHERS?
WORRYING ABOUT THEMSELVES, PROXIMA.
WE NEED TO GET THE HELL OFF OF ZERO SANCTUARY!
AGH!
WE NEED THIS ESCAPE POD.
I COULD HAVE CONVINCED HIM TO GIVE US THE POD, PROXIMA.
WHAT DOES IT MATTER?

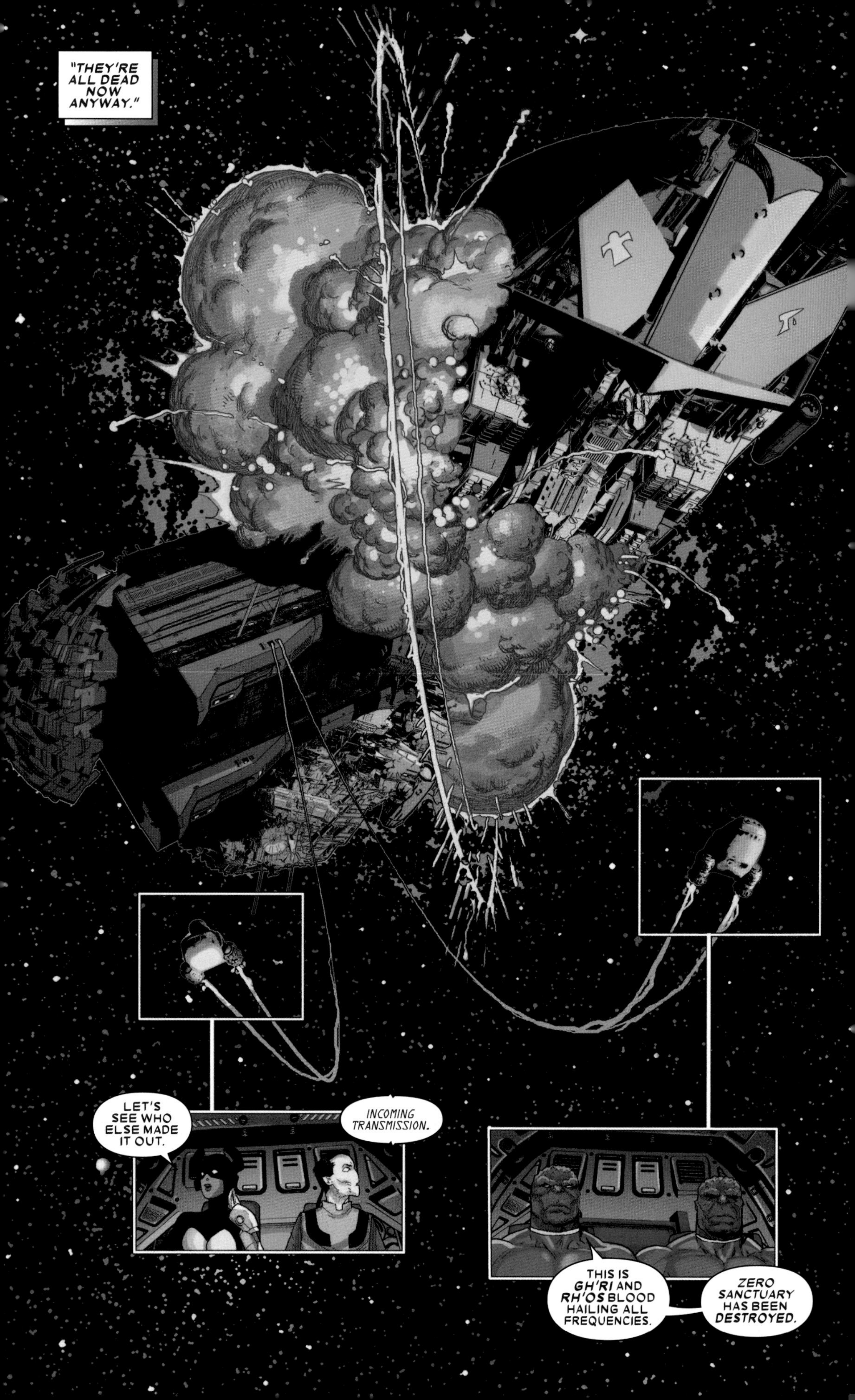
"THEY'RE ALL DEAD NOW ANYWAY."
LET'S SEE WHO ELSE MADE IT OUT.
INCOMING TRANSMISSION.
THIS IS GH'RI AND RH'OS BLOOD HAILING ALL FREQUENCIES.
ZERO SANCTUARY HAS BEEN DESTROYED.

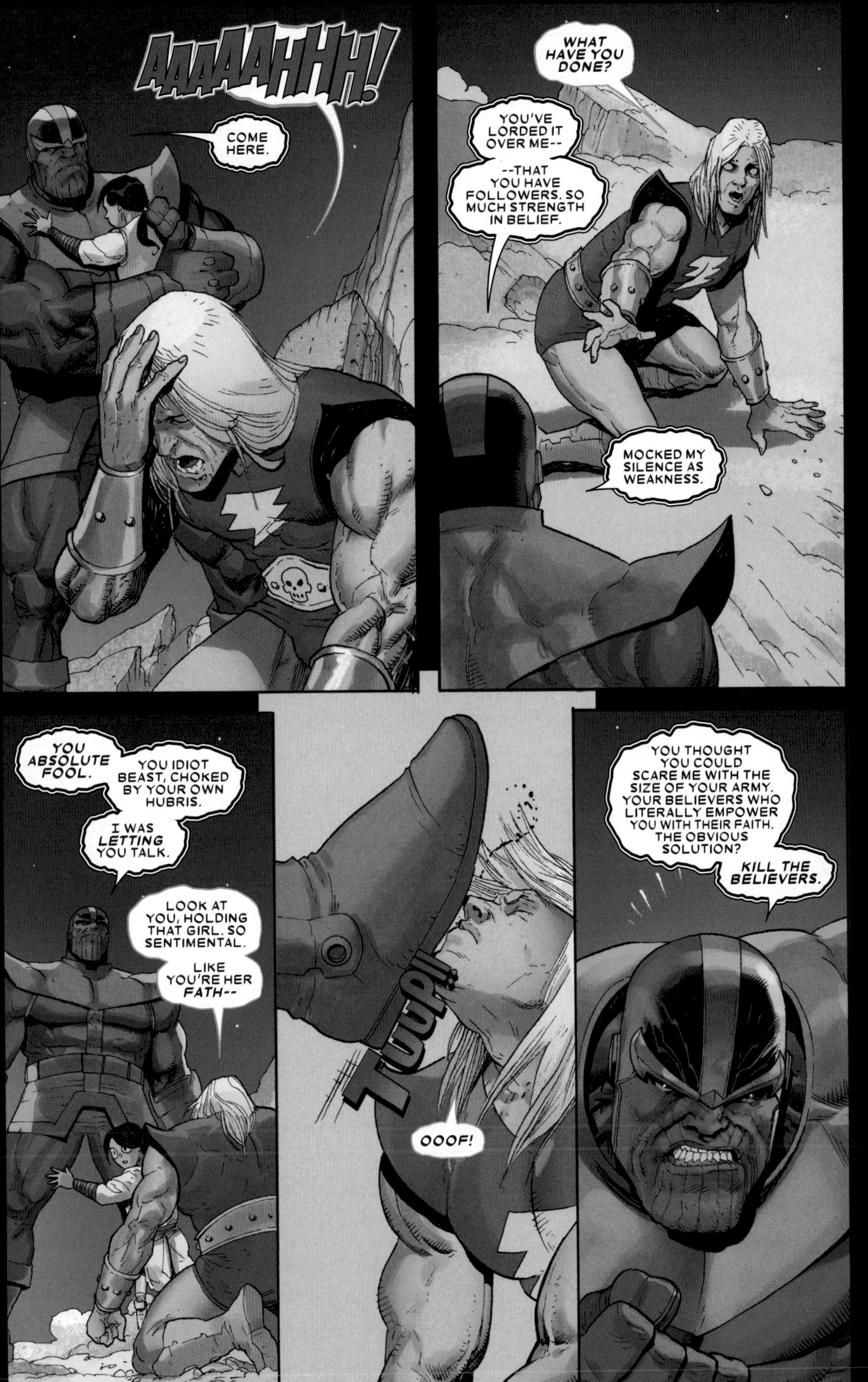
AAAAAHHH!
COME HERE.
WHAT HAVE YOU DONE?
YOU'VE LORDED IT OVER ME--
--THAT YOU HAVE FOLLOWERS. SO MUCH STRENGTH IN BELIEF.
MOCKED MY SILENCE AS WEAKNESS.
YOU ABSOLUTE FOOL.
YOU IDIOT BEAST, CHOKED BY YOUR OWN HUBRIS.
I WAS LETTING YOU TALK.
LOOK AT YOU, HOLDING THAT GIRL. SO SENTIMENTAL.
LIKE YOU'RE HER FATH--
TUUUP!!
OOOF!
YOU THOUGHT YOU COULD SCARE ME WITH THE SIZE OF YOUR ARMY. YOUR BELIEVERS WHO LITERALLY EMPOWER YOU WITH THEIR FAITH. THE OBVIOUS SOLUTION?
KILL THE BELIEVERS.

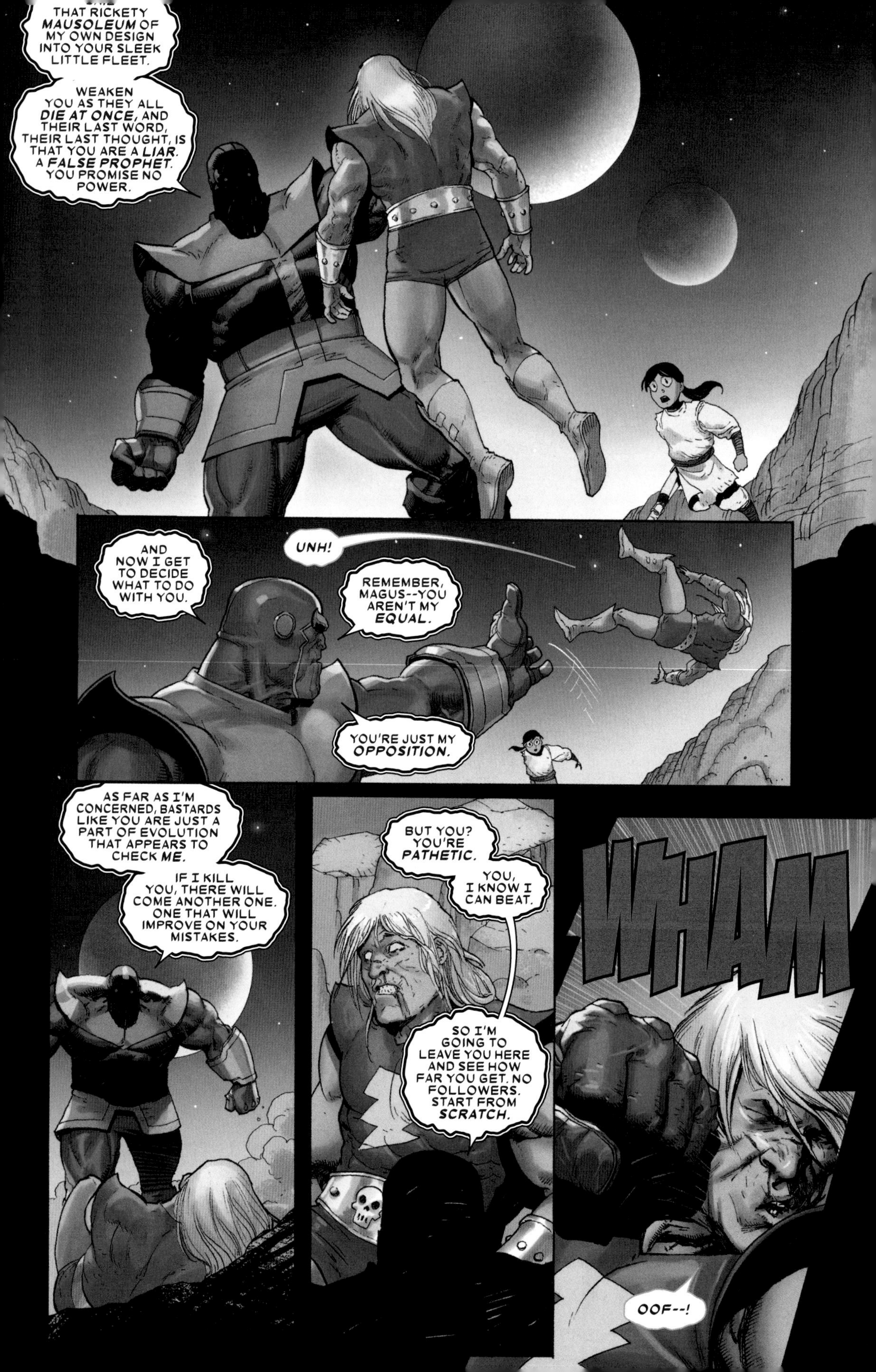
THAT RICKETY MAUSOLEUM OF MY OWN DESIGN INTO YOUR SLEEK LITTLE FLEET.
WEAKEN YOU AS THEY ALL DIE AT ONCE, AND THEIR LAST WORD, THEIR LAST THOUGHT, IS THAT YOU ARE A LIAR. A FALSE PROPHET. YOU PROMISE NO POWER.
AND NOW I GET TO DECIDE WHAT TO DO WITH YOU.
UNH!
REMEMBER, MAGUS--YOU AREN'T MY EQUAL.
YOU'RE JUST MY OPPOSITION.
AS FAR AS I'M CONCERNED, BASTARDS LIKE YOU ARE JUST A PART OF EVOLUTION THAT APPEARS TO CHECK ME.
IF I KILL YOU, THERE WILL COME ANOTHER ONE. ONE THAT WILL IMPROVE ON YOUR MISTAKES.
BUT YOU? YOU'RE PATHETIC.
YOU, I KNOW I CAN BEAT.
SO I'M GOING TO LEAVE YOU HERE AND SEE HOW FAR YOU GET. NO FOLLOWERS. START FROM SCRATCH.
WHAM
OOF--!

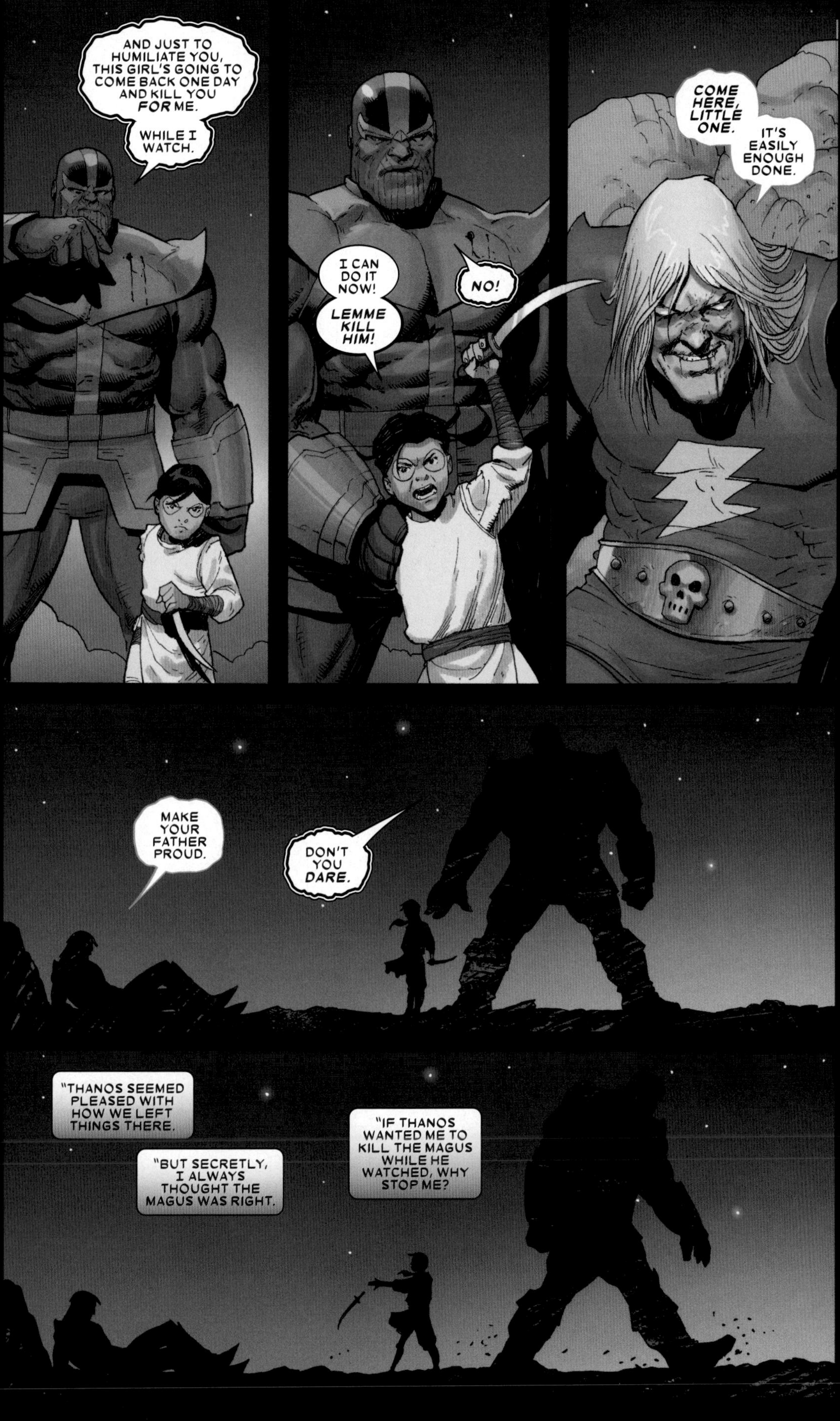
AND JUST TO HUMILIATE YOU, THIS GIRL'S GOING TO COME BACK ONE DAY AND KILL YOU FOR ME.
WHILE I WATCH.
I CAN DO IT NOW!
LEMME KILL HIM!
NO!
COME HERE, LITTLE ONE.
IT'S EASILY ENOUGH DONE.
MAKE YOUR FATHER PROUD.
DON'T YOU DARE.
"THANOS SEEMED PLEASED WITH HOW WE LEFT THINGS THERE.
"BUT SECRETLY, I ALWAYS THOUGHT THE MAGUS WAS RIGHT.
"IF THANOS WANTED ME TO KILL THE MAGUS WHILE HE WATCHED, WHY STOP ME?

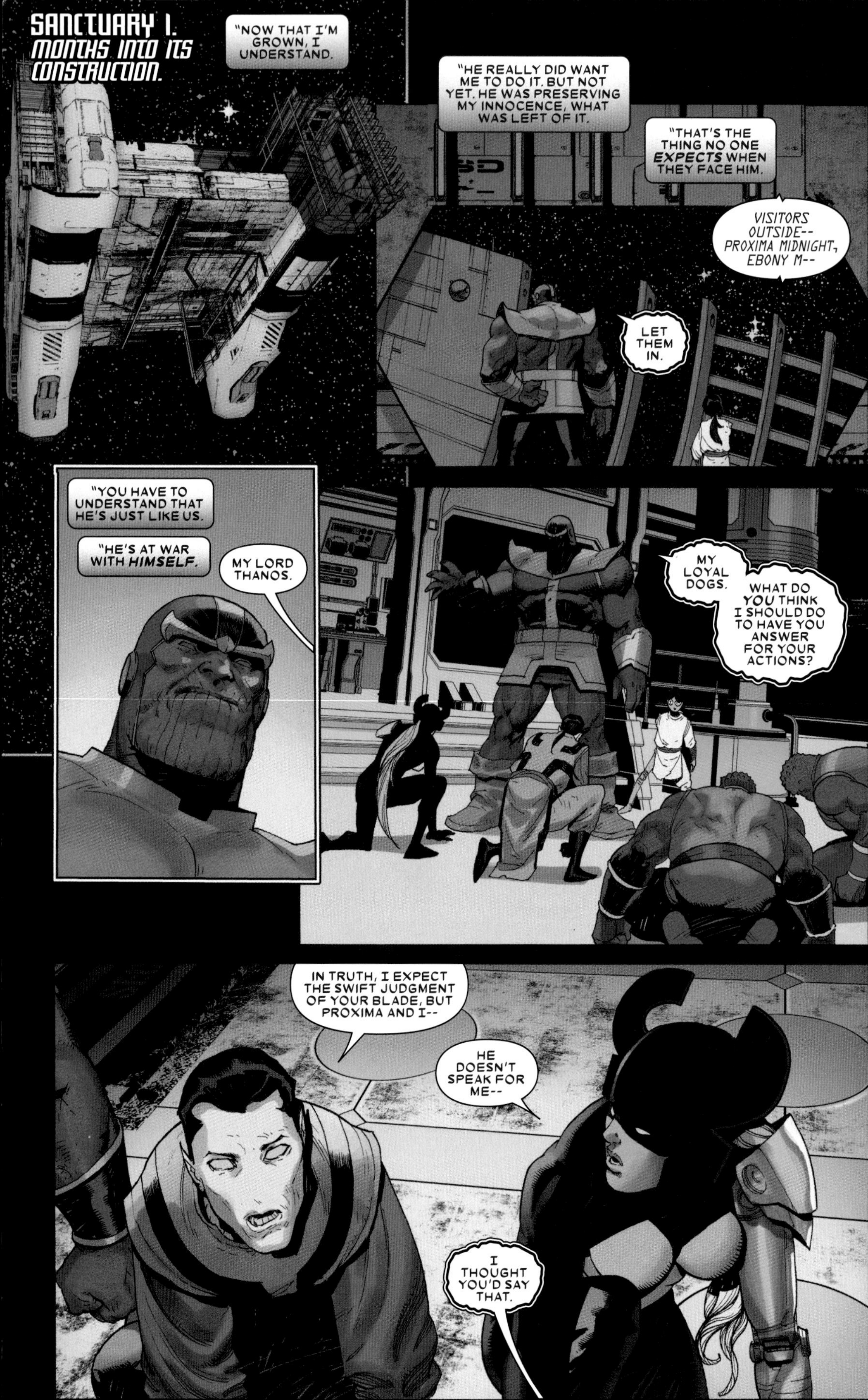
SANCTUARY I.
MONTHS INTO ITS CONSTRUCTION.
"NOW THAT I'M GROWN, I UNDERSTAND.
"HE REALLY DID WANT ME TO DO IT. BUT NOT YET. HE WAS PRESERVING MY INNOCENCE, WHAT WAS LEFT OF IT.
"THAT'S THE THING NO ONE EXPECTS WHEN THEY FACE HIM.
VISITORS OUTSIDE-- PROXIMA MIDNIGHT, EBONY M--
LET THEM IN.
"YOU HAVE TO UNDERSTAND THAT HE'S JUST LIKE US.
"HE'S AT WAR WITH HIMSELF.
MY LORD THANOS.
MY LOYAL DOGS.
WHAT DO YOU THINK I SHOULD DO TO HAVE YOU ANSWER FOR YOUR ACTIONS?
IN TRUTH, I EXPECT THE SWIFT JUDGMENT OF YOUR BLADE, BUT PROXIMA AND I--
HE DOESN'T SPEAK FOR ME--
I THOUGHT YOU'D SAY THAT.

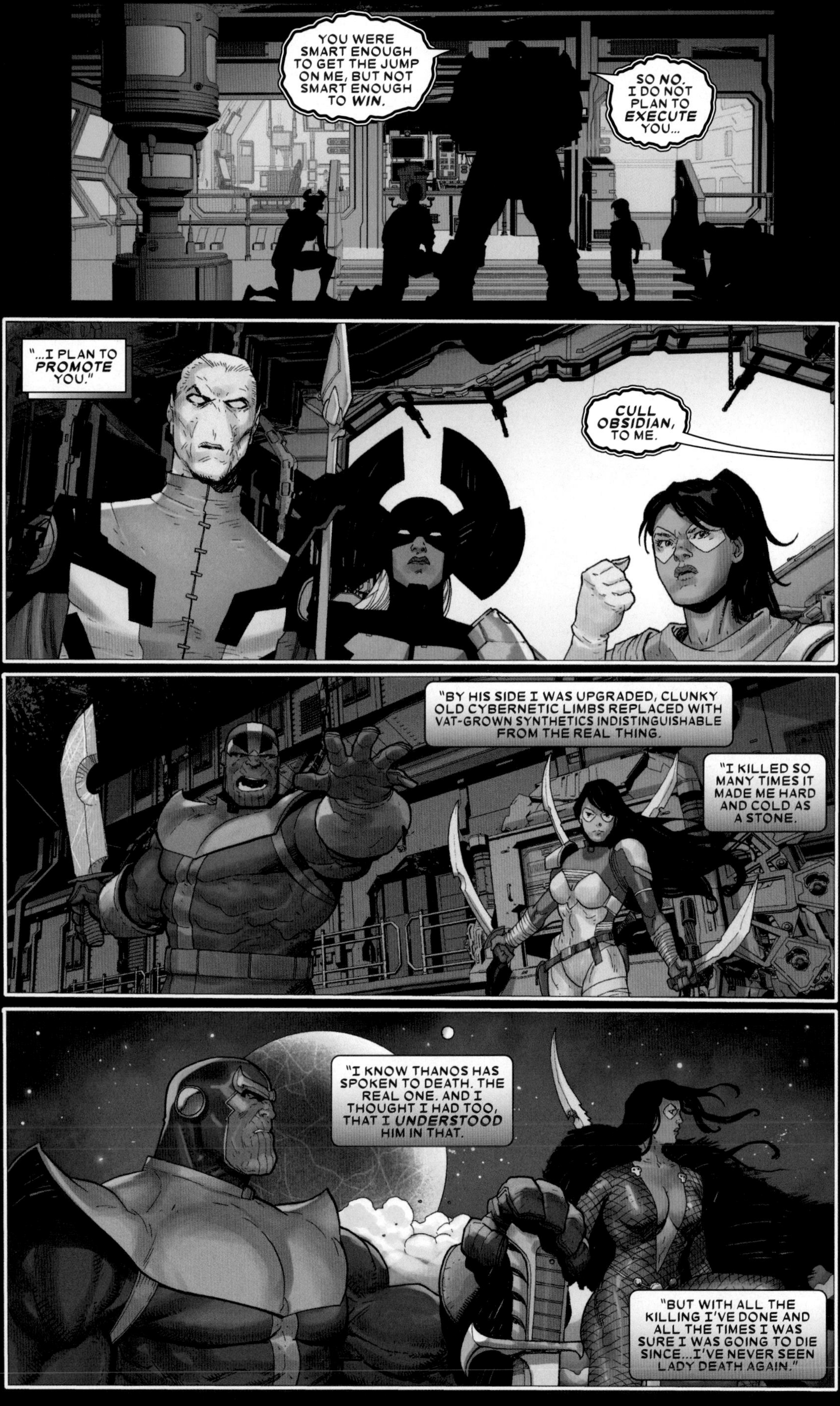
YOU WERE SMART ENOUGH TO GET THE JUMP ON ME, BUT NOT SMART ENOUGH TO *WIN*.
SO *NO*. I DO NOT PLAN TO *EXECUTE* YOU...
"...I PLAN TO *PROMOTE* YOU."
CULL OBSIDIAN, TO ME.
"BY HIS SIDE I WAS UPGRADED, CLUNKY OLD CYBERNETIC LIMBS REPLACED WITH VAT-GROWN SYNTHETICS INDISTINGUISHABLE FROM THE REAL THING.
"I KILLED SO MANY TIMES IT MADE ME HARD AND COLD AS A STONE.
"I KNOW THANOS HAS SPOKEN TO DEATH. THE REAL ONE. AND I THOUGHT I HAD TOO, THAT I *UNDERSTOOD* HIM IN THAT.
"BUT WITH ALL THE KILLING I'VE DONE AND ALL THE TIMES I WAS SURE I WAS GOING TO DIE SINCE...I'VE NEVER SEEN LADY DEATH AGAIN."

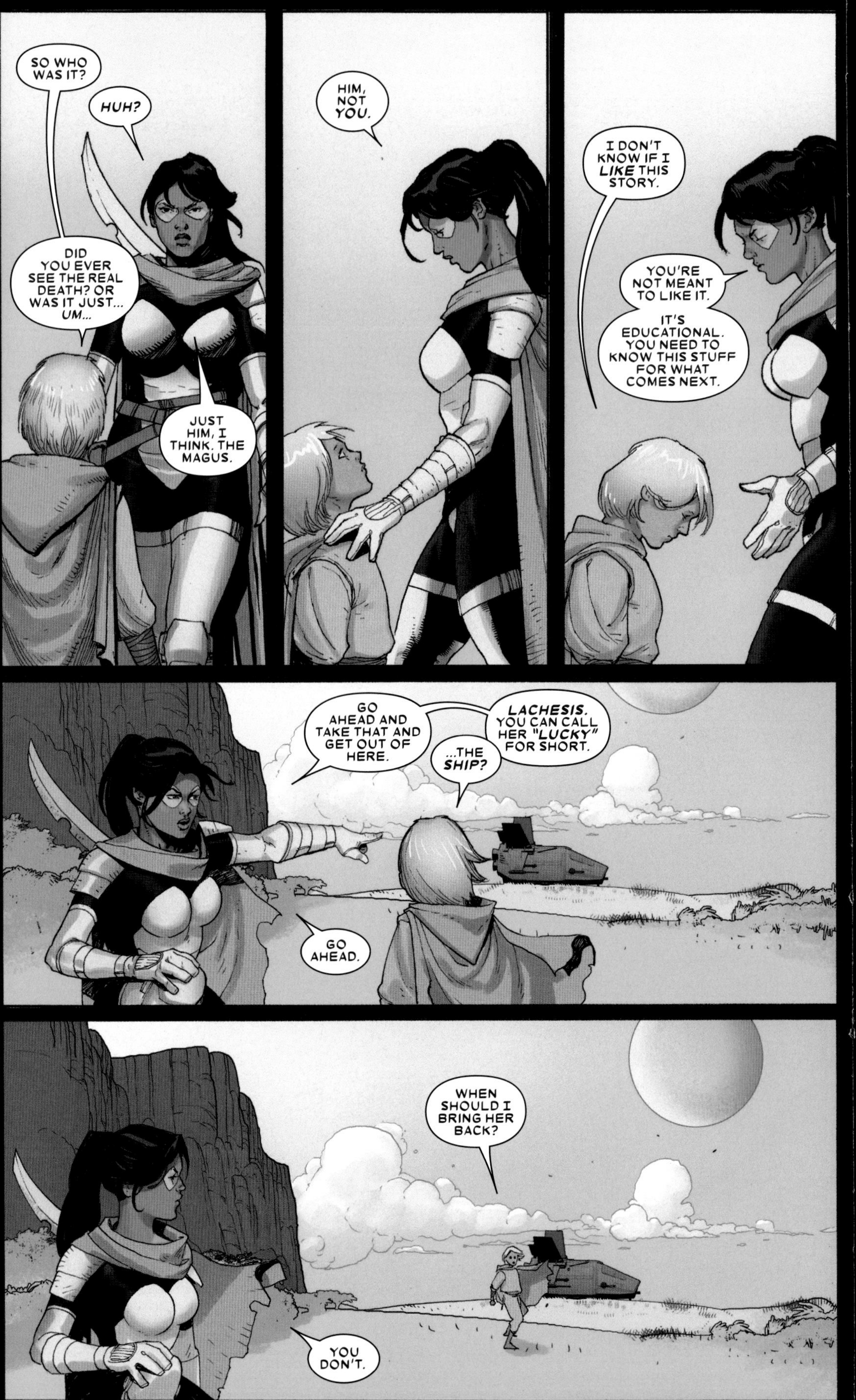
SO WHO WAS IT?
HUH?
DID YOU EVER SEE THE REAL DEATH? OR WAS IT JUST... UM...
JUST HIM, I THINK. THE MAGUS.
HIM, NOT YOU.
I DON'T KNOW IF I LIKE THIS STORY.
YOU'RE NOT MEANT TO LIKE IT.
IT'S EDUCATIONAL. YOU NEED TO KNOW THIS STUFF FOR WHAT COMES NEXT.
GO AHEAD AND TAKE THAT AND GET OUT OF HERE.
...THE SHIP?
LACHESIS. YOU CAN CALL HER "LUCKY" FOR SHORT.
GO AHEAD.
WHEN SHOULD I BRING HER BACK?
YOU DON'T.

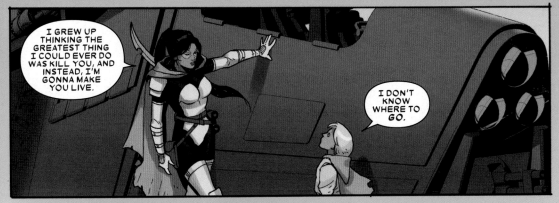

I GREW UP THINKING THE GREATEST THING I COULD EVER DO WAS KILL YOU, AND INSTEAD, I'M GONNA MAKE YOU LIVE.

I DON'T KNOW WHERE TO GO.

IT'S NOT YOUR FAULT, BUT YOU ARE WHO YOU ARE. THAT MEANS YOU HAVE A LOT TO THINK ABOUT.

THERE ARE SOME PEOPLE THAT I THINK CAN HELP YOU--BUT THEY AREN'T ON HALFWORLD.

YOU'VE GOT FOOD AND FUEL IF YOU WANT TO EXPLORE, BUT WHEN THINGS GET TOUGH--HIT THE COORDINATES I PLUGGED IN.

IT'LL TAKE YOU TO A PLACE FOR PEOPLE WHO HAVE BEEN HURT...

...BY THE MAGUS.

I GUESS I CAN BE COUNTED AMONG THEM.

I AM SORRY, YOU KNOW.

BUT I KNOW WHAT I CAN'T DO.

I CAN'T RAISE YOU RIGHT.

I KNOW.

YOU'RE SAVING ME.

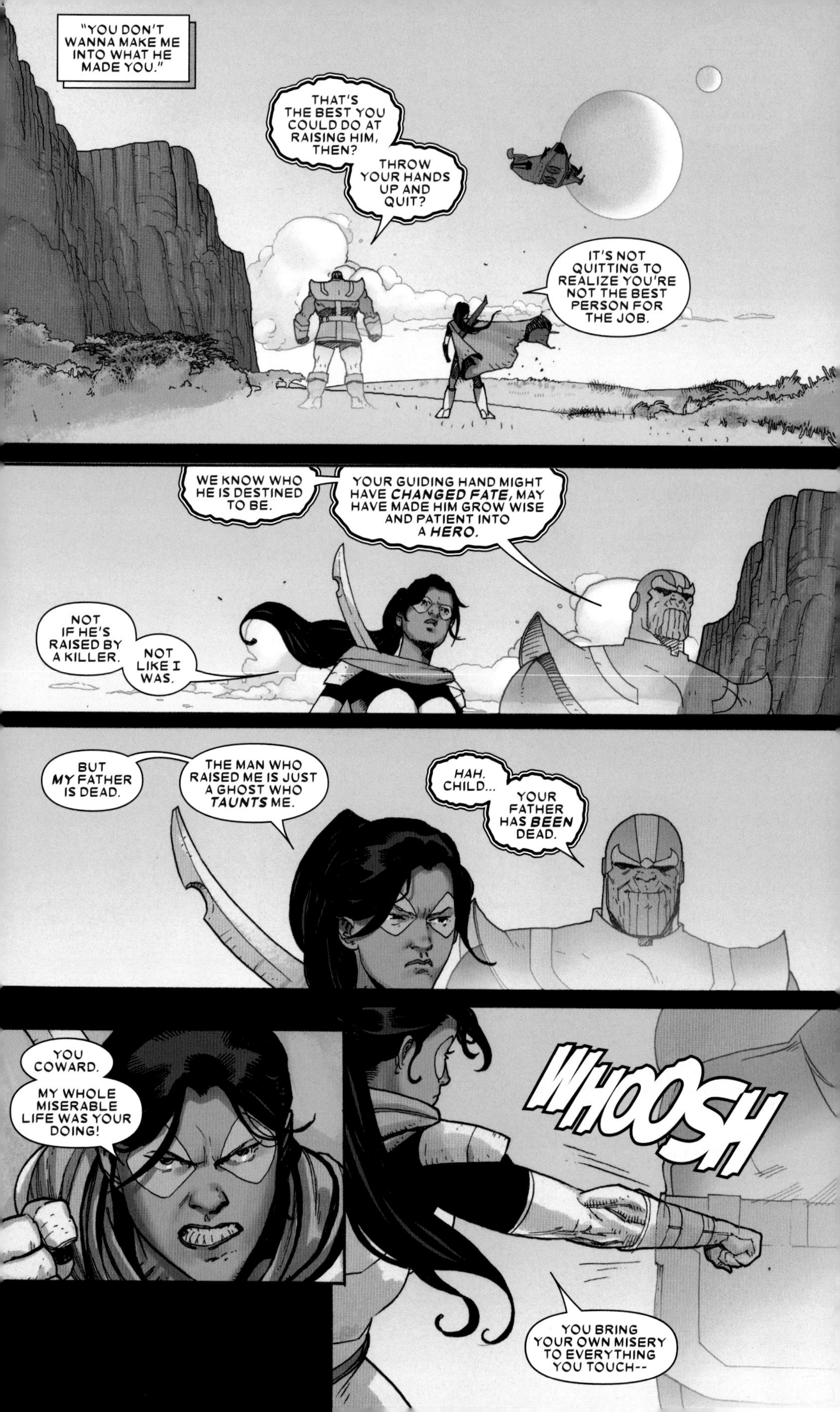
"YOU DON'T WANNA MAKE ME INTO WHAT HE MADE YOU."
THAT'S THE BEST YOU COULD DO AT RAISING HIM, THEN?
THROW YOUR HANDS UP AND QUIT?
IT'S NOT QUITTING TO REALIZE YOU'RE NOT THE BEST PERSON FOR THE JOB.
WE KNOW WHO HE IS DESTINED TO BE.
YOUR GUIDING HAND MIGHT HAVE *CHANGED FATE*, MAY HAVE MADE HIM GROW WISE AND PATIENT INTO A *HERO*.
NOT IF HE'S RAISED BY A KILLER.
NOT LIKE I WAS.
BUT *MY* FATHER IS DEAD.
THE MAN WHO RAISED ME IS JUST A GHOST WHO *TAUNTS* ME.
HAH. CHILD...
YOUR FATHER HAS *BEEN* DEAD.
YOU COWARD.
MY WHOLE MISERABLE LIFE WAS YOUR DOING!
WHOOSH
YOU BRING YOUR OWN MISERY TO EVERYTHING YOU TOUCH--

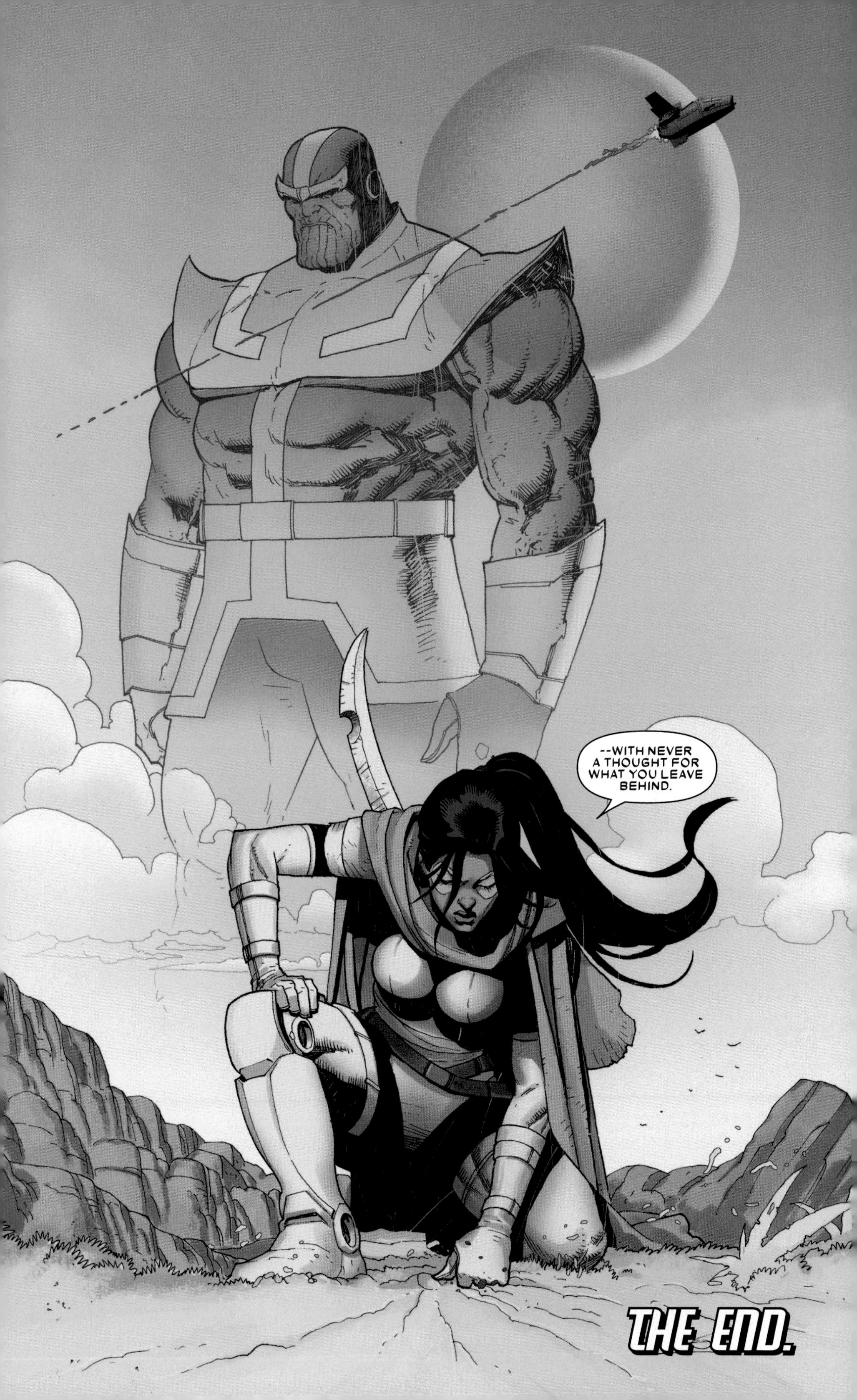
--WITH NEVER A THOUGHT FOR WHAT YOU LEAVE BEHIND.
THE END.

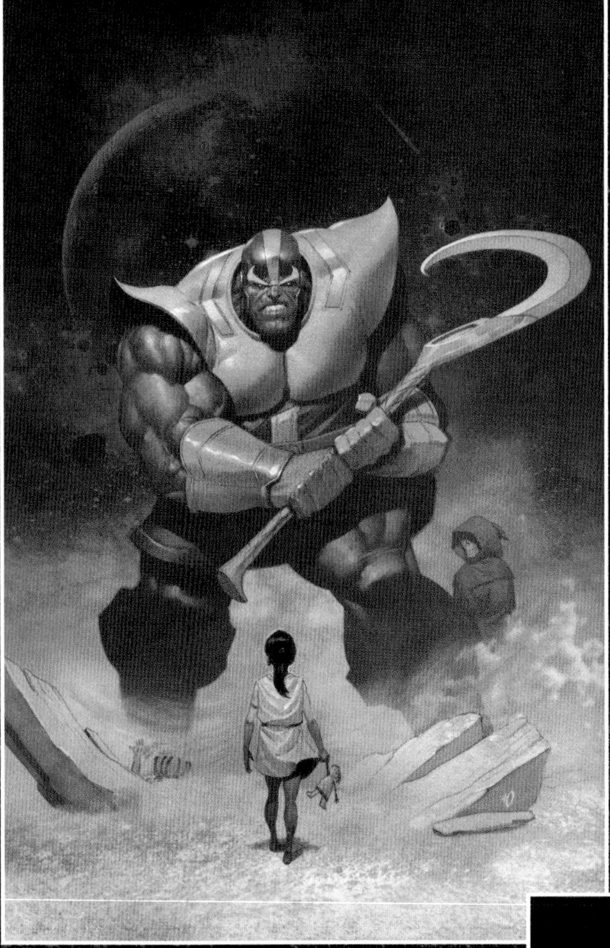

THANOS #1 VARIANT BY
ARIEL OLIVETTI

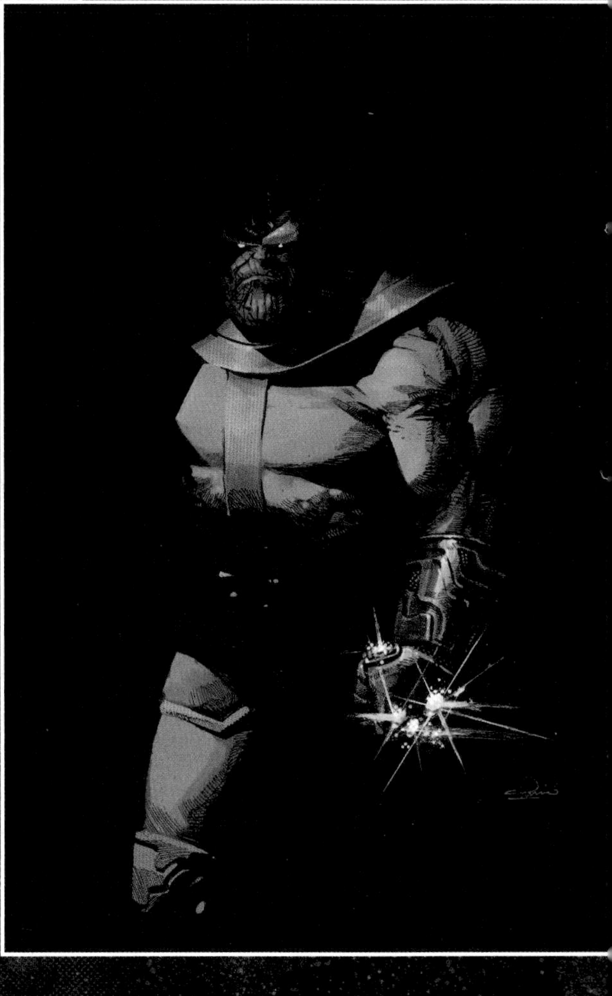

THANOS #1 VARIANT BY
GERARDO ZAFFINO